Michel Tournier

NEW DIRECTIONS IN EUROPEAN WRITING

....

Editor: John Flower, Professor of French, University of Exeter.

As the twentieth century draws to a close we are witnessing profound and significant changes across the new Europe. The past is being reassessed; the millennium is awaited with interest. Some, pessimistically, have predicted the death of literature; others see important developments within national literature and in movements cutting across frontiers. This enterprising Series focuses on these developments through the study either of individual writers or of groups or movements. There are no definitive statements. By definition they are introductory and set out to assess and explore the full spectrum of modern European writing on the threshold of a new age.

ISBN 1350-9217

Previously published titles in the Series:

NEW DIRECTIONS IN EUROPEAN WRITING
....

Michel Tournier

David Gascoigne

BERG

Oxford / Washington, D.C.

First published in 1996 by
Berg
Editorial offices:
150 Cowley Road, Oxford, OX4 1JJ, UK
13950 Park Center Road, Herndon, VA 22071, USA

Berg is the imprint of Oxford International Publishers Ltd.

Library of Congress Cataloging-in-Publication Data

A catalogue record for this book is available from the Library of
Congress.

British Library Cataloguing-in-Publication Data

A catalogue record for this book is available from the British Library.

ISBN 1 85973 024 8 (Cloth)
      1 85973 084 1 (Paper)

Printed in the United Kingdom by WBC Bookbinders, Bridgend,
Mid Glamorgan.

Contents

Preface

The aim of this book is to offer a thematic and structural study of the whole of Michel Tournier's fiction to date. His non-fictional writings are not discussed directly, but I have drawn on them freely where they help our understanding of significant themes and patterns in the novels and stories. I decided from the outset not to write a study in which a chapter was devoted to each work in succession: I had already adopted this chronological approach in an earlier published essay, and there are several studies by other critics which have followed this path more or less successfully. It seemed to me more interesting, and potentially more fruitful, to select a series of major aspects of Tournier's thinking and writing - society, sexuality, religion, the elements, children - and to survey the structures of each across the whole *oeuvre*. This series of thematic chapters (2-6) is preceded by a substantial chapter presenting Tournier's fictions in terms of their construction, since in my view the importance of the artisanal aspect of this novelist's work, his patient elaboration of an inner architecture which structures each narrative, has been considerably neglected and underrated. Chapter 7 examines his novels as narratives of initiation, an aspect which clearly impinges on both theme and structure, while the eighth and final chapter seeks to bring together some of the conclusions of the earlier chapters in characterising Tournier's whole enterprise as an escape from history, an attempt to assert a self beyond time. The particular nature of this study has meant that most attention has been focussed on the novels and more substantial works of fiction, where these dimensions are explored in an extended and wide-ranging way, and that some short stories, and texts for children, have been largely left aside.

Within Chapters 1, 3, 4 and 5 the novels are discussed individually in chronological order, from a particular structural or thematic perspective, so that readers who are interested in one particular text will find an identifiable section on it in each of these chapters. Chapters 2, 6, 7 and 8 offer a more synthesised approach. My aim, self-evidently, has been to respect the specificity of each work, while pushing as far as possible towards a comparative reading of the various texts which aims to bring out the recurrent patterns and resonances between them. This kind of intertextual reading poses, of course, some problems. It will necessarily be of most interest to readers familiar with a number of Tournier's works, and it raises the question: how far is a knowledge of the *oeuvre* as a whole necessary in order to interpret a given work? While each of Tournier's fictions is independent and can be read in its own terms, he nevertheless develops from work to work repetitions and variations on ideas and motifs, and even a certain personal vocabulary, which invite a comparative reading of his fictions. The more Tournier you read, the more manifest certain recurrent structures and preoccupations will become. This study is written in the belief, precisely, that such 'contextual' reading can help a reader to grasp more easily the characteristic structures of a given work, as well as to account for its more problematic features. In writing like Tournier's which is very self-consciously driven by ideas - analyses of experience as well as reflections on culture, tradition and other writings - there may be particular benefits to be gained from a synoptic approach.

When it comes to intertextuality in the wider sense, in relation to writings other than those by Tournier, I have mostly restricted myself to references to texts which Tournier used or may have had in mind. Given the strong sense that Tournier gives in his writing of addressing key issues of modern culture, and of thereby engaging in an open dialogue with the wide range of literature he has absorbed, the critic must of necessity resist the temptation to note and explore every stimulating parallel and contrast that springs to mind. I have tried to retain only those which seemed most stimulating or helpful, for fear that otherwise the main lines of this study would be swamped by comparisons.

One further point as regards the strategy adopted in this book is that in surveying all the novels in each of a number of chapters, from different thematic angles, some repetition is inevitable. In Tournier's works, thematic fields such as sexuality, religion and society are not of course kept separate: they overlap and combine, often in provocative ways. As a result, certain key passages and episodes, for instance, will be examined several times in somewhat different perspectives. To show that they can present a different, but equally scintillating, facet according to the angle of light played on them is the best tribute I can pay to Tournier's often brilliantly polysemic, multi-level fictions.

My thanks are due to the University of St Andrews for granting me the research leave necessary to bring this work to completion, and to colleagues and students who have stimulated and enriched my thinking on these texts. I am particularly grateful to Ian Higgins, who kindly read and commented on the work in typescript; he is of course in no way responsible for any remaining shortcomings. My thanks go also to the staff of the St Andrews University Library and the Buchanan Library, who have been unfailingly patient and helpful. Above all, however, I owe a debt of gratitude to Christine Gascoigne, without whose constant encouragement, support and immaculate proof-reading this book would never have been finished.

David Gascoigne

References to Tournier's Works

The editions used are all Gallimard Folio except where otherwise stated; full details are given in the Select Bibliography. For page references in the text, the following abbreviations are used:

Vendredi ou les limbes du Pacifique	*VLP*
Le Roi des aulnes	*RA*
Les Météores	*Mét*
Le Coq de bruyère	*CB*
Gaspard, Melchior & Balthazar	*GMB*
Gilles & Jeanne	*GJ*
La Goutte d'or	*GO*
Le Médianoche amoureux	*MA*
Le Vent Paraclet	*VPar*
Le Vol du Vampire (Gallimard Idées)	*VV*
Petites Proses	*PP*
Le Tabor et le Sinaï (Belfond)	*TS*
Le Miroir des idées (Mercure de France)	*MI*
Le Pied de la lettre (Mercure de France)	*PL*
Des Clefs et des serrures (Chêne/Hachette)	*CS*
Le Vagabond immobile (Gallimard)	*VI*
Le Crépuscule des masques (Hoëbeke)	*CM*

1

The Craft of Construction

In the introductory essay to his collection of literary reviews and prefaces, *Le Vol du vampire*, Tournier distinguishes two categories of writer: the compulsive writer who is unconcerned by access to a public, as opposed to the artisan, who writes essentially to be published. He places himself cheerfully in the second group, and warmly defends their apparently less high-minded sense of calling: 'Car ils fabriquent très délibérément un objet manufacturé [...]. De l'artisan, ils possèdent l'honnêteté et la conscience professionnelles'(11-12)[1] While the 'objet manufacturé' refers here primarily to the book as object, whose printing, design and marketing matter to these writers, their professional conscientiousness can be understood to extend equally well to the structure of narrative. The narrator in Tournier's story 'Ecrire debout' is a novelist indistinguishable from Tournier himself, who addresses a group of readers in the following terms: 'Un livre, cela se fait comme un meuble, par ajustement patient de pièces et de morceaux. Il y faut du temps et du soin'(*MA* 183). It is proposed here to approach Tournier's fictions in the first instance in this spirit, as the products of workmanship, as 'very consciously manufactured objects'. The purpose of this opening survey is to highlight aspects of the inner architecture of each of Tournier's major fictional structures, to see how the component parts ('pièces', 'morceaux') are arranged and integrated.

Vendredi ou les limbes du Pacifique (1967)[2]

The narrative of Tournier's first novel is in part a recycling of existing materials. It is a version of the story of Robinson Crusoe, borrowing some elements from Daniel Defoe's original novel while transforming their sense and impact in the process.[3] On his compound of materials, of whatever provenance, Tournier imposes a carefully elaborated structure, based on a number of loosely related generating principles.

The first such structural system underpinning the narrative is suggested at the start of the book itself. To the story taken from Defoe,

Tournier has added a kind of prologue, which is set apart by being printed in italics, and by not being given a chapter number. Placed before Chapter 1, it constitutes a 'pre-text', a seminal microcosm of what is to come. It describes how the captain of the storm-tossed *Virginie*, Pieter Van Deyssel, offers a reluctant Robinson a set of predictions based on tarot cards. These can be seen as prefiguring in symbolic form the startling developments in Robinson's life realised in the subsequent narrative. This process of anticipation is quite explicit ('Chaque événement futur de votre vie vous révélera en se produisant la vérité de telle ou telle de mes prédictions'(13)), although the way in which the symbolic configurations which Van Deyssel outlines are realised in the narrative proper is not, as we shall see, a simple or merely sequential one. In the 'prologue', Robinson, in his puritanical distaste at what he sees as a devilish practice of fortune-telling, listens inattentively and sceptically to the prognostications, coming as they do from a shipmate whom he finds disquieting and uncongenial. He is much more preoccupied by the turmoil of the storm raging outside.

The structure of the narrative to come is thus given simultaneously to the hero and to the reader, but the reader is assumed to be more alert to its exposition than Robinson.[4] The hero's inattentiveness is carefully justified; it is a device to free him from any onerous sense of predestination, so that he appears to evolve freely, largely without foreknowledge, only recalling Van Deyssel's words when Tournier feels it appropriate to draw their predictive power once more to the reader's attention. Other reminders are passed direct through verbal cues in the narrative rather than being focalised through Robinson's consciousness: the reader, with the detached and superior insight gained from greater attentiveness, is thus encouraged to relate the stages of the story to the successive phases foretold by Van Deyssel, and to perceive more clearly than Robinson himself the shape and direction of his metamorphosis. This device of the tarot prediction to plot the course of the novel in advance serves a number of functions. It is Tournier's declaration of independence from Defoe, and from any other previous Robinson narrative. It keys into a general popular culture of prediction - astrology, horoscopes, palmistry - which still flourishes in our culture and which aspires to link human lives to shaping metaphysical forces in a non-Christian context: in so doing it attunes the reader to a narrative which is to exploit a number of unconventional initiatic and mythological elements in presenting the hero's development. It also - and this is the immediate concern of this chapter - provides an explicit structural framework which can give shape to a narrative which, for considerable stretches, is to be concerned with inner development rather than external action. In short (as for instance Valéry does very differently in *La Jeune Parque*) it uses traditional mythological elements to dramatise and schematise a process of Becoming.

The main body of the narrative which follows this prologue is divided into twelve chapters, and it can be read in terms of the sequence of eleven tarot cards drawn and commented on by the Captain. If we seek to relate the cards, as glossed by Van Deyssel, to subsequent sections of narrative, the following kind of pattern emerges:

1. The *Demiurge* or organiser, creating illusory order 'avec des moyens de fortune' (7): Robinson, retrieving tools from the shipwreck, first builds a boat which he is unable to launch, and then assembles an elaborate system of order for the island, his 'île administrée', which will eventually be shattered (Chapters 1-3).

2. *Mars*, figure of power and of warfare: Robinson, in his *folie de grandeur*, sees himself as king of the island, possessing total authority over his (imaginary) subjects, and builds military defences when he becomes aware of the existence of neighbouring Araucanian tribes (Chapter 4).

3. The *Hermit*: Robinson descends into an underground grotto, to escape from the oppressive order he has himself created: as Van Deyssel suggests, it is at once a return to origins and a place of metamorphosis (Chapter 5).

4. *Venus*: the Venus who emerges from the waves (Chapter 7) is the youth to whom Robinson will give the name Vendredi, just as Defoe's Crusoe christens his companion Friday. The name, thus transposed into French, derives, as Robinson tells us, from the Latin *veneris dies*, 'day of Venus', and he who bears the name will eventually inspire in his European partner deep love, and wonderment at his beauty.

5. *Sagittarius*: 'Vénus transformée en ange ailé envoie des flèches vers le soleil' (9): Vendredi, fascinated by everything to do with air and wind, shoots elaborate arrows into the sky (Chapter 9).

6. *Chaos*: 'La bête de la Terre est en lutte avec un monstre de flammes. L'homme [...], pris entre des forces opposées, est un fou [...]'(9). The conflict between earth and fire is most evident in the gunpowder explosion at the end of Chapter 8, which wrecks Robinson's edifice of 'civilisation'. It comes about as a result of Robinson's insane rage of jealousy.

7. *Saturn*: a man hanged by his feet, upside down. The giant cedar

tree keels over, its roots in the air, while Robinson learns to walk on his hands (Chapter 9).

8. *Gemini*: the Venus figure becomes a twin brother, the twins being depicted at the feet of an androgynous angel. In Chapter 10, Robinson will pray to be made more like Vendredi, sharing the same features, while the symbol of the 'Ange bisexué'(10) anticipates the vision of Vendredi-Venus smiling and gesturing heavenwards 'comme certains anges sur des peintures religieuses' (221).[5]

9. *The Lion (Leo)*: Two children stand holding hands before the wall of the Solar City, beneath the representation of the Sun God. This card, and Van Deyssel's commentary on it, is quite precisely recalled by Robinson near the end of Chapter 10 (229). This leads into a nocturnal vision of the Dioscuri, mythical heavenly twins blessed by their father the Sun God, which Robinson records in the very last entry in his logbook, to close the chapter.

10. *Capricorn*: interpreted by the captain as the gateway to Death. When Vendredi abandons Robinson, leaving unexpectedly on the departing British schooner *Whitebird* whose offers of rescue he has himself declined, Robinson feels overcome by the weight of years, and prepares to die (Chapter 12).

11. *Jupiter*: a golden child appears from the entrails of the earth to offer the keys of 'la Cité solaire' (13): the red-haired cabin-boy Jaan, whom Robinson will call Jeudi (etymology, *Jovis dies* = Jupiter's day), emerges from a hole in the rocks where he has been hiding, and the two of them climb to the highest point on the island to watch the sun rise (Chapter 12).

To summarise in this way the structural relationship between the tarot predictions of the preface and given moments of the following narrative is an exercise of limited usefulness.[6] It is not evident that the predictions manifest themselves in the order as announced - the explosion (Chaos) precedes the arrow-shooting (Sagittarius). More generally, while a few of them may appear to refer in the first instance to a precise moment or event - the Hermit to the descent into the cavern, or Sagittarius to Vendredi's firing of arrows - for others the precisely corresponding incident cannot be so confidently localised. Far from indicating a tidy series of defined stages, each centred on some emblematic event, they are rather ciphers for forces or patterns which often manifest themselves in Robinson's life and behaviour over a substantial period, in combination or alternation with each other. In this light, the Hermit stands not just for the cavern episode, but for the whole process of inner metamorphosis and maturation of which Robinson is aware between bouts of administration (Demiurge) and authoritarianism (Mars). These different selves will continue to coexist even after Vendredi's arrival, which in fact reawakens the imperial instinct of the would-be colonial master. Vendredi's personas as Venus and Sagittarius similarly coexist; the Araucanian becomes the Other in Robinson's life, the only object of all his capacity for passionate human relationships (Venus), yet at the same time Vendredi deflects that attention upwards, towards the sky (Sagittarius). Yet even this interpretation is over-restrictive, since Venus is present from earlier on, in Robinson's increasing exploration of sexuality, both his own and that of the flora and fauna of the island, and in his constitution of the island as Speranza, female object of his sexual desire and of the erotic invocations taken from the Song of Solomon.

At first sight, then, Tournier is offering us in the prologue a structured matrix with which to decode the narrative. On closer examination, however, its terms prove to be fluid in their realisation, vectors in a play of forces rather than distinct compartments in a fixed series.[7]

More rigour is to be found by looking carefully at the twelve-chapter structure of the narrative itself.

An important indication as to the nature of this structure is provided in the prologue. The prize which Robinson is promised at the end of his turbulent pilgrimage is the keys of the 'Cité solaire'. In his commentary on the ninth card, Leo, Van Deyssel speaks of the 'zénith de la perfection humaine' which the 'City of the Sun' symbolises. The City is 'suspendue entre le temps et l'éternité, entre la vie et la mort' (that is, in the 'limbo' of the novel's title), and its inhabitants are 'revêtus d'innocence enfantine'(12). They have attained a 'circular' solar sexuality: 'Un serpent se mordant la queue est la figure de cette érotique close sur elle-même'(12). The word 'circulaire' is emphasised by being set in roman type. It is rich in resonance, being reinforced by the figure of the snake biting its tail and by the circle of the sun ('sexualité solaire') at its highest point ('zénith'). This emphasis on circularity prepares the reader for a circular structure in the text, constructed as a closed cycle whose tail, like the snake's, leads us back to the head. Four of the names given to the Tarot cards - Sagittarius, Gemini, Leo and Capricorn - are also four of the twelve Zodiac signs,[8] and this in turn suggests the traditional division of the cycle into twelve parts: twelve months in the year, twelve hours on the clock-face.

The clock-face is in fact a useful working model for the structure of this text. It implies a descending first half, followed by an ascending second half, to the final 'zenith'. The half-way point is marked, at the beginning of Chapter 7, by the arrival of Vendredi, who will be the catalyst of the emergence of the 'new' Robinson from the shell of the old, and who will precisely reverse Robinson's downward, earth-directed orientation into an upward, sun-directed one. In this sense the narrative has the structure of a diptych, as the author himself has confirmed: 'Les deux volets de Robinson sur son île, *Avant-Vendredi*, *Avec-Vendredi*, s'articulent parfaitement l'un sur l'autre [...]' (*VPar* 232). As this turn of phrase suggests, some structural symmetries can be seen between the two halves.[9] Chapters 1 and 2 trace the misconceived effort to build a boat, which ends in madness. Cleansed of his derangement by the sea, Robinson finds himself obliged to make a fresh start, with a reversal of strategy: to accept the island rather than seeking at all costs to escape from it. Chapters 7 and 8, the equivalent chapters at the start of the Vendredi hemicycle, likewise recount a disastrous false start, with Robinson seeking to impose a master-slave model on their relationship. This enterprise too precipitates him into a demented loss of control: the resulting explosion purges his old life with fire, and releases him to re-establish his coexistence with Vendredi on quite opposite assumptions. The middle two chapters of each half (Chapters 3-4 and 9-10) present the most stable phase of each hemicycle, as Robinson presides over Speranza or happily shares life with Vendredi. The respective fifth chapters of each hemicycle present a challenge to this equilibrium. In Chapter 5, the interiority of the grotto experience undermines and threatens the external enterprise of the 'île administrée', while in Chapter 11 the arrival of the *Whitebird* calls into question all the priorities Robinson has come to adopt. Chapter 6, closing the first hemicycle, contains an extended reflection on death, and ends in the discovery that Speranza has brought forth mandrake 'children' in the hollow which has received Robinson's semen. Chapter 12, too, begins with a weariness unto death and ends with the discovery of a child, emerging from the entrance to the natal underground cavity.[10]

The arrival of this new companion can be taken to imply a new beginning, the start of a fresh (hemi)cycle, which might be entitled 'Robinson and Jeudi': we are back at the snake's head.[11] This cyclical form corresponds well to the notion of suspension 'between time and eternity' which is the attribute of the 'Cité solaire'. The cycle, of hours, months or seasons, is a figure of human time, yet its infinite repetition gives it a semblance of eternity.

In this light, the significance of the novel's title is multiple. The phrase 'les limbes du Pacifique' is used by Robinson in his 'logbook' in Chapter 6 to describe his sense of being only half alive, aware as he is that the rest of the world will mentally have consigned him to the realm of the dead.[12] This notion of suspension in limbo, 'aux confins de la vie' (130), is, by the end of the Vendredi hemicycle, valorised and exalted into the ideal of the 'Cité solaire'. It can be seen, then, that the second element of the title has, like the tarot headings of the prologue, a fluid, multiple relationship to the narrative: it refers at one and the same time to the geographical remoteness of the island, to Robinson's sense of 'demi-mort' (130) and to a kind of ideal state of being, granted only to the elect. (As Van Deyssel says, 'Il semble que vous soyez appelé à vous élever jusque-là'(12).) Arguably, this same polysemic aspect is to be found in the first element of the title, the word *Vendredi*. Clearly, for Tournier to call his novel 'Vendredi' rather than 'Robinson' is (like the prologue) a declaration of independence from Defoe, and from the many novels since whose titles have included the name Robinson in order to annex a little of its prestige. Critics, however, have not been slow to point out that the claim implied by Tournier's title, that his novel is to break with tradition by telling Vendredi's story rather than Robinson's, is not borne out by the narrative which remains overwhelmingly Robinson-centred.[13] From there it is but a step to accusing Tournier of unredeemed Eurocentrism behind a veneer of Third World sympathy, despite the novel's critique of some European and colonial values. While Tournier's cultural politics are open to debate, it may be that this particular line of attack is misconceived, resting as it does on the identification of the title 'Vendredi' with the character as subject. Just as 'limbo' can be seen as at once a place and an aspiration, so Vendredi is both a character and an ethos, a day of Venus through which Robinson lives and in the course of which he is transformed. Vendredi is perhaps less a character in his own right than a stimulus and instrument of change in Robinson, introduced at the critical point of his metamorphosis and withdrawn again when Robinson is ready for the next stage. The title, according to this view, is not at odds with the perception that the whole text is wholeheartedly concerned with the initiation of the hero.

Le Roi des aulnes (1970)

Tournier's second novel, *Le Roi des aulnes*, focuses almost unwaveringly on the life of Abel Tiffauges: he is present as protagonist or narrator virtually throughout.[14] The career being recounted is far from ordinary: after his schooldays at the Collège St-Christophe at Beauvais, Tiffauges is seen successively as garage proprietor in Paris, detainee, soldier, prisoner of war, game warden and acting head of an SS training school ('Napola'), until his final presumed death in the Prussian marshes during the Soviet onslaught on the crumbling Third Reich in March 1945.

The novel is divided into six substantial sections, each with its own heading. The first of these, 'Écrits sinistres d'Abel Tiffauges', is wholly in diary form, and is made up of eighty-four dated entries, which can in turn be grouped into three sequences: 3.1.1938 - 20.5.38 (thirty-six entries); 3.10.38 - 31.12.38 (eighteen entries); 2.3.39 - 4.9.39 (thirty entries). Curiously, all these groupings - 36+18+30 = 84 - within the first of the six parts of the novel are themselves multiples of six, which seems unlikely, in the hands of such a self-conscious constructor of narrative as Tournier, to be a coincidence.[15] As for the significance of this numerological principle of structure, the key is revealed in the final sentence of the novel, in Tiffauges's final vision of 'une étoile d'or à six branches' revolving slowly in the black sky. The novel thus implicitly presents itself as a narrative replica of that star, its six parts like the six points of the star which, if you follow them round, bring you back in some sense to the starting point. It aspires, like the star, to illuminate the blackness of its setting, in the darkest period of recent European history.

While the *histoire* of the novel, in Genette's sense of the word *histoire*,[16] stretches back to include Tiffauges's schooldays around the time of the First World War, the time-frame established by the *récit* commences with the first diary entry dated 3.1.1938, so that the focus is clearly on the period of the Second World War and its immediate preliminaries. Everything prior to this starting date - Tiffauges's schooldays, his affair with Rachel - is recounted in retrospective narrative (what Genette calls *analepse*)[17] in the first of the six parts of the novel, headed 'Écrits sinistres d'Abel Tiffauges'. This has the effect of characterising these earlier episodes as preliminary to, and in some sense preparatory of, the 'main' events of the period of the *récit*.

This strategy in Part I is of a piece with a narrative in which there is heavy emphasis on the predictive value of events and perceptions: the narrative voice will constantly suggest that the full import of an experience will only become apparent much later, and that it is an element in a pattern which will only gradually be revealed. Part I, easily the longest of the six, ends with the declaration of war and Tiffauges's conscription into the army. From this point on, there is much less oscillation between the narrative present and a past preceding the *récit*, and the remaining wartime narrative is more or less faithfully chronological to the end.

At the start of the text, Tiffauges presents himself twice, in two quite different modes: first as an ogre, a being of mythic status, and then as a Paris garage proprietor. The narrative thereafter grows out of the tension between these two dimensions, the mythological and the realist. For most of the book, each section represents a stage in a physical journey, as well as in a mythological quest. At the start of Part II, 'Les pigeons du Rhin', Tiffauges leaves Paris for service with the army in Alsace. The opening pages of Part III, 'Hyperborée', transport him to the prisoner-of-war camp at Moorhof. Part IV, 'L'Ogre de Rominten', finds him in Goering's game reserve, and Part V, 'L'Ogre de Kaltenborn', at the SS training school. In the sequence of titles, alongside the place-names marking the realist journey are set other elements - 'écrits sinistres', 'ogre', 'hyperborée' - which emphasise the metaphysical itinerary, culminating in the title of the final section, 'L'Astrophore'.

Part I is distinguished from the others not only in its time structure (use of *analepse*) and its Paris setting but also in its narrative mode, being the only one composed entirely of diary entries. The diary form of first-person narrative characteristically involves both a record of events and the reflections of the diarist. It foregrounds the act of writing - the recording of an event at some point after it has happened - and most of all it foregrounds the process of interpretation. The diarist selects which events and thoughts to record, and their choice and presentation will imply certain priorities and preoccupations, the eliciting of pattern and the creation of meaning. In the sequence of diary entries the interest can be in the unfolding of the story, but it can also be in the discourse of the diarist-narrator, as he (in this case) develops and reinforces a certain kind of interpretation, a particular understanding of his life. By this means characterisation is achieved as much through the *act* of narration as through the information we are given. In his 'Écrits sinistres', Abel Tiffauges cultivates and projects a certain image of himself, his importance, evolution and destiny as he sees it, and his narrative will develop a rhetoric of persuasion designed to recruit the reader into some degree of complicity with this view.

The second dated entry in the diary provides a good example of this technique. It gives an account of two episodes, narrated in retrospect. The first is a trivial accident at the garage in which he sprains his right wrist, but this 'incident banal' (16) yields the revelation that he is endowed with a natural gift for writing fluently with his left hand. The words 'révélation'(16) and 'événement bouleversant'(17) already indicate the weight of supernatural significance which he will build on this discovery, which inspires him to start writing the diary. Thus the narrative accounts for its own genesis, and the decision to start writing is itself an element in the constructed edifice of significance which the text will proceed to erect. This sense of an unforeseen gift, of a different and special mode of writing, will be only one of many aspects of his life which he will see as supernaturally ordained, marks of some special favour, signs of a privileged destiny. The term 'sinistre' is of course self-consciously used in a double sense, meaning not only 'left' as opposed to right (from Latin 'sinister'/ 'dexter') but also 'of ill omen', implying a dark side to the story to be told, and to the enterprise of writing thus begun.[18] This is but an early example of a series of related binary oppositions (benign/malign, symbolic/diabolic, light/heavy...) to be presented as keys for decoding experience and generating significance.

The second, more substantial, episode to be recounted in retrospect is the collapse of his relationship with Rachel, his independent-minded Jewish lover. The fact that she is a Jewess is not at this stage given great weight, except insofar as it adds an extra dimension of inscrutability to her person in the eyes of her ruminative French partner. This marker will however be massively reactivated by the final revelations about Auschwitz vouchsafed by the symmetrically placed figure of the Jewish waif Ephraim in the final part of the novel. Rachel's teasing accusation, recorded in the opening line of the novel, that Tiffauges is an ogre becomes a grim premonition of the process by which Jewish flesh will be preyed on by the ogre figures of the Third Reich. This element thus links the end of the narrative to the beginning, a link implied in the figure of the six-pointed revolving star. It is, in another sense, a 'trait' which links first to last, Alpha to Omega.[19]

By the end of Part I of *Le Roi des aulnes*, Tournier's narrative has fulfilled the reader's expectations of a realist novel, constructing a highly individual narrator-protagonist, and conferring on him a well-defined situation and biography in a precise and documented historical situation. Within these mimetic conventions of the historical novel, Tournier also alerts us to the problematic generation of patterns of meaning. The relatively conventional narrative mode contains an eccentric prioritisation and interpretation of events. As Tiffauges leaves Paris and civilian life behind him at the end of Part I, the suspense which carries the reader forward to the next episode concerns in part the conventional desire to know what will happen next, what role this unorthodox individual is going to play in the extraordinary period of European history looming up. What it also centres on, more significantly, is the premonitory, prophetic aspect of the narrative, designed to provoke curiosity as to whether, and in what form, the projected patterns of meaning are to be realised. A narrative machine of considerable complexity and power has been set in motion.

At this point there is a significant shift in narrative voice. Following the long opening section in diary mode, Parts II, III and IV move to third-person narrative. The reader, having been thoroughly immersed for two hundred pages in Tiffauges's view of himself and the world, is now placed in a potentially more detached relationship to the character. The narrative is no longer retrospective but calmly chronological. The ruminative-confessional mode gives way to a more picaresque framework, with Tiffauges's latent sense of his own destiny set within a wryly drawn picture of the oddities and idiocies of war.

At the end of Part IV Tiffauges obtains his transfer to Kaltenborn, his *terre d'élection* and final destination, and for the remaining two parts of the novel the narrative will be in mixed mode, alternating the diary mode of the 'Écrits sinistres' with the third-person narrative adopted for the intermediate stages, between Paris and Kaltenborn. A clear three-phase structure of narrative mode thus emerges: Part I in diary mode; Parts II-IV in third-person narrative; Parts V-VI in mixed mode. These three substantial sections into which the narrative is divided represent, as it were, a thesis-antithesis-synthesis progression in narrative mode.

This formal division corresponds to the changing focus of the narrative. The first, diary-mode section presents an autobiographical reading of private events, coupled with a caustic commentary on the newspaper reports on public affairs from which the diarist feels totally alienated. The central section, starting from Tiffauges's recruitment to the army, adopts the external narrative of history: it depicts the individual caught up in the eddies of the tide of war, each successive wave carrying him willy-nilly further eastward. The final, mixed-mode section poses the question of the synthesis of (auto-)biographical and historical focus, of the relationship between the individual and the collective story, between the defeats and disasters which overtake nations and the paradoxical apotheosis of an individual. The juxtaposition of narrative modes in the first two sections leads to their rapid alternation in the third, as this confrontation of perspectives becomes acute. It is in the counterpoint between these narrative modes that the questions arise regarding the coherence and significance of the interpretative patterns elicited in both modes from the material of private and public events.

Tournier has declared his allegiance to nineteenth-century narrative forms: 'Mon propos n'est pas d'innover dans la forme, mais de faire passer au contraire dans une forme aussi traditionnelle, préservée et rassurante que possible une matière ne possédant aucune de ces qualités' (*VPar* 195). It is true that he meets a good many of the demands made on the writer of realist fiction *à la* Zola: chronological narrative, with clearly marked time relationships; highly developed characterisation; conventional narrative modes, including an omniscient narrative voice; historical and geographical realism backed by substantial documentation. One of the features that marks this text's modernity, however, is that, from the moment Tiffauges recounts the genesis of his own diary, the text self-consciously poses and re-poses the question of decoding, of the attribution of meaning and the perception of pattern. The diary develops an idiosyncratic interpretation of history which the text, to a great extent, seeks to lure the reader into accepting. The dual narrative mode, however, leaves space open for the reader to question this promotion of personal vision into generalised, symbolic truth, a point to be taken up again in the concluding chapter of this study.

One further structuring principle in this text deserves attention, that of music. The title of the novel ('The Erlking') will recall for many not just the poem by Goethe quoted in the text but also the setting of those words by Schubert in one of his most famous lieder. This is not the only musical association suggested by Tournier: in *Le Vent paraclet* (125-30) he recounts how two other pieces of German music, one old and one very modern, played a significant role in the genesis of the novel.[20] The modern piece, Karlheinz Stockhausen's *Gesang der Jünglinge*, was for four years the 'accompagnement obsédant' of his composition of the novel. The music is inspired by the story, as told in the book of Daniel (Chapter 3), of how King Nebuchadnezzar threw three Jews, Hananiah, Mishael and Azariah, into a 'burning fiery furnace' when they refused to worship his golden image instead of their own God. An angel preserves them from the fire, and they can be seen walking unscathed in the midst of the flames.[21] Stockhausen, as Tournier points out, gives the story a further slant by making the three Jews boys rather than adult administrators, thus offering an even more powerful stimulus to Tournier's wartime narrative and its final view of the Holocaust through the eyes of Ephraim. Tournier's Jewish boy is, like his three Biblical counterparts, a miraculous survivor and steadfast in his Jewish faith, chanting the Haggada as the castle of Kaltenborn burns around him.

The parallel is not only thematic but also structural. For the youths, Stockhausen uses a single voice, multiplied through multi-track recording. Likewise, in Tournier's text, the various boys who play such an important role in Tiffauges's life are essentially anonymous, interchangeable units in a series, from Jeannot the garage apprentice (130 ff.) to Étienne at the Louvre (141), from the boy skaters of the Palais de Tokyo (171 ff.) to the trio of Haio, Haro and Lothar and their four hundred companions forming and re-forming on parade at Kaltenborn and singing their Nazi songs. This is one aspect of a special relationship between singular and plural: the singular is not specific but representative, symbolic. It is considered not in its unique physical reality but as a momentary incarnation of a type or a principle: not 'un enfant' but 'l'Enfant'. This can of course release the narrator from any sense of moral responsibility to the individual, but it is also reminiscent of the way in which, when the metaphysical meaning takes over, the actions or sufferings of an exemplary individual - a legendary hero, a saint or Christ - can become the embodiment of the experience of all.

The second piece of music which Tournier mentions as influencing the genesis of his novel is Bach's *The Art of Fugue*. Fugue as a musical form implies a play of identity and repetition: a single theme, with perhaps a second or counter-theme, keeps returning in different voices, at different pitches, in different combinatory patterns. Tiffauges evokes in passing this image of counterpoint, when he makes the acquaintance of the schoolgirl Martine: 'Quand elle m'a dit qu'elle avait trois soeurs, j'ai tressailli de curiosité. Comme je voudrais connaître ces autres versions de Martine - à quatre ans, à neuf ans, à seize ans - comme un thème musical repris par des instruments et à des octaves différents! Je retrouve là mon étrange incapacité à m'enfermer dans une individualité, mon irrépressible inclination à rechercher, à partir d'une formule unique, des variations, une répétition sans monotonie'(182-83). We are thus back with the idea of the multi-tracked voice, of each voice being not a unique utterance, but taking its significance from its place in a sequence of exchanging and interchanging voices.

The fugal principle might be seen as operating on a structural level too, in the thematic organisation of the novel. It is possible to see the novel as constructed around two related themes, that of the ogre (announced at the start) and that of 'la phorie', the act of carrying (introduced soon after), both implicit in the title, and each represented, developed and commented on at regular intervals throughout the text, in a dynamic combinatory dialogue. In formal fugue, the fugal subject can occur in inversion, so that for instance an ascending motif becomes a descending one, and this notion of inversion is of course strongly developed in the novel, with both figures, the giant and the act of 'phorie', appearing in a variety of benign and malign manifestations. Another possible variant is that the fugue subject can be heard 'cancrizans', or backwards, a device which has become even more frequent in serial music by twentieth-century composers since Schoenberg. There is indeed a principle of reversal as well as inversion in the counterpoint of the novel, with a regressive movement back to mythic origins which finally takes precedence over the simultaneous forward movement of historical time.[22]

Les Météores (1975)

It is suggested above that, in terms of narrative mode, *Le Roi des aulnes* has a tripartite structure, with the third section functioning as a synthesis of the first two. A similar structure, operating on various levels, can be detected in *Les Météores*. The twenty-two chapters of *Les Météores* can be divided into three distinct sequences of seven chapters each, plus a final concluding chapter.

The first sequence, which we shall call sequence A, starts in the first chapter and continues in Chapters 3, 6, 8, 10, 12 and 14. It offers an account of the life from earliest childhood to young manhood of the identical twins Paul and Jean Surin and of the very particular psychological bond between them which gives them the sense of a single shared identity (Jean-Paul). This sequence ends at the point at which Jean, less and less content within the closed binary cell of twin bonding which his brother is intent on preserving, finally leaves the family home on an odyssey that will take him round the world. The house on the Breton coast, La Cassine, where 'Jean-Paul' grows up with an unnumbered clutch of elder brothers and sisters, is presided over by their imperturbable and prolifically fertile mother, Maria-Barbara. This household is just one element of a complex small community, Les Pierres Sonnantes, which also comprises the family textile factory and an institution for handicapped and deformed children run by nuns. The twins' father, Edouard Surin, owns the factory but spends a good deal of time living a pseudo-bachelor life in Paris, with his mistress Florence, a nightclub singer.

A second, interwoven sequence (sequence B, covering Chapters 2, 4, 5, 7, 9, 11 and 13) concerns Alexandre, Edouard's brother (and thus the twins' uncle). Alexandre is regarded, both by Edouard and by his other brother Gustave and their families, as a black sheep, because of both his open homosexuality and his reluctance to pursue a career. When, however, Gustave dies unexpectedly, Alexandre is persuaded to take on the management of his major refuse-disposal business. This sequence of chapters recounts Alexandre's life from this point on, depicting his reaction to his newly inherited empire of refuse dumps and his adventures as a gay hunter-seducer, cruising for partners until his death in a knife-fight in the dangerous dockside quarter of Casablanca.

The third sequence (C), running uninterruptedly from Chapter 15 to Chapter 21 inclusive, follows Paul's journey round the world in the footsteps of his errant twin, from Venice (Chapter 15) to Tunisia (Chapter 16), then to Iceland (Chapter 17), Japan (Chapter 18) and Canada (Chapters 19-20), ending with his return to Europe to keep a rendez-vous in Berlin (Chapter 21).[23] His arrival there coincides with the erection of the Berlin Wall, and he barely survives a last-minute attempt to escape from East to West Berlin via a precarious underground tunnel, in which his body is crushed and mutilated. In the concluding chapter of the novel he has returned to the family home in Brittany, where he interprets the mutilation and its effects as opening up to him a new and enriched mode of being in the world.[24]

Sequences A and B are thus intertwined and presented in parallel, despite the narrative links between them being relatively weak: while they deal with branches of the same family, these have little or no contact with each other (it is not until the final chapter of sequence B, Chapter 13, that Alexandre sees the twins in Casablanca, and they are apparently unaware of his presence). It is worth noting that sequence A and sequence B are not presented entirely in symmetrical alternation. Because both Chapters 4 and 5 are devoted to Alexandre, sequence A both begins (Chapter 1) and ends (Chapter 14) the intertwined series, and thus the twins' story encloses that of their uncle, which starts in Chapter 2 and ends in Chapter 13. There are a number of possible reasons for this distribution. Since the whole final section of the novel is concerned with the abandoned twin's pursuit of his brother, Tournier needs to maintain the twins, and notably Paul, as the clear central focus of the novel. It is thus appropriate that the opening chapter, 'Les Pierres Sonnantes', should concern them and their origins, in symmetry to the closing chapter 'L'âme déployée', which presents Paul's return to Les Pierres Sonnantes and his intuition that the space of his missing arm and leg makes possible the reincorporation of his absent twin within himself. It is also appropriate that the final chapter of sequence A, Chapter 14, which recounts the splitting apart of the twins and Jean's flight, should precede without interruption the entry into sequence C, Paul's pursuit, so that narrative momentum at this crucial pivotal point is not lost. Finally, the enclosure of Alexandre's story by that of the twins helps to keep it within the bounds from which it is always threatening to break, given the dynamism and prestige of the portrait of this flamboyant, astute and cynical character developed in sequence B.[25]

Sequence C is by contrast a single linear movement leading toward the metaphysical conclusion, and the implication is that, on an ideological if not on a purely narrative level, it represents a synthesis of the two preceding strands. The thesis of the condition of twinship, *la gémellité*, presented in sequence A, is placed in opposition to and in dialogue with the antithetical experience of the (homosexual) non-twin, the *sans-pareil*, as recounted in sequence B. The standard majority experience, that of the heterosexual non-twin, is exemplified in Edouard, whose life can be seen as a kind of 'control' in this socio-personal investigation, a conventional norm against which the specificity of the other, non-standard conditions can be measured. Once all of these experiences (twin/non-twin, homosexual/heterosexual) have been followed through to their breaking-point, then the final sequence C, which concerns Paul's subsequent life as a twin bereft of his partner (*jumeau déparié*) can be read as a synthesis of these antithetical elements of twinship and singularity leading to possibilities and insights not available to either.

Within this pattern of chapter sequences it is also instructive to examine the interplay of narrative voices. Most of the novel is recounted by one or other of the participants: Tournier retains the compound of third-person and first-person narrative found in his two previous novels. The mix has become more complex, however: whereas previously the first-person narrative derived from a single all-pervasive viewpoint - Robinson, Tiffauges - here it is shared by six characters. Of these, three are central to the plot (Paul, Jean, Alexandre), while the others are secondary characters, whose voices are heard in one chapter only (Sophie in Chapter 14, Hamida in Chapter 16, Shonïn in Chapter 18).[26] Alexandre is sole narrator of his own life throughout sequence B. It is only in the last few pages of this sequence, in Chapter 13 after Alexandre's death, that Paul takes over the narrative, to react to this death, and to reflect on the might-have-beens of his relationship with both uncle and father. It is thus in part because Alexandre wholly controls the telling of his own story, with an incisively and often aggressively analytic tone, that he acquires such prestige in the narrative. By contrast, Edouard is allowed no share of narrative voice; his story is told partly by Paul, but mostly by an impersonal narrative voice in Chapters 1, 10 and 12, in an analysis which stresses his good-natured weakness, his capacity for self-delusion, his seemingly inevitable destiny as the plaything of circumstances which conspire to frustrate his aspirations to heroism or even dignity.

Besides assuming responsibility for Edouard's story, the impersonal narrative voice establishes the historical framework of the narrative, providing authoritative background information on, for example, the early months of the Occupation in France (Chapter 12) and the measures taken during the construction of the Berlin Wall (Chapter 21). At the opening of the text it sets down the precise date and time, given in the playful opening paragraph, as the starting point of the chronology of the narrative - 25th September 1937, 17h19. What it describes here - thereby fulfilling the expectations of the title -is a meteorological phenomenon, the arrival and effects of a wind blowing from the Atlantic.[27] The narrative voice of the opening sentences thus establishes the intersection of chronology and meteorology which is to be one of the novel's main themes.[28] Besides this opening chapter of sequence A, the only subsequent chapter which is entirely narrated by this impersonal voice is Chapter 21, the final chapter of sequence C, entitled 'Les emmurés de Berlin'. The narrative voice thus frames the three-sequence structure, encouraging us to see the final Chapter 22 as the potential start of a new sequence which moves beyond the scope of the narrative: the shift from closure, implicit in the three-sequence x seven-chapter structure and in its implied thesis-antithesis-synthesis, to a new openness is itself conveyed by the contrasting titles of the last two chapters, 'Les emmurés de Berlin' and 'L'âme déployée'. In a Hegelian dialectic, the synthesis, once established, becomes a new thesis, and thus the potential starting point for a fresh cycle of change.

The only protagonist's voice to be heard with regularity throughout the text is that of Paul, and especially so, of course, in sequence C, in which he narrates all or part of every chapter except the last (Berlin) chapter of the sequence. In his first intervention as narrative voice in sequence A, in Chapter 3 (70 ff.), it is quickly made clear that Paul's narrative here is a retrospective one, written some time after his accident in the Berlin tunnel. Within a few pages he refers to 'cette [...] blessure [...] me clouant sur cette chaise longue, face à la baie de l'Arguenon' (75) - a reference to his situation in the final chapter of the novel. Further references to his double amputation and to the chaise longue in Chapter 6 (180,184) confirm this retrospection.

The alternating - one is tempted to say competing - narrative of Alexandre in sequence B is organised on a quite different principle. At the start (Chapter 2) he recounts and reflects on a sudden change that has taken place in his life - his inheritance of the SEDOMU refuse-disposal empire - just as Tiffauges reflects at the start of *Le Roi des aulnes* on the ending of his affair with Rachel and his discovery of his *écriture sinistre*. For Alexandre as for Tiffauges, this initial rite of passage (the 'sacre' of the chapter heading) stimulates him to evoke at some length his experiences at boarding school, in which he traces the origins of his personal and sexual orientation. Once this overture to his story has been played, however, Alexandre's narrative unambiguously takes the form of a diary recording events, reflections on them and elements of his philosophy of life, comparable, in fact, to Tiffauges's 'Ecrits sinistres' and to Robinson's 'logbook'. From the second chapter of his sequence (Chapter 4) onwards, his writing is close to the events he records. He notes in the present tense the sounds he can hear from his newly rented room in the Hotel Terminus (86), and his subsequent attraction to and pursuit of first Eustache and then Daniel are recorded stage by stage, as the chase develops. This cumulative autobiographical record comes to an end, logically enough, with the final entry before he leaves his hotel room in Casablanca on his last fatal excursion.

In this way, Tournier has skilfully differentiated the narratives of Paul and Alexandre in mode as well as in substance, and one can conclude also that the greater immediacy of Alexandre's mode of narrative is another factor in its considerable impact on the reader. The question becomes more complex, however, when a similar scrutiny is made of the status of Jean's narrative voice in sequence A. Jean's voice first intervenes in Chapter 6 (176 ff.) with a commentary on what Paul has just written regarding Jean's compulsion to run across the wet beach at low tide. Jean's first words are 'Sur ce point au moins,

Paul n'est jamais allé au fond des choses'. His next contribution (273 ff.) similarly takes issue with Paul on the part played by the turbulent factory-girl Denise Malacanthe in Jean's emotional life. The emergence of Jean's voice in the text proffering a discourse independent of that of Paul, the self-appointed keeper of the indissoluble twin-cell, itself dramatises the coming scission. The more complex question, however, is to determine when, with respect to the time-frame of the narrative, this critical discourse is produced. If, as has been shown, Paul's narrative is retrospective, then so must be Jean's commentaries on it. If this is accepted, then logically the passages expressing in the present tense his frustration and anger at being locked within the twin cell with Paul as his jailer ('La prison, oui, l'esclavage gémellaire! Paul s'accommode de notre couple, parce que c'est toujours lui qui mène la danse. C'est lui le maître' (273)) would have to be taken as a vivid reliving of the emotions he had experienced at that point. This precarious hypothesis collapses, however, when we reach Chapter 14, 'La malencontre', the last chapter of sequence A, which recounts the crisis precipitated by the arrival of Jean's fiancée Sophie at La Cassine. While Paul's narrative continues for the moment firmly in retrospective mode ('*Pour autant que mes souvenirs ne me trahissent pas*, Sophie n'était pas exceptionnellement jolie [...]' (391 - my italics)), Jean's is written *in medias res*, as he contemplates his next move: 'Si Paul s'imagine que tout va rentrer dans l'ancien ordre après le départ de Sophie, c'est que son obsession gémellaire a oblitéré certaines cases de son cerveau!' (417); 'Je serais allé à Venise avec Sophie. J'irai à Venise sans elle'(418). As though by force of attraction, Paul's final entry in this chapter is pulled into the same time-frame: 'Petit Jean je sais où tu es! [...] *A l'heure où j'écris ces lignes*, tu descends de ton train à la Stazione Santa Lucia'(423 - my italics). This chapter stands therefore as a crisis not only in the plot but also in the collision of two incompatible modes of narration, the immediate and the retrospective. It can now be seen that this schism in narrative mode had been prepared, by the interpolation of Jean's more immediate narration into Paul's would-be monolithic retrospective account. Following this crisis chapter, Paul's writing moves into the mode announced by a phrase such as 'à l'heure où j'écris ces lignes', that is, into the diary-form present tense which has hitherto largely been the prerogative of Alexandre's narrative. Paul's narrative in the following Chapter 15, the first of sequence C, begins: 'Lorsque j'ai atterri ce matin à l'aéroport Marco Polo [...]'(424). As Alexandre's traveller's tale falls silent at his death, Paul's begins. To borrow the terms Paul learns from the Venetian meteorologist Giuseppe Colombo, he falls from the calm stratosphere of retrospective contemplation into the troposphere - the 'sphère des troubles' (447) - of immediate events, recorded in all their day-to-day unpredictability. He falls, in short, into time.[29] The twin, bereft of his partner ('déparié'), senses that he is now obliged to embark on an 'apprentissage de la vie sans-pareil' (420), and one immediately apparent feature of this apprenticeship is that he inherits from his 'sans-pareil' uncle the restless urge to travel and the narrative mode appropriate to translate this journey into words. This journey and this mode of narrative will carry him forward until the story he tells finally reaches the vantage point in time, as he lies on the chaise longue overlooking the bay, from which he had given us his retrospective account of the twin-cell phase. In other words, the narrated time of Paul's story reaches the point of narration of his sequence A account, and the circle of his narrative is complete. On a literal level Paul, after the abrupt discontinuities of his journey round the world, has returned to his origins, in the house in Brittany. The sense of apotheosis which he conveys at the end is reinforced also by this metaphorical 'homecoming' in narrative mode, by the sense in which his narrative regains, after a lapse into immediacy, the vantage-point from which he can again command a confident overview of his life.

The choice and deployment of narrative modes in *Les Météores* is thus governed less by the demands of internal coherence, which is not always respected, than by a powerful overarching structural design which holds sway, to a surprising degree, on both a thematic and a technical level. This formidable narrative machine allows the participating voices only a limited autonomy and blurs the relationship between them, subordinating them to its own grand design.

Le Coq de bruyère (1978)

This collection of fourteen short fictions (of which the last, 'Le Fétichiste', is actually a script of a play for one character) has no explicit overall structure.[30] The items are arranged to move, broadly, from shorter to longer texts, and from *contes* drawing on myth and fairy-tale to more realistic *nouvelles* with a contemporary setting.

Some thematic groupings can be discerned. The first three stories offer revised views of the archetypes of Adam and Eve, Robinson Crusoe and Father Christmas. The next three, 'Amandine ou les deux jardins', 'La fugue du petit Poucet' and 'Tupik', all focus on children growing up in a restrictive adult environment. In 'Que ma joie demeure' and 'Le Nain rouge' the protagonist becomes a clown, and finds a way of expressing his true nature. In 'Tristan Vox' and 'Les Suaires de Véronique' a man's life is taken over by the power of his own image: in the first, the married life of a radio personality is blighted by the charismatic presence of his seemingly distinct personality as a radio voice, while in the second, the avant-garde photographer Véronique literally corrodes the body of her young lover in her dangerous experiments to produce photographic images of him by direct bodily contact.[31] 'La jeune fille et la mort', the tale of a young woman's obsessive death-wish, develops further the link between death and eroticism suggested in 'Véronique', and the notion of a final 'transfiguration' (when her suicidal intent is overtaken by a heart-attack) comparable to that of Raphaël Bidoche in 'Que ma joie demeure'. The final three pieces, 'Le Coq de bruyère', 'L'aire du Muguet' and 'Le Fétichiste', are all linked by the theme of men seeking love and sexual fulfilment outside the area (literal or metaphorical) prescribed for them: the adulterous philanderer, the lorry-driver venturing off the motorway into confusing countryside lanes, the young man obsessed with lingerie. All these vagaries are cruelly punished.

Despite these elements of thematic linking and grouping, the diversity and relative discontinuity of this collection is in sharp contrast to the monumentally ordered structures of the three novels which precede it, and the book thus represents a different strand of Tournier's creativity. It is however a feature of his subsequent extended fictions - *Gaspard, Melchior & Balthazar*, *La Goutte d'or* and *Le Médianoche amoureux* - that Tournier will seek to reconcile the two patterns, of monolithic novel and loose-knit anthology, by placing short, autonomous tales within a controlling overall structure which sharpens their contextual significance.

Gaspard, Melchior & Balthazar (1980)

Gaspard, Melchior & Balthazar (hereafter referred to simply as *Gaspard*) represents a further stage in the movement towards a more dispersed form of novel structure. Compared to the integrated, linear plot development of Tournier's first two novels, *Les Météores* had already presented a more complex and open construction. This could be summed up as having two phases: an initial antiphonal section of two intertwined sequences recounting different lives over the same period of time, followed by a second section (sequence C plus epilogue) which both carries the story forward chronologically and represents a synthesis and apparent resolution of the ideological issues raised in the first two.

These two phases are present also in *Gaspard*. In the logic of the story of the Magi, this novel starts with a series of three narratives, one for each Wise Man, covering his previous life and his journey. The independent stories of the Magi converge as they meet each other, just as, in *Les Météores*, the paths of Alexandre and the twins cross in Casablanca. The parallel stories merge and are carried forward to the Nativity and beyond, and the final extended story of the apocryphal fourth Wise Man, Taor, can be read as an ideological resolution to the whole text. In this respect, then, there is a very broad likeness in structure between this novel and its predecessor. The fragmentation of the structure, however, goes much further since between the stories of the third and fourth Wise Men three further sections are interpolated: the *conte* entitled 'Barbedor', the story of Herod, and the reflections of the Ox and the Ass. This is an amplification of the minor role of subordinate narrators (Sophie, Hamida, Shonïn) in *Les Météores*. The first three sections, related by the Magi, are consistent in tone and complementary in their perspective, as each King pursues his particular dream of human fulfilment, in love, in artistic creation or in the exercise of power. The second three sections are, by contrast, quite disparate in tone and content. 'Barbedor', a tale told by Herod's court storyteller, is reminiscent of the world of the *Arabian Nights* and in its timelessness is quite independent of the Nativity chronology. Herod's narrative is by contrast an historical account of his ruthless dealings to ensure his own political survival, including the elimination of his entire family. In the section which follows, the Ass's story offers an oblique angle of vision on the Nativity itself, combining whimsicality with a naïve sense of wonder. This sixth, Nativity chapter can be seen as a synthesis of, on the one hand, the fairy-tale aspect of Barbedor and, on the other, the brutality which pervades Herod's narrative and which is familiar to the donkey and all his kind. This sequence of sections, each with a distinctive narrative tone, thus prepares and presents the Nativity as a junction of the most wondrous magic and the most sordid reality. The final section, the story of Taor, synthesises elements of both previous sequences (the Magi stories and the Herod/Nativity stories). Within the account of the fourth Wise Man is found the closure of the narratives of the first three, as they tell their fellow pilgrim of what they have seen, and how each of them has found the particular revelation he sought. In addition, Taor's story brings together once more the elements of fairy-tale wonder and brutal cruelty in a still more dramatic juxtaposition, in the pivotal episode when the fabulous feast offered by Taor to the children of Bethlehem coincides with the massacre of baby boys by Herod's men.

The relationship of the sections can be expressed in another way. In the sequence of the narratives of the three Wise Men, each is darker than the last. While Gaspard's choice of a fair-skinned blonde girl as his favourite causes jealousy, his absolute authority is never questioned, and no bloodshed results. Balthazar's love for his museum, however, sparks off a dangerous revolt of iconoclasts, in which the collection is destroyed and its guardians killed. Balthazar's authority is brought into question, if not actually threatened, by this movement of religious fanaticism. Prince Melchior, for his part, is a fugitive, pursued by his unscrupulous uncle who has seized the throne from him by treachery, abduction and murder. These three stories thus plot a progression from effortless, unthreatened autocracy to brutal civil strife. Sections four and five (Barbedor and Herod) can be inscribed at opposite ends of this spectrum: King Nabounassar, in 'Barbedor', lives in a world of fable where (even more than in Gaspard's Méroé) the monarch is universally beloved, and political issues, while present, are remote, save for the question of the succession to the throne. Herod's story is, in contrast, a saga of treachery and violence which outweighs even Melchior's experiences. These five stories thus establish a range of narratives focusing on power and its limits. At one extreme, the tale of *Barbedor* told by the skilled storyteller at Herod's behest finds favour because it encapsulates the wish-fulfilment dream of the sovereign - the absolute love and allegiance of his subjects retained without effort, and a fantasised solution to the problem of a successor: the next king is to be himself, reborn to a new life and a new reign. At the other extreme is the nightmare of retaining power in a historically real, turbulent situation, where the cost of maintaining the authority which can ensure peace and stability for the populace is internecine strife in the ruling family, including the death of all heirs, and the devastation of the monarch's own life. The Nativity, recounted through the eyes and voices of the most powerless witnesses of all, the animals, brings its response to this insistent question about the ends and means of power: the King of Kings has put off his power to become a tiny baby, while Gabriel promises an end to animal sacrifice, heals the donkey's wound and foretells the glorious moment when an ass will bear Jesus into Jerusalem on Palm Sunday.

The story of Taor is the only one told by an impersonal narrator, and it thus acquires an air of independent authority in relation to the individual voices which have each told their own story in preceding sections. It recapitulates the experience of, and debate about, power implicit in the text so far. Taor's initial existence in his kingdom of Mangalore is akin to the effortless self-indulgence of Barbedor or Gaspard, and his quest - for the recipe for Turkish delight - is of a fairy-tale frivolity. The nearer he approaches his destination, however, the more he suffers difficulties and losses, and the enterprise loses all its air of insouciant hedonism. The conjunction of the feast and the Massacre of the Innocents ends this self-centred 'Age du sucre', and he enters the 'Enfer du sel' in which, divested of all wealth and status, he will surrender himself as a prisoner in the salt mines in place of a father of four children condemned for debt. The divine food of the first Eucharist, vouchsafed to him at the end, is the reward for this absolute renunciation of power.

Gilles & Jeanne (1983)

The 'récit' *Gilles & Jeanne*, which associates the story of the mass murderer Gilles de Rais with that of his contemporary Joan of Arc, is much shorter than the fictions so far discussed, and it is also less formally structured. It is made up of twenty-seven unnumbered sections, and the voice throughout is that of a conventional third-person narrator. Apart from a retrospective survey of Gilles's early years in section 2, the narrative is broadly chronological.

Nevertheless, within this apparently straightforward linear movement it is possible to identify a characteristic, if quite sketchy, architecture. The twenty-seven sections suggest a division into three sequences of nine sections each, and the shape of the text does support this grouping. The first nine sections could be called the Jeanne sequence, covering Gilles's meeting with Jeanne, his life at her side, and his response to her terrible death. The second sequence (sections 10-18) is dominated by the Renaissance alchemist Prelati, brought back from Florence by Gilles's confessor Blanchet who is in despair at his patron's state of mind and soul. The third sequence (sections 19-27) - let us call it the Judgment sequence - succinctly relates Gilles's trial and death.

Some symmetry can be seen in the structure of the first two sequences. In section 1, Gilles meets Jeanne, an encounter which founds the title and the central dialectic of the text. In section 10, the first of the Prelati sequence, Blanchet meets Prelati in Florence. These two encounters are complementary. Jeanne, at this stage, epitomises 'la sainteté', while Gilles will plunge into crime and degradation. Similarly, the abbé Blanchet's orthodox piety contrasts with the renegade priest Prelati's enthusiasm for the black arts. Jeanne and Gilles discuss the 'voices' which have whispered to them, voices of holy exhortation or of temptation respectively: Blanchet and Prelati are themselves the voices which, in the second sequence, vie for Gilles's allegiance to orthodox belief or to devil-worship.

The central (fifth) section in each of the first two sequences presents a crucial turning-point: the death of Jeanne in section 5, and the first meeting of Gilles and Prelati in section 14. Similar parallels can be suggested for the last three sections in the Jeanne and Prelati sequences. Section 7 describes Gilles's cult of the Holy Innocents (the victims of the Massacre of the Innocents), for whom he builds a chapel. He recruits choirboys for its liturgy, as much for their physical beauty as for their voices. In section 16, Prelati sees Gilles grasping a boy in a menacing embrace, surrounded by other mesmerised children 'dans un silence de mort' (105). These sections are thus linked both by paedophile desire and by murderous intent. Section 8 describes how the rumours of Gilles's preying on young children circulate, and ultimately find their way into legend, in the story of Tom Thumb and the ogre. In section 17, the equivalent chapter in the Prelati sequence, the Italian predicts the future canonisation of Jeanne. Both chapters thus speak of posterity and the way in which Gilles and Jeanne respectively will be accorded a kind of immortality, diabolical or saintly. The final section in each sequence is, naturally, transitional: in section 9, Blanchet is sent to Florence, thus preparing the Prelati sequence, while in section 18, Gilles is arrested as a prelude to his judgment.

The final Judgment sequence is, as we have come to expect from Tournier's structures, in some sense a synthesis. In its first section (section 19) the prosecutors reflect gloomily on the link that is bound to be made between the fate of Gilles and that of Jeanne: this bond was of course stressed in the Jeanne sequence, leading up to Gilles's reiteration of Jeanne's dying cries of 'Jésus!' in section 9. In section 26, the penultimate section of the *récit*, Prelati gives evidence to the court. The final Judgment sequence thus not only sums up what has gone before by revealing in retrospect the full truth about Gilles's abuse and massacre of children: it is also framed by references back to the two dominant phases of influence in his life, Jeanne and Prelati.

What we find in *Gilles & Jeanne* overall is a marked shift to a simpler style and a less visible formal structure. Closer examination suggests, however, that many of the same principles of fiction-building are being used, behind a more artless facade, and that these principles continue to be concerned with the rhythms of opposition and convergence in the ideology of the text.

La Goutte d'or (1986)

While *La Goutte d'or* is longer than *Gilles & Jeanne*, it is similar in structure. It also is divided into a large number of unnumbered sections - twenty-six, in fact. Here again, as in *Gilles*, this seemingly informal distribution of material is symmetrically planned. The book can be partitioned into two halves. The first thirteen sections tell of the Berber boy Idriss's decision to travel from his home in Algeria to Paris, and of his journey there. The second half (sections 14-26) is set entirely in Paris, and deals with his encounters with Western urban culture. Each half contains one section which consists wholly of an Oriental *conte* on the lines of 'Barbedor' in *Gaspard*. The fourth section, 'Barberousse ou Le portrait du roi', recounts how Barbarossa, pirate turned king, is ashamed of his red hair and beard until a Scandinavian tapestry-maker depicts it in the glorious autumn colours of a European forest. The tale of the 'Reine blonde' which forms the penultimate section of the book (section 25) is also concerned with a monarch's hair. It tells how the blonde hair of the queen in question is considered a mark of hereditary disgrace, and how the portrait of this beautiful but unhappy woman mesmerises and destroys all those who gaze on it, until a young man learns how to decompose it into its constituent lines, each the inscription of a proverb in Arabic script, and thereby neutralise its maleficent power. These two interpolated stories, one placed near the beginning of the first (journey) sequence, the other near the end of the second (Paris) sequence, are evidently designed to counterbalance each other. Each is concerned with cultural prejudice directed at a physical characteristic (hair) and with the role of the artistic image and its perception in dealing with the resulting humiliation and pain. These similarities encourage the reader to compare them, and at this point significant differences emerge. 'Barberousse' celebrates the beneficent prestige of the image: the king's portrait is a catalyst to his passage to a new sovereign status, it enables him to value himself as he is and it founds a new, confident sense of identity.[32] 'La Reine blonde', in contrast, proclaims the maleficent tyranny of the image, until it can be decomposed by language.

This polarity, distilled in the two interpolated stories, underlies the two halves of the book. The fifteen-year-old shepherd boy Idriss is photographed by a blonde Frenchwoman passing through in a jeep, and his subsequent obsession with the idea of finding this photograph leads him to leave his home to travel to Paris. Idriss, like Barbarossa, looks for an image which will confirm his status and his acceptance in the world at large. This dream of salvation through the image is however betrayed at every turn. The mocking delivery-man Salah Brahim brings him a picture of a donkey in place of the promised photo; an emotionally disturbed bereaved mother, Lala Ramirez, shows him the photo on her son Ismaïl's tomb, and tries to cajole Idriss into replacing him and taking on his identity in her life. Even the photomat machine delivers photos of someone quite different, which are then attached to Idriss's passport. His identity and status, far from being confirmed or reinforced, are distorted and undermined by these images. These attacks on his identity move progressively from the farcical to the serious. The donkey postcard merely injures his self-esteem by making him an object of fun. Lala Ramirez, however, seeks to erase his real identity and to make him someone else's ghost, while the false passport pictures, accepted without comment by the immigration officer, seem to deny him any specific identity at all. In the 'regard de l'autre' he is always something or someone else, caricature or stranger, never himself.

The Parisian sequence of the second half explores the insidious exploitative power of the image in Western life. In the culture of visual allure Idriss is a victim in two senses, as consumer mesmerised by shop-window or peep-show, and increasingly as an accessory to the marketing industry, recruited as an extra for TV adverts or as a model for department-store display dummies. Here again, the sequence of sections is structured to show the increasing threat to Idriss's integrity and even to his person. The TV producer, Achille Mage, uses him as an ingredient in a colonialist exotic fantasy, turning him from a person into a mere cultural signifier. The camel, who serves the same purpose and thus mirrors Idriss's own situation, is destined for the abattoir, until Idriss takes it to the zoo instead.[33] The analogy with the fauna of Africa is continued in the figure of the 'femme-lionne' who writhes and snarls in the peep-show. The climax to this theme of imprisonment and transformation into an object of display is reached in section 22, describing how a mould is made of Idriss's body in order to manufacture polyester shop dummies from it. Naked like the woman, chosen like her for his 'exotic' appearance, he is placed in a tank which is then filled with a glutinous liquid. The procedure is not without its danger, and he loses his eyebrows and eyelashes in the process. The shop-manager then suggests employing him to stand motionless in the window alongside the dummies, made up like them, making a few jerky gestures to attract passers-by, but forbidden to blink. Idriss draws back from this threat of ultimate robot-like enslavement. While the 'journey' sequence deals with the more abstract question of identity and self-image, in the Paris sequence it is the body itself which is in question, and the peril is corporal as well as spiritual.

The final four sections make up the response to and resolution of this crisis. 'La Reine blonde' is a parable both of the devastating power of the image and of its antidote. It is central to the teaching of the master calligrapher Abd Al Ghafari, and encapsulates his lessons of detachment, self-discipline and adherence to timeless wisdom. The arabesques of traditional Arab calligraphy represent the presence of the desert, the infinite, 'l'espace pur'(202). This pure space of sign unlocks the imprisoning space of the enslaving image. When Idriss, armed with his pneumatic drill, breaks through the tarmac surface of Paris, he has rediscovered this liberating space in his own culture. This gesture represents an imaginary realisation of a famous slogan of May 1968: 'Sous les pavés, la plage.'[34]

This evocation of the desert creates an obvious sense of symmetry with the opening of the book, and thereby a sense of formal closure. This is reinforced by the similarly symmetrical evocation of two formidable women performers: the belly-dancer Zett Zobeida and the Egyptian singer Oum Kalsoum. The punning and enigmatic song which surrounds Zett Zobeida's performance suggests that the dancing wings of the butterfly ('libellule') can become a lampoon ('libelle') to outwit death, just as the chirping of the crickets ('criquet') becomes a text ('écrit') revealing the secret of life. This refrain, recalled at intervals throughout the book, anticipates the final triumph of the sign over the life-threatening image, just as the song of Oum Kalsoum can bring a miracle of colour into the life of the blind man listening to her. The closure, and symmetry of beginning and end, is clinched by the 'goutte d'or' of the title, a perfectly formed jewel worn by the dancer and found by Idriss after her performance. He loses it to a platinum-blonde prostitute in Marseilles, in a symbolic surrender of his childhood and his cultural independence, but will find it again in the final section, in the window of a prestigious jewellery shop in the Place Vendôme. In the vibration from his pneumatic drill, the window shatters, and the jewel becomes accessible again, as a symbol of his newly restored cultural identity.

One last thematic network woven into the structure of the novel deserves mention. The text offers an ongoing reflection on the use and abuse of representation, centring on four individuals whose names all begin with the same letter: Mogadem, Mustapha, Mage and Milan. The first two belong to the journey sequence, the second two to the Paris sequence, and here again symmetries can be perceived. Mustapha, 'artiste photographe'(82), persuades his tourist customers to stand in front of a painted backdrop striking heroic poses: he and Mage, each in their way, use the camera to encapsulate the stock-in-trade fantasies of their public. Mustapha stands Idriss in front of a 'fantaisiste' panorama representing Paris-by-night (87), just as Mage creates an equally strip-cartoon image of the Sahara for his viewers. They thus represent complementary aspects of the play of cultural stereotype between Europe and Africa. The other two, Mogadem and Milan, are contrasted rather than complementary. Mogadem, Idriss's uncle at Tabelbala, keeps a photo of himself as a soldier in the war, but he is superstitiously distrustful of the power of the uncontrolled image. Etienne Milan also looks back to an earlier period in his life, by collecting dummies from the 1960s which resemble the ten-year-old he then was. When he photographs the dummies arranged in a real setting, alongside real children, he is indulging in a perverse game with just that corrosive power of the image of which Mogadem warns Idriss. Mogadem asserts that men can lose their lives if they lose possession of their photograph; in Milan's photographs, the real world and real people lose their solidity and their status: 'C'est absolument la réalité sapée à sa base par l'image'(181). This 'trompe-l'oeil' mixture of the real and the fabricated is a 'mise en abîme' of the novelist's own procedure. Oum Kalsoum, incorporated in the fiction, existed in real life, as Tournier's post-scriptum emphasises, and the figure of Etienne Milan has an appropriately ambiguous status, being a transparent encoding of the name and work of the artist Bernard Faucon (both surnames referring to birds of prey). By this device, as when Tiffauges meets Goering, the real is fictionalised, and the imagined draws sustenance from the life-blood of the real. A fundamental device especially of historical fiction, it is another aspect of the 'vampirism' of fiction which Tournier refers to in the title essay of *Le Vol du vampire*.

Le Médianoche amoureux (1989)

Le Médianoche amoureux is Tournier's second collection of short fictions, but unlike his first such anthology, *Le Coq de bruyère*, it has an explicit, if rather loose, framework which implies a certain unity and progression in the sequence of stories. *Le Coq de bruyère* took its title, in conventional fashion, from that of the longest story it contains. The title *Le Médianoche amoureux* is on the contrary an autonomous global title, and refers to the fictional frame established in the first section, 'Les amants taciturnes'. The lovers in question are Yves and Nadège, a married couple, from different backgrounds: she a shipowner's daughter, he a deep-sea fisherman. Since his redundancy, they have moved away from their common element, the sea, only to find that they have less and less to say to each other. They decide to hold a midnight feast to announce their separation to their friends, and at this dinner the guests recount the nineteen stories which follow. '[C]es récits étaient tantôt des contes inaugurés par le magique et traditionnel "il était une fois", tantôt des nouvelles racontées à la première personne, tranches de vie souvent saignantes et sordides'(46-47).[35] The stories have a cumulative influence on the couple: while the pessimistic and corrosive *nouvelles* tend to aggravate the divisions between them, the *contes* (especially the last one of all) serve to reinforce and renew their relationship. In accordance with the scheme implied here, the first ten (including the initial 'frame' story) of the component stories can broadly be seen as *nouvelles*, the second ten as *contes* - the reverse of the progression seen in *Le Coq de bruyère*.[36] The whole collection which makes up *Le Médianoche amoureux* is thus announced as a single systole-diastole movement of dissolution followed by regeneration, marked by the passage from one fictional genre to another.

Within the first sequence, that of the *nouvelles*, smaller groupings can be seen. The first three stories told, 'Les mousserons de la Toussaint', 'Théobald ou Le crime parfait' and 'Pyrotechnie ou La commémoration', set the negative, corrosive tone. In the first, a wealthy socialite, with two failed marriages behind him, rediscovers with pleasure the countryside of his youth in Burgundy, but his impulsive plan to buy and renovate the now dilapidated family home founders on his insensitivity and impatience, and a possible chance of renewal in his life is lost. The other two stories are both tales of carefully calculated revenge. In 'Théobald', a headmaster frames his promiscuous wife and her current lover for his own murder, because she is pregnant; in 'Pyrotechnie', a man violently avenges the public humiliation of his mother, thirty years before, at the hands of a local Resistance leader. The next three stories, 'Blandine ou La visite du père', 'Aventures africaines' and 'Lucie ou La femme sans ombre', all concern the repercussions of a sexual, or potentially sexual, relationship between an adult and a child. Blandine, pre-pubescent and coquettish, charms her way into the life of a bachelor photographer, only to be followed by her father who tries to exploit the relationship to obtain accommodation for his family in the bachelor's house. 'Aventures africaines' recounts two contrasting liaisons between the narrator and young boys in Morocco: the father of one wishes to encourage the adoption of his son by the affluent visitor who can offer him so much, but the narrator is still preoccupied by another youngster who, after sharing his hotel room, has robbed him and disappeared.[37] In 'Lucie', a man tells how, as a little boy, he was infatuated with his primary school teacher (the Lucie of the title) with whom he spent a night after his own mother had left home. The resulting scandal has led to her dismissal, and dried up the well-spring of emotional generosity in her which had enriched those around her. In all these stories, the adult-child relationship in question, which is presented as potentially life-enhancing for both, is not free to blossom, whether because of the adult's own perverse preference, or because others exploit or wilfully misinterpret it. The final three stories in the 'nouvelle' sequence, 'Écrire debout', 'L'auto fantôme' and 'La pitié dangereuse', are slight, pseudo-autobiographical anecdotes; the last of them describes how the attachment of a doctor to an incurably sick woman patient devastates his life. The sequence ends characteristically on a note of disaster and failure, and the thinness of these last three texts, after the richness of 'Lucie', seems calculated to testify to an exhaustion of the *nouvelle* genre and of the realist and quasi-autobiographical mode it takes here.

The first story of the second half, 'Le mendiant des étoiles', effects the transition from *nouvelle* to *conte*. The narrator and a friend on a visit to Calcutta witness the crowds of destitute people huddled under Howrah Bridge. They decide to return there on Christmas night to distribute fruit and delicacies, only to find that the intended recipients have gone, so that they must eat their feast themselves. The first, daytime visit to the colony of paupers is thus 'realist' - it is reminiscent of television or press reportage, and stimulates a corresponding gesture of practical charity. The second visit, by night, confounds this realist scenario. The protagonists, moving through the night towards the river, speak of ancient myths of the Underworld, of Homer, Rembrandt and Don Juan, but when they find themselves cheated of their role as heroic dispensers of largesse, they recall instead first a Charlie Chaplin film, then the Biblical parable of the rich man who sends his servants forth to compel the poor and the crippled to partake of the supper which his friends have disdained. These chastening comparisons lead them to a less noble definition of the role of the rich, as the 'prostitutes' of the poor. The disruption of realist logic and the infiltration of myth and intertext lead to a surprising and unforeseen insight, and the story ends with the poetic vision of a single beggar perched above them like a stylite on a pillar, 'sa main ouverte vers le ciel scintillant d'étoiles' (207).

The Christmas theme continues in the next two stories. In 'Un bébé sur la paille', the French President uses his Christmas broadcast to the nation to make a revolutionary suggestion: that expectant mothers should be able to choose any place they wish for the birth, so that babies are imprinted at birth with many different environments, and not invariably a hospital one. The first response he receives is from a certain Marie, who opts for a stable, with an ox and an ass standing by... This whimsical anachronism leads us smoothly into 'Le Roi mage Faust'. King Faust finds that all his erudition is of no avail in his effort to come to terms with the death of his son and heir; following the comet of his son's soul to Bethlehem, he finds the answer in the innocent, confident gaze of the Christ Child which envelops him. These three Christmas stories move the reader progressively away from the anguish of contemporary reportage and towards the spiritual solace of myth. With the withdrawal from realism, the stories generate positive, not negative conclusions. Just as King Faust is enabled to overcome bereavement, the child Angus in the next story derives strength and maturity from the utmost horror.[38] In a notional medieval Scottish setting, Angus is born into a noble family as the consequence of a savage rape by a brutal neighbouring seigneur, Tiphaine. From a young age, the boy, unaware of his father's identity, is charged by his maternal grandfather with the task of challenging and killing Tiphaine in single combat. This he achieves, but only because Tiphaine wishes at all costs to avoid hurting him. Tiphaine's life of brutality is by implication redeemed by his love for the child, and Angus's recognition of this love, and what he owes to it despite everything, assists him in his transition to manhood. Angus, heir to both estates, reconciles in his person father and grandfather, and the conflicting claims of two attachments which seemed irrevocably opposed. A similar emotional synthesis takes place in the next, infinitely gentler *conte* 'Pierrot ou Les secrets de la nuit', based on the traditional figures of the commedia dell'arte, and a work to which the author himself is particularly attached. Pierrot, the pale-faced village baker in white garb, is in love with the laundress Colombine; she however is seduced by the infinitely more colourful Arlequin, an ambulant house-painter, and they elope together, to Pierrot's despair. With the coming of the winter snow, however, Colombine's thoughts turn again to the village, and she returns to take refuge in Pierrot's warm bakehouse. Arlequin follows her, and the *conte* ends with all three sharing a brioche baked by Pierrot as a homage to Colombine, in the shape of her body. In the realist mode of the earlier *nouvelles* 'Théobald' and 'Lucie', a woman's sharing of intimacy with more than one partner leads to pain and disaster; in 'Pierrot', by contrast, Tournier can present as perfectly unproblematic the erotic 'ménage à trois' which is at once knowingly suggested in the concluding tableau and neatly defused by the 'faux-naïf' narrative style. What makes this *conte* a tour de force is that the final communion of the three protagonists is not just the reconciliation of two love-affairs, but a synthesis of many other polarities deftly established in the text between the nocturnal, moonstruck, domestic existence of the white-clad Pierrot, and the diurnal, sunny, nomadic nature of the gaudy Arlequin. Not least, while Arlequin is the persuasive talker, Pierrot expresses his feelings through writing, and Colombine is seduced by language, listening to one and reading the other. While spoken language is like Arlequin's paintwork (Tournier implies), dazzling but impermanent, the written word can be savoured and digested like Pierrot's nourishing bread sculpture.[39]

The ending of 'Pierrot' is an apotheosis of the senses - the sight of the golden loaf, its touch as Colombine clutches it to herself in delight, its smell and its taste. The four short 'legends' which follow each focus on different senses. 'La légende du pain' (following on naturally from 'Pierrot') offers a light-hearted account of the origins of the loaf (hard without and soft within) and the 'pain au chocolat' (soft without and hard within) as the reconciliation between rival traditions in neighbouring villages. The next two legends move from touch and taste to hearing and smell respectively. 'La légende de la musique et la danse' and 'La légende des parfums' recount in very similar terms the Fall of Man as a fall into creativity: when Adam and Eve forfeited the scents of Paradise and the music of the spheres, they set in motion the endless invention of new musics and new perfumes by their successors. The last of this group, 'La légende de la peinture', completes the spectrum of creativity by looking at the confection of visual delight. In a competition between two artists, a Chinese painter presents a delightful mural of an idyllic garden, while his Greek rival unveils, on the opposite wall, a huge mirror in whose reflection the whole company present appears to be standing in the painted garden: the Greek thereby wins the contest.[40] The stated moral of this tale is that art and communication are interdependent: the painter's work is enhanced by being projected to involve the public. This ties in with Tournier's insistence, noted at the start of this chapter, on the value of writing for publication, rather than simply as a private activity.

The final story, 'Les deux banquets ou La commémoration', pursues the idea of copy and duplication. In another competition, this time between two chefs, the second contender wins by exactly reproducing the exquisite meal presented by the first. The caliph who judges their efforts declares that by 'commemorating' the first meal, the second accorded to it a new and higher dimension, just as historical events are made significant by memory. It is through ritual repetition that the sacred finds expression.

This concluding notion of an added significance being achieved through repetition is apparent in the structure as well as the thematics of the text. The final story, 'Les deux banquets', ends with the same sentence as the opening frame-story 'Les amants taciturnes'. Nadège's invitation to Yves to be 'le grand prêtre de mes cuisines et le conservateur des rites culinaires et manducatoires qui confèrent au repas sa dimension spirituelle'(49) gains in importance when we realise, at the end of the collection, that she was in fact repeating and adopting the final words of the last story. Thus the fiction of 'Les deux banquets' infiltrates and transforms the life of the listeners: it is a metaphor for the power of imagination and language. Just as Colombine is moved by reading Pierrot's letter, and Pierrot by listening to Arlequin's song 'Au clair de la lune', leading to the communion of all three, Nadège and Yves are reconciled by the *contes* they hear.

The relationship of the two halves of the diptych structure, the *nouvelles* and the *contes*, is in the end quite a subtle one. To confront contemporary reality directly, without mediation, as in the *nouvelles*, is to register discord and failure. In the *contes*, by contrast, many of the same negative factors - loss, bitterness, revenge - are coped with by drawing on the resources of myth, poetry, legend and fantasy. The extent to which the second half operates as a kind of therapeutic reprise of the first can readily be seen by taking the three themes implicit in the title *Le Médianoche amoureux* - love, night and eating. In the first half, the different love affairs in 'Théobald', 'Lucie' and 'Blandine' all end in bitterness and separation, while the togetherness of the couple in 'La pitié dangereuse' is destructive of one of them. In the second half however, in 'Angus', 'Pierrot' and 'La légende du pain', rivalries are reconciled. This theme of the healing of division is extended from love to other areas: in the legends of music and perfume, the disaster of the Fall is compensated by the assertion of mankind's creative powers, while in each of the two final *contes*, the two contestants, the innovator and the 'copyist', are seen as mutually indispensable: the caliph offers both chefs employment. The other two aspects of the title, night and eating, are linked in the first of the guests' stories, in which the narrator drives at night from Paris to Burgundy to collect mushrooms, and to rekindle memories of his youth. He shares a mushroom omelette at dawn with a childhood friend but, once back in Paris, the only legacy he retains from this interlude is a few rotting mushrooms in a bag which he dumps in a rubbish bin. In 'Le mendiant des étoiles', the feast which the two friends plan by day to give to others, they consume themselves at night. In 'Pierrot' too the final scene is a 'médianoche', in which the food is, in symbolical form, Colombine's body: when she exclaims 'Comme je suis savoureuse! Vous aussi, mes chéris, goûtez, mangez la bonne Colombine! Mangez-moi!'(276), the subtext is both erotic and eucharistic. There is an echo here of Taor's arrival at night at Joseph of Arimathea's house (*GMB* 271): the Last Supper was also a 'médianoche amoureux'. This eucharistic aspect of the nocturnal feast is the therapeutic or redemptive response to an earlier *nouvelle*. In 'Lucie ou La femme sans ombre', the motherly teacher gives her body at night to comfort the distressed child[41] but in the contemporary world, and in the realist mode of narrative, such a gesture is ruthlessly punished. As the reformed 'femme sans ombre', she subsequently loses this capacity for tenderness, associated with inner darkness and night.[42] The final story, 'Les deux banquets ou La commémoration' adds to this theme of the shared feast the notion of ritualistic repetition, further reinforcing the link to eucharistic communion.

Despite its very different format, *Le Médianoche amoureux* distantly resembles *Vendredi* in structure, with its 'negative' first half and its regenerative second half. Following as it does, however, on Tournier's reflections in *La Goutte d'or* on image and sign, it is more self-consciously reflexive than his first novel. *Le Médianoche* is about the regeneration of language by dwelling in the house of words: 'la littérature comme panacée'(49). Apart from this characteristic defence of writing as a source of revitalisation, the twin figures of innovator and copyist in 'Les deux banquets' define the parameters and priorities of the writer's function, as Tournier sees it: whatever he finds that is new will only be given significance in the repetition of past creations, his own or others. The structural features of *Le Médianoche* underline the extent to which, as an earlier critic has remarked, 'Tournier's aesthetic endeavour is to reconcile imitation and repetition with originality and creation'.[43]

In the ordering of his fictions, then, Tournier can be seen to oscillate between two different structural principles: symmetry and synthesis.

In *Vendredi*, the Robinson hemicycle of the first half is structurally mirrored by the Vendredi hemicycle of the second half. This symmetrical pattern is significantly repeated in the two sequences (the journey, and Paris) of *La Goutte d'or*. The structural similarity between these two texts is quite appropriate, in that Tournier saw the later text (the non-European encountering European culture) as itself a symmetrical counterpart to *Vendredi* (the European encountering non-European culture).[44] This symmetry of form also characterises *Le Médianoche amoureux*, as we have just seen. In each case this binary form is found appropriate for a narrative which turns on a process of dismantling (first half) and reconstitution (second half). In *Vendredi* and *La Goutte d'or* what is being thus transformed is an identity (colonialist to pantheist, African village-boy to self-assured immigrant worker); in *Le Médianoche amoureux* it is at once a human relationship (the marriage of Yves and Nadège) and a narrative genre (the shift from *nouvelle* to *conte*).

In contrast, it is the ternary rhythm of thesis-antithesis-synthesis which most frequently prevails elsewhere. We have seen how, in different ways, it is apparent in the use of narrative modes (first-person/ third-person) in *Le Roi des aulnes*, fundamental in the three-sequence structure of *Les Météores*, and arguably implicit in the construction of both *Gaspard* and *Gilles & Jeanne*. While the symmetrical rhythm is of destruction-construction, the ternary structure suits a different form of creative evolution, whereby two apparently opposite elements combine. In *Les Météores* the separate perspectives of the twin and the non-twin merge (as in the Jumo binoculars) to compose the transcendent vision of the *jumeau déparié*. In *Gilles et Jeanne*, the destinies of the saint and the mass-murderer merge into the same pattern of ordeal and even salvation.

What is common to both forms is that they reflect a model of growth and development. After examining a number of the most important thematic strands in Tournier's fiction, we shall return to look specifically at an initiatic pattern of growth in these works, and the final chapter will consider the balance they suggest between static and dynamic elements.

Notes to Chapter One

¹ See also *PL* 11: 'Cette appartenance à la catégorie artisanale me paraît tout à fait honorable, et d'autant plus juste que l'écrivain non seulement écrit de ses mains, mais solitairement, chez lui; bref, il relève de la catégorie la plus pure du genre: c'est un artisan en chambre.'

² Referred to hereafter simply as *Vendredi*. It is not, however, to be confused with a simpler version for children which he published in 1971 under the title *Vendredi ou la vie sauvage*.

³ The precise relationship of Tournier's text to Defoe's has been much analysed. See in particular Lynn Salkin Sbiroli, *Michel Tournier: la séduction du jeu* (Geneva, Slatkine, 1987); Arlette Bouloumié, *Vendredi ou les limbes du Pacifique de Michel Tournier* (Paris, Gallimard, 1991), 100-11; Margaret-Anne Hutton, *Tournier: Vendredi ou les limbes du Pacifique* (Glasgow, University of Glasgow French and German Publications, 1992), 3-13; Margaret Sankey, 'Meaning through intertextuality: isomorphism of Defoe's *Robinson Crusoe* and Tournier's *Vendredi ou les limbes du Pacifique*', *Australian Journal of French Studies*, vol.18, no.1 (1981), 77-88; Anthony Purdy, 'From Defoe's *Crusoe* to Tournier's *Vendredi*: the metamorphosis of a myth', *Canadian Review of Comparative Literature*, 11 (1984), 216-35.

⁴ The term 'hero', which imputes some exemplary status to a main character, can justifiably be applied to Robinson, as to some other Tournier protagonists, in the light of the initiatic status of the narratives in question: see Chapter 7.

⁵ Tournier speaks elsewhere of Leonardo da Vinci and of the 'mystérieux sourire de son saint Jean-Baptiste levant l'index vers le ciel' (*VV* 68). This picture, in the Louvre, is often linked to that of the *Angel* (after Leonardo) in Basle, by art critics who have frequently commented on the hermaphroditic appearance of both figures. See for instance Cecil Gould, *Leonardo: the Artist and the Non-Artist* (Boston, New York Graphic Society, 1975), 122-27.

⁶ Successive critics of *Vendredi* have (rightly) become increasingly sceptical about the possibility of seeing a precise sequential pattern in the narrative corresponding to the tarot card series. Compare Salkin Sbiroli, *Michel Tournier: la séduction du jeu*; Bouloumié, *Vendredi de Michel Tournier*, 23-37; and Hutton, *Tournier: Vendredi*, 75-8.

⁷ Tournier in fact wrote this section last of all, after the rest of the novel (see Françoise Merllié, *Michel Tournier* (Paris, Belfond, 1988), 175). This implies that the prologue, with its tarot sequence, was drafted to reflect the subsequent narrative, not the other way round.

⁸ These zodiacal names attributed to them by Van Deyssel are not the original titles of the tarot cards, which have often been ignored or changed. For a full account of the original cards, their titles and meanings, see Salkin Sbiroli, *Michel Tournier: la séduction du jeu*.

[9] This kind of structural symmetry was, it seems, a deliberate objective, according to an interview Tournier gave in 1970: 'L'un des secrets consiste à écrire la fin du roman avant le début. [...] Je procède ensuite à un découpage rigoureux. Le livre se compose toujours de deux versants séparés au milieu par unè crise (la déclaration de guerre dans *Le Roi des aulnes*). Pour obtenir les correspondances, il suffit de travailler simultanément à chacun des versants.' See the interview with Jean-Louis de Rambures, 'Je suis comme la pie voleuse' (for which full details are given in the bibliography).

[10] Bouloumié and Hutton have shown that a case can be made for other possible structural divisions, into three or four sections, but for the purposes of this mainly thematic study I have found this circular model the most flexible and fruitful.

[11] As Colin Davis suggests, the word 'désormais' and the future tense used in the last paragraph of the novel - 'Désormais, lui dit Robinson, tu t'appelleras Jeudi' (*VLP* 254) - indicate the start of a new cycle of initiation and discovery. See Davis, *Michel Tournier: Philosophy and Fiction* (Oxford, Clarendon Press, 1988), 32.

[12] In *PL* 119, Tournier defines 'limbes' as 'Séjour des âmes des justes morts avant la venue de Jésus-Christ, ainsi que des enfants morts avant le baptême'. Limbo, in Catholic theology, thus provided an appropriate destination after death firstly for unbaptised children, and secondly for the righteous of the Old Testament or noble heathens. It is in just such a limbo, idealised and de-Christianised, that Tournier places his final couple, Jeudi the unbaptised child and Robinson, the would-be Old Testament patriarch now turned noble heathen. See my essay 'Michel Tournier' in Michael Tilby (ed.), *Beyond the Nouveau Roman* (Oxford, Berg, 1990), 64-99 (72-3).

[13] In the words of Gérard Genette, for instance, 'la narration reste pour l'essentiel [...] focalisée sur Robinson [...] qui demeure le foyer - je dirais volontiers le *maître* du récit, et d'un récit qui raconte son histoire, non celle de Vendredi'. See Genette, *Palimpsestes: la littérature au second degré* (Paris: Seuil, 1982), 424.

[14] The only significant exception is the first-person account of the life of an officer at the Napola, Stefan Raufeisen (416-21).

[15] The six factor continues as regards the diary entries of the 'Écrits sinistres' when they return in sections 5 (thirty entries) and 6 (six entries).

[16] See Gérard Genette, 'Discours du récit' in *Figures III* (Paris, Seuil, 1972), 72. Genette uses the term *histoire* to refer to the 'signifié' or content of a narrative, and *récit* to refer to the 'signifiant' or narrative discourse itself. While borrowing these basic terms, I am not here proposing a Genettian analysis.

[17] Genette, 'Discours du récit', 82.

[18] See Tournier's note on 'La droite et la gauche' in *Le Miroir des idées* (209-12): 'Traditionnellement le bien est à droite, le mal à gauche. Par exemple, sur le Calvaire, le bon larron se place à la droite du Christ, le mauvais larron à sa gauche. Lors du Jugement Dernier, les élus iront se placer à la droite du Père, les réprouvés se rangeront à sa gauche'(*MI* 209).

[19] See pp. 63, 92, 577. Cf. Revelation 1:8 : 'I am Alpha and Omega, saith the Lord.' This 'trait' is further discussed in Chapter 3.

[20] In a note headed 'Musique' (*PP* 225-9), Tournier speaks of the pervasive influence of music on his writing. For him, as for the hero of Sartre's *La Nausée*, music represents a model of rigour and necessity.

[21] Another reference to this story is to be found in 'Lucie ou La femme sans

ombre' (*MA* 168-9).

[22] Some of these points on fugal structure are covered in Bouloumié, *Michel Tournier: le roman mythologique* (Paris, Corti, 1988), 73-80, and in Susan Petit, *Michel Tournier's Metaphysical Fictions* (Amsterdam, John Benjamins, 1991), 34-7. The idea of Bach's *Art of Fugue* as a model for the writer to follow had already been invoked in André Gide's novel *Les Faux-monnayeurs*. See Gide, *Romans, récits et soties, oeuvres lyriques* (Paris, Gallimard (Bibl. de la Pléiade) 1958), 1,084; and Alain Goulet, *Lire les* Faux-monnayeurs *de Gide* (Paris, Dunod, 1994), 144.

[23] This narrative sequence, with one chapter for each staging-post of an extended journey, is in this sense comparable to *Le Roi des aulnes*, where the first five sections recount Tiffauges's life in five different places: Paris, Alsace, Moorhof, Rominten, Kaltenborn. The structure is in each case that of the initiatic journey (see Chapter 7).

[24] For an entirely different interpretation of the structure of *Les Météores* based on the twenty-two cards of the tarot, see Marie Miguet, 'Le Tarot et *Les Météores*', in A. Bouloumié and M. de Gandillac (eds), *Images et signes de Michel Tournier* (Paris, Gallimard, 1991), 341-65.

[25] Tournier has commented on this problematic aspect of the ordering of chapters in *Les Météores*: 'Chronologiquement les deux premiers chapitres auraient dû être intervertis. Le récit y aurait trouvé l'avantage d'un départ plus rapide. Mais le déséquilibre en faveur d'Alexandre se serait encore aggravé, objection décisive'(*VPar* 258).

[26] Each of these three secondary characters is of less importance on the level of plot than the last. Sophie, as Jean's short-lived fiancée, is the catalyst of the separation of the twins - the catalyst rather than the cause, it is clear, of a split whose roots lie deeper and which is prepared much earlier in the narrative. Hamida is one of a series of female 'signpost' characters - Hamida, Selma, Kumiko - who direct Paul in the footsteps of his brother. Shonïn is Paul's Zen master in Japan, and is present in the text only as the spokesman for a philosophy of life, a voice in an East-West dialogue reminiscent of Malraux's *La Tentation de l'Occident*.

[27] At one level the opening can be read as an amiable pastiche of the opening paragraph of Robert Musil's *Der Mann ohne Eigenschaften (The Man Without Qualities)* whose equally playful, ironically pretentious meteorological opening leads also, circuitously, to a chronological placing: '[...] it was a fine August day in the year 1913', the eve of an earlier World War, we might note. See Musil, *The Man Without Qualities*, Vol. I (London, Picador, 1979), 3.

[28] It also, in a playful *mise en abîme*, separates narrative voice from the person of the author since the wind 'tourna huit pages des *Météores* d'Aristote que lisait Michel Tournier sur la plage de Saint-Jacut': the reader of Tournier's novel *Les Météores* is thus afforded a glimpse of its author reading (another) *Les Météores*, and Tournier becomes at one and the same time author of the text, object of the narrative (having the same status as, say, Maria-Barbara on whom the wind blows in the second paragraph) and intertextual link (between his own novel and its Aristotelian namesake).

[29] Compare Paul's intuition on the effect of the previous disaster, the arrest of Maria-Barbara: 'Mais la dévastation des Pierres Sonnantes n'était que l'envers d'une réalité plus profonde: le départ de Maria-Barbara venait de douer d'*immédiateté* notre relation fondamentale' (365 - italics in text).

[30] One critic has sought to read the fourteen stories of *Le Coq de bruyère* as illustrating the Seven Virtues and the Seven Deadly Sins - an ingenious

interpretative key, but one which is more persuasive for some stories than others. See Petit, *Michel Tournier's Metaphysical Fictions,* 101-109.

[31] The theme most obviously common to both these pairs of stories is that of the power, positive and negative, of the 'alter ego' or the 'double': Raphaël Bidoche ('Que ma joie demeure') the would-be concert pianist inadvertently falling into a brilliant career as comic entertainer; Lucien Gagneron ('Le Nain rouge') the sinister dwarf turned children's clown; the unglamorous Félix Robinet alias Tristan Vox, charismatic radio personality; Hector, the photographer's subject, literally consumed by the images drawn from his body, the copies destroying the original. On this theme of the double, richly developed in Tournier's work, see Bouloumié, *Michel Tournier: le roman mythologique,* and Nicole Guichard, *Michel Tournier: autrui et la quête du double* (Paris, Didier, 1989).

[32] On the function of the image of the political leader, see Tournier's introduction to a volume of photographs by K.R. Müller, *François Mitterrand* (Paris, Flammarion, 1983).

[33] The camel is neatly made symbolic of a European attitude to immigrants in general, when one of Mage's assistants points up the analogy: 'On croyait les avoir loués et pouvoir les renvoyer chez eux quand on n'en aurait plus besoin, et puis on s'aperçoit qu'on les a achetés et qu'on doit les garder en France'(*GO* 151).

[34] Tournier is very impressed by the lapidary power of this slogan: 'Trouver des images percutantes, des formules "à l'emporte-pièce" ou "frappées comme des médailles". Trouver la formule qui s'inscrit instantanément dans toutes les mémoires. Qui ne se souvient de *Sous les pavés la plage* de Mai '68? C'est trop peu dire que ces cinq petits mots résumaient Mai '68. Il faudrait dire plutôt que tout le remue-ménage de ce bruyant printemps fut suffisamment justifié par l'invention superbe et anonyme de ces cinq mots.' See his preface, 'Quand le peintre parle', to Liliane Thorn-Petit, *Portraits d'artistes,* (Paris/Luxemburg, RTL Edition, 1982), 11.

[35] For a more developed account by Tournier of the distinction he makes between the genres of 'nouvelle', 'conte', and 'fable', see 'Barbe-bleue ou le secret du conte' (*VV* 38-43) and 'Le fantastique et le mythe: deux réalités', *Bulletin de l'Académie Royale de langue et de littérature françaises* [Brussels], t.LVI, no.3-4 (1978), 307-316.

[36] This formula, of a collection of tales told to each other by a group of people, is of course reminiscent of Boccaccio's *Decameron* or Marguerite de Navarre's *Heptaméron,* even respecting the convention of grouping the stories in tens.

[37] This story strongly recalls the first African episode in Gide's *L'Immoraliste,* where the narrator, Michel, prefers the Arab boy who steals scissors from their house to the other more well-behaved ones. See André Gide, *Romans,* 394-5.

[38] The subject-matter of this story grew out of a narrative poem by Victor Hugo. This is discussed further in Chapter 6.

[39] A perceptive analysis of 'Pierrot' forms part of an excellent doctoral thesis by Martin Roberts, which forms the basis of his recent book *Michel Tournier:* Bricolage *and Cultural Mythology* (Stanford, ANMA Libri (Stanford French and Italian Studies 79) which at the time of writing I have not been able to consult. See also J.-B. Vray, 'L'habit d'Arlequin' in *Sud* (special issue on Tournier, 1980), 149-166.

[40] This commixture of real people and a fabricated background in a single composition recalls Mustapha's photographs in *La Goutte d'or.*

[41] Among Lucie's first words to the boy when he arrives are 'As-tu mangé?'. He does not eat then, but later the emotionally deprived child feels nourished by his night in her arms: 'Je crois que je buvais directement à sa source le lait de tendresse [...]'(159).

[42] In Hugo von Hofmannsthal's story 'Die Frau ohne Schatten' ('The Woman without a Shadow'), from which he drew the libretto for the opera of the same name by Richard Strauss, the shadow is also associated with fertility and maternity.

[43] See Davis, *Michel Tournier: Philosophy and Fiction*, 164.

[44] The immigrant population in France were the implicit dedicatees of *Vendredi* (see *VLP* 236).

2

The Writer as Delinquent

For Tournier, the true writer is necessarily a dissident. 'Nous subissons tous la pression du corps social qui nous impose comme autant de stéréotypes nos conduites, nos opinions et jusqu'à notre aspect extérieur. Le propre des créateurs est de résister à cette sujétion pour remonter le courant et mettre en circulation leurs propres modèles'(*VV* 25). By temperament or experience, the creative individual is set at odds with the social fabric: surveying literary geniuses of the past, Tournier concludes that 'une certaine dose de malheur, d'inadaptation, de marginalité, voire de délinquance potentielle constitue en l'occurrence un atout presque obligé'(*VV* 313). It is the writer's task, he argues, to question the status quo of conventional values, and the tonic value of this function should be evident to a free society. 'Un écrivain doit être *contre*. [...] [Il] est fait pour lutter en faveur du désordre contre l'ordre. [...] Mais dans une société intelligente on comprend la fonction essentielle des fauteurs de désordre, des fauteurs de troubles.'[1] Even in an authoritarian regime, the writer can make an impact. Why should a tyrant, like Napoleon, fear a writer like Mme de Staël? It is because the power which he wields rests not just on armed force and physical repression but also on 'un ensemble d'artifices psychologiques destinés à emporter le consentement moral des "sujets"'(*VV* 94). It is this consensus, and the mechanisms which maintain it, which the writer is capable of undermining. The most powerful writers, in Tournier's view, characteristically revisit and renew the great myths and archetypes of our cultural tradition, and these myths are themselves figures of disorder and revolt, whose function seems to be, precisely, to 'sauvegarder une certaine *inadaptation* de l'individu dans la société'(*VV* 34).[2] Drawing on this granary of seminal myths, the writer, as an apologist of disorder, non-conformist, marginal, writing 'against the current', is likely to cause consternation if not outrage. 'Good literature is inventive and any invention amounts to a perversion.'[3]

'Malheur, inadaptation, marginalité, délinquance' - those features which Tournier saw as near-indispensable elements of the creative writer's posture in relation to the social and cultural environment can readily be identified in the make-up of his own fictional characters. Robinson the castaway is 'marginal' in the most literal sense, expelled to the furthest edge of the inhabited world, brutally detached from a society whose values, inscribed within him, 'suffer a sea-change into something rich and strange'.[4] Idriss, in *La Goutte d'or*, moving in the opposite direction from the margin to Europe, is profoundly 'inadapté' to all he sees, as he encounters an urban society whose values he rejects to the end. In other major characters, an unconventional destiny is built on a socially idiosyncratic inner orientation, towards paedophilia (Abel), extrovert homosexuality (Alexandre) or the enclosure of identical twinship (Paul). The causality underlying this state of 'inadaptation' remains of course complex. In *Vendredi* it is initially external - exile through the accident of shipwreck - before being adopted by choice when the *Whitebird* arrives. The causes of Idriss's displacement in *La Goutte d'or* are both inner and outer: his inherently restless temperament is provoked into departure by the passage of the woman who photographs him, and who thereby concretises his desire (for the photograph and the identity it confers, as well as for herself as erotic icon). The socially 'anomalous' state of others - Abel, Paul or Alexandre - is likewise fostered by the apparent complicity of external events.

There is of course nothing original in this view of the writer, and of fictional heroes, as misfits or rebels - from Rousseau to Rimbaud, from Werther to Maldoror, it is a commonplace of the Romantic movement. What is of interest is to define what cultural codes are being attacked or rejected, and what principles, if any, are being proposed in their place. Caution must be exercised in seeking to adduce from a body of fiction a coherent ideology, and Tournier has, like many another author, quite reasonably protested about being attacked for opinions expressed by one or other of his characters.[5] That said, the heterodox and dissident views expressed and explored by his major characters are often in unison with opinions and analyses he has himself forcefully and consistently disseminated in many interviews and articles. For the most part there is arguably no difference in kind, though sometimes in the degree of virulence, between the ideology developed in the fictions and the agenda of Tournier himself as social and cultural commentator.

Tournier's indictment of the structure and ideology of society is mediated through those fictions which have a modern setting - notably *Le Roi des aulnes*, *Les Météores*, *La Goutte d'or* and some stories from *Le*

Coq de bruyère and *Le Médianoche amoureux*.[6] A characteristic image of contemporary society as he sees it is to be found in a passage from *Les Météores* where Paul, travelling across Canada by rail, records the impressions he has gleaned from an extended exploration of the train from end to end: 'J'ai regagné mon trou solitaire avec la conscience nouvelle de la société bigarrée que nous formions dans ce train. Mais ce que je retiens surtout dans mon exploration, c'est l'isolement des groupes, leur exclusion réciproque, et combien les compartiments du train répondent à un compartimentage de la société'(*Mét* 568). This compartmentalisation of society is, Tournier argues elsewhere, a by-product of affluence: he finds in the Third World, or in the working-class suburbs of Naples, a solidarity and sense of community which is entirely lacking in the classy apartment blocks of the '16e arrondissement' in Paris, where 'il [...] est de bon ton d'ignorer jusqu'au nom des voisins de palier' (*VPar* 224). In 'La fugue du petit Poucet' (*CB*), the boy's father, 'le commandant Poucet', extols the virtues of contemporary compartmentalised living, when he decrees that the family should exchange their little house and garden in the country for a neon-lit, sound-proofed, air-conditioned flat on the twenty-third floor of a tower block, with non-opening windows and lifts instead of stairs. Little Pierre's instinctive reaction to this urban dream lifestyle is to leave home, with his rabbits, to find an alternative place to live in the 'forêt de Rambouillet'. In 'Amandine ou les deux jardins', the ten-year-old Amandine's diary describes her parents' house and garden in terms which discreetly suggest a more subtly oppressive and enclosed environment. In the house, Mummy's realm, the temperature is the same summer and winter, and you must wear slippers to protect the parquet floor. In the garden, Daddy's domain, the grass is always green and immaculately trimmed, and smokers must use the ash-trays provided. For the child, this highly controlled and unvarying order is 'rassurant' but also 'un peu ennuyeux' (*CB* 36), and like Pierre Poucet, she is instinctively impelled to break out and find an alternative space, the overgrown garden next door, which will give her the freedom she needs to grow and to be herself. In these two cases, the compartmentalisation is at once spatial (the flat, the house and garden) and social (the cell of the nuclear family). Tournier clearly sees the order of the closed family unit as hostile to personal, and especially sexual, development and freedom: as a story of a young boy's sexual and emotional growth disastrously distorted by well-meaning parents, 'Tupik' is in the lineage of Gide's *Les Faux-monnayeurs*, and Tournier could be seen as echoing his predecessor's famous outburst, 'Familles, je vous hais!'.[7]

The barriers created by the family and social order in these fictions are sense-deprivations, maiming by a system of taboos the individual's capacity for sensory exploration of his or her environment. One of the polemics most frequently reiterated in Tournier's writings is directed against our culture's puritanical insistence on looking, not touching: '[...] Nous vivons dans un monde où l'image visuelle envahit tout par la photo, le cinéma, la télévision. En même temps, on jette sur les sens du contact immédiat - le toucher, le goût, l'odorat - une condamnation absurde qui appauvrit affreusement notre vie. "Ne touche pas!" L'odieuse recommandation qui a empoisonné notre enfance se prolonge [...]'(*PP* 223).[8] Two manifestations of this thwarting of desire which Tournier refers to more than once are the shop-window and the peep-show. In 'L'aire du Muguet' Pierre, the young long-distance lorry-driver, reflects how objects gain a spurious charm by being placed behind a window, and that viewing a landscape only through a windscreen from the motorway has the same effect. When he stops in the lay-by of the story's title, he sees a teenage farm-girl and talks to her through the perimeter fence, but cannot touch her or sit beside her. His later gloomy reflections make the link: 'Le paysage derrière un pare-brise, les filles derrière une clôture, tout en vitrine. Pas touche, défendu, bas les pattes! C'est ça l'autoroute!' (*CB* 284). At the end of the story he will lose his life crossing the motorway in a desperate attempt to find a way through the barrier to the land of desire beyond. *La Goutte d'or* is Tournier's most systematic exploration of the image as screen, as barrier. Idriss moves into a culture where seductively framed and stereotyped visual images are designed as a substitute for complexity and contact, and thus threaten every mode of being in the world beyond that of passive spectator and programmed consumer. Sometimes, however, an act of transgression, breaking through the partition, can be successfully accomplished: 'Parfois, tout de même, un pavé vole dans une vitrine et un jeune corps se rue sur les fruits défendus...'(*CS* 26/*PP* 116). This exemplary smash-and-grab is indirectly achieved by Idriss on the final page of *La Goutte d'or*, when the window of the exclusive jewellery shop in the Place Vendôme shatters under the vibrations of his pneumatic drill, to lay bare the 'goutte d'or', the golden droplet pendant which has symbolised the perfect fulfilment of his desire throughout the narrative.

In a more general sense, Tournier's heroes celebrate the richness of the non-visual senses. Robinson experiences his solitude, the absence of society, as a loss of sight: 'Ma vision de l'île est réduite à elle-même. Ce que je n'en vois pas est un *inconnu absolu*. Partout où je ne suis pas actuellement règne une nuit insondable [...] Les phares ont disparu de mon champ [...] Les ténèbres m'environnent' (*VLP* 54). (In this he is following a fundamental metaphor of our culture, in which understanding and rational control are equated with sight: 'I *see* what you mean.') At the same time the substitution of touch for sight when he wallows in the mud-pool is experienced as a degradation. Later, descending into the grotto, he accepts darkness and blindness as the route to a different mode of being. Released from that self-conscious condition of 'watching oneself see' which he posits as founding the traditional view of perception[9] he attains a different 'vision' of the island as an entity existing independently of his capacity to perceive it. By the end of the text he has become 'heliotropic', like plants who thrive only when bathed by the sun's warmth, and his sensory relationship to Speranza has long since ceased to be primarily visual. In *Le Roi des aulnes*, Abel Tiffauges is myopic by nature, and the other senses are by way of compensation highly developed in him. 'La phorie' is an act of direct contact, and his intense attraction to children is mediated through every sense. It is scent and sound that draw him powerfully towards the room full of naked small girls, assembled for examination and induction into the Hitler youth movement: 'Tiffauges monta le large escalier menant à la salle des mariages, tiré en avant par une odeur d'une exquise fraîcheur printanière où il y avait du poivre et de la semence [...] Il entendait comme un gazouillis de volière, et les tendres effluves l'enveloppaient avec insistance'(*RA* 367). When challenged by an indignant matron, he can only stammer 'C'est l'odeur... Je ne savais pas que la chair de petite fille sent le muguet...'(*RA* 368).[10] Another of many possible examples of this non-visual excitation comes as Tiffauges waits in the hot shower, blinded by the steam, for the arrival of the cadets: 'J'étais couché nu sous un jet brûlant, suffocant et aveuglé déjà, quand la musique de leurs voix claires mêlée aux tapotements de leurs pieds nus sur la pierre a empli l'escalier.' In the 'ténèbres laiteuses' of the steam he is 'maintes et maintes fois piétiné broyé par le poids des corps mouillés [...]' (*RA* 516). On his final journey into the marshland, Ephraïm on his back, he walks with hands outstretched 'comme un aveugle'(*RA* 580) and feels rather than sees the alder trees and the bog beneath him. The final 'vision' of the six-pointed star acquires all the more force, and the suggestion is that, like Robinson's vision of Speranza from the darkness of the grotto, the spectacle in question is for this blind seer a product of the mind's eye.

Let us take just two further examples of this emphasis on the non-visual senses. Firstly, in *Gaspard*, Taor sets out not to see the Saviour, like his three fellow Magi, but to taste the most delicious sweetmeat in the world. It is implicit in the hierarchy of the senses that this at once seems a less noble aim, but it leads to the Eucharist, in which the despised act of eating, the ignoble sense of taste, is promoted as the medium of communion with the Almighty.

Secondly, in *Les Météores* (96-8), Alexandre prides himself on the sharpness and sensitivity of his sense of smell, which sets him apart from the mass of humanity in which this olfactory flair has atrophied. While his eyesight discerns clearly only the objects of his desire, his smell gives him a rich appreciation of the ingredients and nuances of his different refuse dumps, and thus a personal geography of society from the point of view of its waste products. Alexandre's appreciation of the heterogeneous nature of his raw material gives him a special horror of the incineration plant which he visits. This destroys the texture and variety of the waste and amounts in his eyes to 'l'uniformisation, le nivellement, l'élimination de tout ce qui est différent, inattendu, créateur'(*Mét* 140). Here the suppression of the rich diversity of sensual stimuli is equated with society's hostility to any non-conforming, creative originality. This destructive process of 'uniformisation', described as 'infernal' by Alexandre, and in the chapter heading, is the culmination of society's morbid obsession with purity, which in other circumstances can lead to the genocide of 'inferior' or 'degenerate' races and categories of people in the name of racial 'purity'. *Le Roi des aulnes* anticipates this theme of purification by fire, in a tirade in Abel's 'Écrits sinistres': 'La pureté est horreur de la vie, haine de l'homme, passion morbide du néant'(*RA* 125). Purification, whether political, religious or racial, engenders crimes without number, and its preferred instrument is fire, symbol of purity and of hell. In due course Blättchen provides the racial theory for such an obsession and Auschwitz bears witness to its consequences. The warning is in Van Deyssel's last words to Robinson, in the prologue to *Vendredi*: '[...] [g]ardez-vous de la pureté. C'est le vitriol de l'âme' (*VLP* 14).

There is in *Les Météores* an image of the revenge of the rejected against what Tiffauges calls 'les démons de la Pureté' (*RA* 163). During a dustmen's strike in Roanne Alexandre revels in the sight of the rubbish piled up in the streets, and the rats it attracts. He finds not only a certain perverse pleasure in the 'exuberant' sculptural constructions that are thereby created in the gutter, but a heady joy at the notion that, momentarily, 'les oms [ordures ménagères] tiennent le haut du pavé' (*Mét* 210), and that the ruling bourgeoisie are at the mercy of what they most despise and reject. As Tournier has written elsewhere, 'Pauvre pollution, si cruellement calomniée! Savez-vous que les hommes ont pour vous un goût inavouable? Savez-vous qu'ils admirent [...] les sculptures volubiles composées par l'entassement des ordures ménagères (que nos villes deviennent belles sous le coup d'une grève des éboueurs!) [...]'. He notes that perfume-makers put putrid aldehydes into their products to avoid the scent becoming too sickly sweet. 'Rien ne se crée dans la nature ou la société sans un minimum d'ordure.'[11] The polarity is clear: purity prescribes destruction; impurity is the mark of the creative.

Abel, Paul and Alexandre all recognise that they are real or potential victims of this purifying destruction. When Blättchen declares, 'Le mauvais sang n'est ni améliorable ni éducable, le seul traitement dont il est justiciable est une destruction pure et simple', his collaborator Tiffauges recalls that he is himself of the race of Abel, a stateless nomad, a prime candidate for 'treatment'. When Blättchen speaks of 'Blut und Boden', the soil of Germany fertilised by blood, the Bible tells Tiffauges that it is Abel's lifeblood, spilt by Cain, that the earth will receive (*RA* 432-3). Paul, in *Les Météores*, notes how little attention is paid by the world at large to the death of the handicapped children whom Franz took out in the boat, and suspects that it is a cause of general satisfaction rather than grief. As a twin, and thus a 'monstre', Paul sees himself part of the same 'tribu à part'(*Mét* 163) as those children, feared, scorned and detested by others. In a later episode, when Alexandre reports to the police the discovery of a corpse in the refuse dump, he finds them unconcerned with what they take to be the death of some vagabond or immigrant worker. 'J'ai bien compris que nous ne faisions pas partie de la société' (*Mét* 307). In the coming war, Alexandre resolves, 'nous autres, les marginaux' will stand on the sidelines keeping the score. These novels thus constantly present the reader with characters who feel alienated and threatened by the prevailing exclusive social culture.

Abel is wrongly accused of rape, since in the eyes of the police his responsibility for this crime follows with inexorable logic from his record of eccentric (if largely harmless) behaviour towards children. Alexandre is ambushed by police acting to harass or arrest homosexuals meeting in the park at night. In each case the arrest and ordeal derives from public, and officially sanctioned, hostility to their unorthodox mores, and both in consequence bear no allegiance to the social and political establishment, which they despise. Abel rails against the penal code as the basis of French law, prizing property above people (*RA* 202-3), and develops a fantasy counter-code whereby all politicians, dignitaries and wearers of uniform can be summarily shot (*RA* 121-3). He is particularly horrified by the glorification of bloodshed, manifest in the streets named after military leaders responsible for massive butchery (*RA* 83,123-4) and in the huge crowd that gathers to revel in the public execution of Weidmann.[12] Through Abel's voice here, and through Alexandre's in *Les Météores*, a fiercely anarchist polemic is unfurled against the dominant culture and the powers that enforce what are seen as its hypocritical and indefensible values. The spectacle of the *débâcle* of 1940, bringing the ignominious collapse of the social order they detest, finds Alexandre surprised at his own residual patriotism: 'Cette débâcle a beau [...] conclure une querelle d'hétérosexuels qui ne me concerne pas, je ne peux me défendre d'un serrement de coeur devant ce désastre historique essuyé par mon pays' (*Mét* 335). Abel, on the other hand, takes vengeful delight in France's humiliation, seeing in it 'la condamnation d'un ordre injuste et criminel'(*RA* 250). It is Abel's reaction which is closer to that of the author himself, as an adolescent: 'Je sais personnellement avec quelle jubilation dyonisiaque [*sic*] un jeune garçon en pleine révolte contre son milieu assiste à l'effondrement de son pays, et voit jetées cul par-dessus tête ses institutions et sa "morale": j'avais quinze ans en 1940...'(*CM* 68).

In seeking some pattern in these various anti-authoritarian stances, it is useful to turn to Tournier's review of Gilles Lapouge's book *Utopie et civilisations*.[13] Lapouge distinguishes three types of man in the world of politics: the political leader, who makes history through *realpolitik*; the utopian, with a formula for human happiness, who seeks to halt the disastrous course of history and take over from the political leader; and, lastly, the common enemy of both these, the counter-utopian - vagabond, hippy, poet, detesting organisation and concerned only with the individual. 'C'est un nomade, un pasteur, un descendant d'Abel, il mange les fruits du Bon Dieu, il ne connaît pas les frontières, et toute la terre lui appartient' (Lapouge's words, quoted by Tournier). The utopian and the counter-utopian are both opposed to the status quo, but the former opts for the organisational, the latter for the organic; the utopian's ideal is equality, the counter-utopian's liberty. Surveying utopianism from Plato and Augustine to Sade, Marx and Fourier, Tournier concludes that one could readily analyse current political reality in terms of these three categories, whose permanence attests to their being basic mental structures.

It is instructive to plot Tournier's fictional characters in these terms. Robinson is in Utopia in a double sense: the term is derived from the Greek, meaning 'nowhere', and Robinson experiences his 'limbo' as a non-place. More importantly, Thomas More coined the term to signify a system or plan that seems impossible to realise, and Robinson's utopian 'île administrée' - organisational rather than organic - is finally non-viable. The collapse of this system leaves him open (after a process of initiation) to the freewheeling individualism of the counter-utopian. Abel, by his first name, seems destined to be a counter-utopian, but is drawn into the inferno of systems and organisations of an increasingly brutal (dystopian) kind, until his release from them at the end. Paul is rigorously utopian: of this category, Tournier says (in the same review) that 'l'un de ses soucis majeurs, c'est d'enfermer sa cité dans un milieu clos, à l'abri des infiltrations historiques [...]'. This sums up Paul's project to maintain the closed twin cell. Only when this closed, self-sufficient, utopian male bond is shattered by the departure of the partner is the hero able (again after a process of initiation) to open himself to the world, in an asocial cosmic individualism that moves beyond all politics.

Alexandre by contrast remains counter-utopian throughout: nomadic, prizing freedom and 'disponibilité' above all, gratuitously undermining his own authority over his employees. The purest prototype of the counter-utopian in Tournier's fiction is Logre, the gentle hippy giant in 'La Fugue du petit Poucet' (*CB*), the embodiment of the 1960s apostle of drug culture, free love and a nomadic lifestyle. For little Poucet he is the positive counterweight to the utopian tendencies of Poucet *père*, the tree-feller, who dreams of a family life insulated from nature, and of a Paris devoid of trees. At the end of the story Logre is arrested, like Alexandre and Abel, as a result of his nonconformist mores: to the police captain, the sampler which reads 'Make love, not war' is itself ample evidence of guilt.

There can be little doubt that the central current of Tournier's thinking and writing is essentially counter-utopian. Alexandre espouses this stance; Robinson moves progressively to embody it. The utopian systems which his characters initiate and struggle to maintain - Robinson's 'île administrée', Tiffauges's colony of boys at Kaltenborn, Paul's closed twin cell, Gilles's castle devoted to alchemy and the rituals and science of death - all end as dystopias, which can only be maintained by power and domination, not by love or consent, and the heroes in every case find a kind of redemption only when they renounce the poisoned politics of the utopian system in favour of its opposite. Salvation is only ever found once politics has been stripped away. In *Gaspard*, Herod the political leader is the furthest from salvation, and each of the first three kings struggle with the politics of government (Melchior), art (Balthazar) or of interpersonal relations (Gaspard's love for a slave). The accolade is reserved for Taor, whose quest is absolutely non-political, and who renounces power even over his own life and body.

The hostility to politics and to power structures in Tournier's work stems from a fundamental ultra-libertarian, even anarchist stance, in favour of the maximum freedom for personal growth, uninhibited relationships with others and the removal of taboos in sensual and sexual pleasure. Much of what he abhors is summed up in an image which recurs in his writing: that of glass partitions. It is present in his diagnosis of the isolation of individuals in our culture: 'Oui, nous vivons enfermés chacun dans notre cage de verre. Cela s'appelle retenue, froideur, quant-à-soi. Dès son plus jeune âge, l'enfant est sévèrement dressé à ne pas parler à des inconnus, à s'entourer d'un halo de méfiance, à réduire ses contacts humains au strict minimum'(*VPar* 222-3).[14] 'Il faudrait briser la cage de verre. Et pour cela en prendre d'abord conscience [...]' (*VPar* 225). The fundamental figure of the glass cage of compartmentalisation and sensory deprivation generates the Poucets' high-rise flat with its hermetic windows, Pierre's windscreen in 'L'aire du Muguet', and the shop-window or peep-show aperture in *La Goutte d'or,* all of which amputate desire from its object. At its worst the glass cage can become a metaphor for the total devaluation of the individual. The 'cellule de moulage' in which Idriss is placed to make a body mould for mannequins resembles 'une étroite cabine téléphonique de plexiglas'(*GO* 185), but even this oppressive experience seems benign besides Ephraim's account of the containers in which victims were placed at Auschwitz for appalling experiments in depressurisation, a process observers watched through 'hublots vitrés' (*RA* 559-60). In 'La fugue du petit Poucet' the counter-image to the glass-cage is the tree, the central subject of Logre's counter-utopian sermon, which he celebrates as mediator between earth and sky, living and breathing in constant interchange with the elements.

Charged by an interviewer that his work is 'less edifying than it tried to appear', Tournier responded vigorously: 'Ah, pardon! Je veux être un auteur édifiant! Mais d'une vraie morale, vous comprenez? Je ne suis pas un casseur. Je veux être constructif, et je prétends que mes livres font du bien.'[15] As the image of the tree suggests, this 'vraie morale', which Tournier seeks constructively and edifyingly to communicate, is not to be found in any reform of politics or social structure: it is individualist, metaphysical, quasi-religious. A reading of 'La fugue du petit Poucet', a text for children in which this opposition is most simply spelt out, serves to show how this project of subversive edification is carried as much through intertext as through direct textual statement. Its young readers may already be familiar with the standard version of 'Petit Poucet' (Tom Thumb) popularised in Perrault's *Contes*. Tournier's version takes over many of the ingredients from this model, but playfully transforms the significance of the narrative. While Perrault's ogre and his seven daughters are cruel cannibals, Tournier's Logre, despite his name, is a kind-hearted vegetarian, and his daughters' interest in Poucet is joyfully carnal rather than carnivorous. In Perrault's version, Petit Poucet steals the giant's seven-league boots, which are symbols (as are the German jackboots worn by Tiffauges in *Le Roi des aulnes*) of his sinister, predatory power. In Tournier's reworking, the boots are made of suede, soft, decorated, unthreatening - 'des bottes de rêve' (*CB* 65), conferring access not to power but to a world of imagination, and they are given by the giant as a Christmas present, not stolen from him. Logre's gentle eyes, long hair and silky beard recall conventional portraits of Christ, and his words as the police arrive - 'Les soldats de Yahvé viennent m'arrêter' (*CB* 63) - evoke the calm acceptance with which Jesus allowed himself to be arrested by 'the chief priests, and captains of the temple' (Luke, 22:52). This analogy emphasises to what extent the import of the tale has been turned inside out, with Perrault's Ogre transmuted into a Christ-like victim of a Pharisaic society. It is not just in the explicit preaching of Logre, or in the binomial structures of the narrative that it is subversive: it is in the very act of taking a familiar children's tale and turning its lesson from one of fear of the stranger into one of openness, contact and tolerance.

Notes to Chapter Two

[1] Interview with Alison Browning: 'Une conversation avec Michel Tournier', *Cadmos* 3me ann., no. 11 (Autumn 1980), 5-15 (p.9).

[2] The quotation is from an essay on the Tristan myth (*VV* 28-37), which usefully develops this important point.

[3] Interview with Nina Sutton: 'The offal truth: Michel Tournier and the

perversions of fine literature', *Guardian* (10.2.71), 8.

[4] Shakespeare, *The Tempest* I.2: another tale of Europeans shipwrecked and transformed in an encounter with the elements.

[5] 'Je suis de ceux,' Tournier has declared somewhat disingenuously,'qui ne se mettent jamais en scène eux-mêmes dans leurs propres romans.' See 'L'étrange cas du Docteur Tournier', *Sud* (special issue, 1980), 11-16 (15), reprinted in *CM* 11-19 (18).

[6] *Vendredi*, for its part, obviously presents, in Robinson's colonial posturing and his grandiose Penal Code and Constitution, a broad satire on the post-Enlightenment social contract (see D. Gascoigne, 'Michel Tournier', 67). The anti-colonialist aspect of the novel is however quite superficial. As Tournier himself has stressed, the importance of the Robinson-Vendredi opposition lay for him not in racist or colonialist stereotypes (although there was some mileage to be got out of these) but in the aspects of myth, archetype and the elements. See his essay 'La Dimension mythologique', *Nouvelle Revue française* 238 (Oct.1972), 124-9.

[7] See Gide, *Les Nourritures terrestres*, in *Romans, Récits et soties*, 186. The whole passage in which this exclamation occurs exudes a similar resentment of the 'foyers clos, portes refermées, possessions jalouses du bonheur'. On this anti-family stance in Gide and other writers, see Alain Goulet, *Fiction et vie sociale dans l'oeuvre d'André Gide* (Paris, Minard (Lettres Modernes), 1985), 229 ff.

[8] See also the article 'Toucher' in *CS* 25-6 (reprinted in *PP* 115-16), and his comments on the 'pseudo-morale du "bas-les-pattes"' in *VI* 45.

[9] This conventional mode of perception he calls 'connaissance par autrui', and by implication it is at two removes from real contact or identification with the object perceived. He dreams instead of a kind of salvation in which the self as perceiver would be disqualified entirely in favour of the reality of the rich aura of signals emitted by the island. See *VLP* 95-100, and discussion of this passage in Davis, *Michel Tournier*, 16-17.

[10] In the story 'L'aire du Muguet'(*CB*), the lily-of-the-valley has been wiped out by the building of the motorway, but the name remains to symbolise the irresistible attraction of the adolescent farm-girl.

[11] See the text accompanying a volume of photographs by Arthur Tress: *Rêves* (Brussels, Edns Complexe, 1979), 38-40, 36-8. Notwithstanding these eulogies to waste products, Tournier claims to be a strong anti-pollution campaigner. See e.g. the interview with Browning, 'Une conversation avec Michel Tournier', 8.

[12] Abel speaks of his disgust at the 'abject' President Lebrun's refusal to grant Weidmann a reprieve; declining to prevent judicial murder is itself, in his eyes, the most abominable of crimes (*RA* 185). Tournier shares this view. In an interview he refers to an appeal he himself published in *Le Figaro* for a young murderer to be reprieved, in which he declared: 'Si le Président de la République refuse sa grâce à ce condamné, il devient de ce fait même un déchet d'humanité irrécupérable.' See Alain Poirson, 'Une logique contre vents et marées: entretien avec Michel Tournier', *La Nouvelle Critique* 105 (June-July 1977), 47-50 (50).

[13] 'Clés pour l'histoire', *Quinzaine littéraire* (16-30 April 1973), 25-26 [review of Gilles Lapouge, *Utopie et civilisations* (Paris, Weber, 1973)].

[14] A first draft of this passage is to be found in the article 'La Leçon que nous donnent les pays pauvres', *Paris-Match* no.1,432 (6.11.76), 102. There he

describes the glass cage as 'invisible, mais incassable'. The later rewriting extends the list of gatherings which break through this deadening isolation, from the spiritual community of Taizé and the fraternity of motor-cyclists, to pop festivals and the 'fêtes érotiques' of the Bois de Boulogne.

[15] Interview reprinted in Jean-Louis Ezine, *Les Ecrivains sur la sellette* (Paris, Seuil, 1981), 223-8 (224).

3

Channels of Desire

'La femme est adaptée aux besoins de l'ovule plutôt qu'à elle-même.
De la puberté à la ménopause elle est le siège d'une histoire qui se
déroule en elle et qui ne la concerne pas personnellement.' '[...] [T]out
son organisme est orienté vers la perpétuation de l'espèce.' So writes
Simone de Beauvoir on the subjugation of woman to the propagation
of the species, what she calls 'le conflit entre ses intérêts propres et
celui des forces génératrices qui l'habitent'.[1] Tournier, recapitulating
in *Le Miroir des idées* his preferred myth about the origins of gender as
derived from Genesis and from Plato,[2] makes a similar point: '[...] [E]lle
[la femme] a été formée autour de son propre sexe. Elle est plus
substantiellement soumise à la féminité que l'homme ne l'est à la
virilité. Ce que les scolastiques exprimaient par la formule: *tota mulier
in utero* (toute la femme est dans son utérus)'(*MI* 17).

While Tournier advocates a quite different shift in contemporary
values to that proposed by Beauvoir, his writings like hers suggest the
negative consequences that these blindly self-perpetuating imperatives
of the race have for individual human wellbeing. While Beauvoir
focusses particularly on the burden of this 'destiny' of procreation
placed upon women, Tournier presents (heterosexual) men as victims
in their turn of the procreational imperative. His eulogy of the boy-
child's innocence and physical beauty (whose importance is explored
in Chapter 6) has as its counterpart Tiffauges's desolate view of the
male's fall from grace as the procreative imperative takes him over:
his body succumbs to 'toutes les hideurs de la virilité', and he enters
the marriage trap to be 'attelé avec les autres au lourd charroi de la
propagation de l'espèce' and to make his contribution to global
overpopulation (*RA* 154).[3] Furthermore, Tournier sees Western society
as constantly seeking to regulate the sexual life of individuals to
conform to this procreative vocation. This tribal concern of the
collectivity with its own survival and socio-economic structure explains
its traditionally repressive attitudes towards sexualities which do not
serve this end and which divert libidinal energy elsewhere. Hence its
conventional hostility towards adolescent sexual experimentation,

towards sexualities that are non-heterosexual or non-genital and towards sexual self-expression outside the monogamous couple, designed as the prototypical, child-producing unit.[4] Male sexual desire and potency, however, vastly exceeds what is required to produce two or three children in a lifetime, and yet a puritanical morality strives hopelessly, and destructively, to contain it within this narrow channel of 'acceptable' expression. 'Lorsque la morale victorienne condamne tout acte sexuel qui n'est pas accompli dans les conditions et dans le but de la procréation, c'est tout simplement à l'érotisme qu'elle s'en prend', eroticism being 'la sexualité même, considérée [...] dans son refus de servir la perpétuation de l'espèce', sexual pleasure as an end in itself (*CS* 103/*PP* 151).[5] Eroticism is then for Tournier a positively-charged term, a free expression of the self which is healthily subversive of a repressive social order.[6]

One consequence of this collective code of sexuality which arouses Tournier's deepest indignation is the prolonged sensual and emotional deprivation which it imposes on children and adolescents. From the moment the child is no longer allowed access to its parents' bed ('A ton âge tu ne peux pas décemment...'), the youngster's openness to and need for emotional and physical contact with others is, Tournier argues, crippled by social taboos (external and internalised) and by the watchful surveillance of adults. 'On arrive à cette chose absolument ahurissante que l'enfant et l'adolescent, c'est-à-dire l'être le plus tendre et l'être le plus ardent de tous les êtres qui forment une vie humaine, sont dans une espèce de désert physique créé artificiellement par la société.'[7] This sense of deprivation is inscribed in the psyche of Tournier's first hero, Robinson, and there its effects are far-reaching. As we shall see, the figures of desire in *Vendredi* spring from the emotional legacy of Robinson's childhood of which the narrative affords revealing glimpses, and which is the problematic starting point for the metamorphosis in his sexuality. Before investigating Robinson's family 'pre-history', it will be helpful to trace the figures of (pseudo-) birth and (pseudo-)parenthood as they develop in the text, starting from the key concept of metamorphosis.

Vendredi ou les limbes du Pacifique : Beyond Patriarchy

The concept of metamorphosis is established early and is prominent throughout. Van Deyssel's interpretations of the tarot take the form of coded indications of successive transformations of the self. Throughout the novel Robinson's development is presented in terms of biological imagery: 'Indiscutablement il venait de gravir un degré dans la métamorphose qui travaillait le plus secret de lui-même [...] La larve avait pressenti dans une brève extase qu'elle volerait un jour'(94). The word *métamorphose* in particular recurs frequently in the text (110, 125, 133, 191, 217, 226, 234), and the concept is first introduced by Van Deyssel when he speaks of 'Vénus métamorphosée en tireur à l'arc'(10). Indeed it is foreshadowed by him even earlier, when he interprets the Hermit card: '[...] [E]n s'enfonçant ainsi au sein de la terre, [...] il est devenu un autre homme'(8). It is easy to see why this term holds such attraction for Tournier. On one level, it has a mythological dimension, referring to the magical transformation of gods or human beings into plants, animals, rocks, fountains, stars or other natural forms: an anthology of such legends can be found most notably in Ovid's *Metamorphoses*. Tournier comes close to the world of Ovid when he describes, in a matter-of-fact way, how Robinson awoke one morning to find his beard taking root in the earth (138). Alongside this fantastical meaning, metamorphosis refers to the very physical process of marked natural change vividly exemplified by the larva becoming a butterfly, the image used by Tournier both in the passage already quoted and in *Gaspard*, in the words of Maalek: 'Quant à la métamorphose qui fait de la chenille un papillon, elle est évidemment exemplaire. [...] Peut-on imaginer plus sublime transfiguration que celle qui part de la chenille grise et rampante, et s'achève dans le papillon?'(*GMB* 64-5). The notion of metamorphosis, and especially the metaphor of the butterfly larva, implies a process of dramatic change akin to birth, or rebirth.[8] Combining in itself the mythological and the biological, the term thus ideally encapsulates the notion of an organic change within the individual which is also related to cosmic, supernatural forces.

What Robinson describes in his 'logbook' as 'cette création continuée de moi-même' (118) involves a series of such rebirths. His violent, involuntary expulsion from the protective cocoon of the *Virginie* at the end of the Prologue is the first and most radical of them: Robinson is being expelled, not just from a boat, but from human society and what he knows as civilisation, from the whole matrix of his life so far, and he will come to realise how much it was the external pressure of the presence of others that held his sense of identity and meaning in place (see e.g. 38).[9] Washed up on to the shore of the island, he at first refuses to accept his 'birth' into this new world, convincing himself that he is bound to be rescued soon, and that any efforts to establish a way of life there for the longer term are not only pointless, but somehow even jeopardise the chances of the longed-for rescue. All his energies are channelled into the construction of a boat in which to escape. This project comes to naught when he fails to launch it, and he lapses into a mud-pool and into despair (a literal Slough of Despond, to match Bunyan's allegory in *Pilgrim's Progress*[10]). In an onset of delirium, he sees a mirage of a galleon sailing into the bay, swims after it, and is washed up on to the beach for a second time. This second ejection from the water represents a second, and this time decisive, metaphorical rebirth: 'Une ère nouvelle débutait pour lui - ou plus précisément, c'était sa vraie vie dans l'île qui commençait [...]'(45).

The third 're-birth' sequence occurs in Chapter 5. Robinson descends (as Van Deyssel predicted from the Hermit card) into an underground cave for several days, having removed all his clothes and smeared himself with goat's milk, to slip more easily head first down the narrow passage which leads to it. The cave has obvious affinities with the womb, and his condition, on re-emerging into the dazzling light of day, is that of a tiny infant: 'Il était nu et blanc. Sa peau se granulait en chair de poule [...] Son sexe humilié avait fondu. Entre ses doigts filtraient des petits sanglots [...]' (110). This episode constitutes the most extended and literal birth metaphor in the novel, and it prefigures two comparable pivotal moments later in the narrative. The first is the explosion of gunpowder which blows both Robinson and Vendredi out of the entrance to the cave at the end of Chapter 8. Like a new-born child, Robinson opens his eyes to see a face leaning over him, and both men soon stand naked, shedding their irreparably scorched clothes. This 'twin' birth is prefigured by the tarot card of Gemini (10). The dual role of parent and twin thus implied for Vendredi is characteristic of the polyvalence of his relationship to Robinson, who will later come to see in him 'mon fils et mon père, mon frère et mon voisin' (224).[11] The last occurrence of this cyclical birth motif occurs in the final pages, when Jaan, the cabin-boy who has absconded from the *Whitebird*, emerges from his hiding place among the rocks at the same spot: '[...] [U]n corps obstrua le faible espace noir. Quelques contorsions le libérèrent de l'étroit orifice, et voici qu'un enfant se tenait devant Robinson [...]' (252).

Each of these five birth-events can be seen as marking a crucial transition in Robinson's progressive metamorphosis. After the initial expulsion from the cocoon of society into the 'limbo' of the title, the second (after the mirage) initiates the project of the 'île administrée', and the third (after the hermit experience) the contrary perception, of the 'other island' as the locus of gratification and plenitude. The fourth (the explosion) shatters the 'île administrée' and transforms the relationship between Robinson and Vendredi. The final 'birth', of the child Jaan, saves Robinson from mortal despair and leads directly to the apotheosis of the final page.

If, then, the prologue can be read as a primal birth-scene, establishing a pattern of similar points of passage from one phase of Robinson's life to another, then the ramifications of this symbolism merit closer scrutiny. A birth implies parents, progenitors. In the birth scenario of the prologue, the 'mother' is necessarily the boat,[12] with her 'panse courte et rebondie', risibly dumpy and slow, 'un sujet de gaieté dans tous les ports'(10), but reliable and plucky in adversity: '[...] [L]a paisible *Virginie* luttait bravement de tous ses faibles moyens [...] elle traçait sa route avec une obstination fidèle' (11), so that her 'gémissements' (10) do not evoke undue concern from the men. (That this mother-ship should ironically be called *Virginie* need not surprise us: it hints semi-seriously at the notion of a Virgin Birth.) The 'father' presiding at the birth has to be Van Deyssel, observing *Virginie*'s travail with 'une larme d'attendrissement'(11). His reading of the tarot cards is thus analogous to the predictions made by soothsayers or astrologers about a child's future at the moment of its birth: mention is made in the text of 'les évolutions d'une poignée d'étoiles qui dansaient dans le champ du hublot situé au-dessus de la tête du capitaine'(10), so that he is associated with the whirling constellations. Robinson resents this 'pseudo-father' who insists on offering him paternal advice, and chooses to view him as a 'diable d'homme' playing a 'jeu maléfique'(9). The ship is enveloped by a 'nuit de soufre'(10), while in Robinson's ears the storm resounds like a 'sabbat de sorcières'(9). This overheated satanic imagery is the product of Robinson's piously superstitious mentality, and its virulence emphasises the irrational intensity of his rejection of this father-figure. His first significant action on the island will be to kill a goat, the form traditionally taken by the Devil in satanic rites, and which here could be taken as a totemic representation of Van Deyssel as diabolical father-figure. He first mistakes the motionless goat for a log ('une souche à peine plus bizarre que d'autres' (17)) - but the word 'souche' can also mean ancestor, progenitor.[13] This gratuitous killing could thus be read as a symbolic Oedipal parricide. Alongside and distinct from this diabolical coloration deriving from Robinson, the text offers us a rather different and more whimsical portrait of the captain: '[Il] se pencha par-dessus sur son ventre' (7), 'tassé sur son siège, comme un bouddha' (8), 'ce gros silène néerlandais, tapi dans son matérialisme jouisseur'(9). The non-Christian references, to Buddha and Silenus (chief of the satyrs), reinforce the vignette of a man with very different notions of pleasure or of salvation to those of Protestant Christianity, and his plump Bacchic physique (the common factor to these comparisons) anticipates that of the equally obese Nestor in *Le Roi des aulnes*. The analogy with Nestor is instructive: each bequeaths to his protégé a set of values which will play an essential role in his further development, enshrined in a discourse, a voice, which will continue to resonate in the younger man's consciousness.[14] In his first phase of life on the island, Robinson, bereft of both 'parents', indeed 'orphelin de l'humanité' (47), will reject the father's voice in favour of a desperate attempt to build *L'Evasion*, a boat in which to escape from the island, a replica in miniature of the maternal security afforded by *Virginie*. Once the project of *L'Evasion* - and of evasion of the real issues confronting him - proves unworkable, he begins to accept the island as his real environment. What is interesting here is that while all the protagonists of Robinson's Pacific adventure are male, the feminine principle is powerfully present, first in *Virginie*, and then in Speranza. The all-male cast have their being in a female environment.

The relationship between prologue and narrative is thus a complex and multiple one. 'Le petit discours que je vous ai tenu est en quelque sorte chiffré, et la grille se trouve être votre avenir lui-même' (13). This is the guidance Van Deyssel offers to Robinson, on how to decode his discourse. It could also be taken as a metatextual hint from Tournier to the reader as to the decoding of the whole prologue, not just the captain's predictions. Encoded into it are themes of birth, paternity, maternity and the powerful emotional nexus around them which the remainder of the text (the 'future' of the reader in the text) will uncover and develop.

In particular, the narrative will vouchsafe at intervals Robinson's memories of his early life, and of his real parents. These vignettes are richly suggestive of the primal emotions which underpin Robinson's mentality. The first such memories emerge when he has lapsed into despair following the failure of *L'Evasion*. He is wallowing in the mud-pool, and has surrendered all rational control, a situation which permits deep-seated memories to surface into consciousness. His first recollection is of hours spent as a child tucked away among the rolls of cloth in his father's drapery shop. The milieu is one of protective, womb-like enclosure, 'une forteresse molle qui buvait indistinctement les bruits, les lumières, les chocs et les courants d'air'(39).[15] As in the captain's cabin, there is only one other human being with whom to share this protective space: here it is his real father. The portrait inscribed on Robinson's memory is again a negative one, although in a different vein: it is that of 'un petit homme timide et frileux'(39) perched on a high stool, poring over his business accounts. Robinson would like to believe that he has inherited nothing from his father save his red hair, but he becomes aware on reflection that he is more like his father than he had thought, in his 'facultés de repliement sur lui-même et de démission en face du monde extérieur'(39). It is fitting that this image of 'repliement' and 'démission' invested in the father comes to Robinson in the mud-pool, at a time when he is himself a prey to these forces. The father can be seen to have bequeathed to Robinson his fear of real confrontation with the elements, his obsession with administration, order and book-keeping, and even (as a draper!) his refusal of nudity. Many of Robinson's life-denying attitudes are thus placed beneath the sign of the weak, conventionally pious father, while, in contrast, Van Deyssel's alternative paternity is characterised by a robust materialism and a hedonistic taste for the good things of life. Robinson's evolution can be understood in part as a swing from the orbit of his real father towards the subversive values of the new pseudo-father.

It is worth recalling at this point that Defoe's *Robinson Crusoe* also places great stress on patriarchy. Defoe's hero interprets his shipwreck and exile as a punishment visited on him by God for disregarding the advice of his father who enjoined him not to undertake hazardous ventures overseas, but to accept the modest and secure career mapped out for him at home. Crusoe calls his heedlessness 'my original sin'.[16] The opening pages of Defoe's novel report at length the father's counsel to his son. (Arguably, Tournier's prologue parodies this opening with a pseudo-father's very different discourse, while the man squinting at ledgers from his high stool is the ghost of Defoe's father figure.) Defoe's Robinson will subsequently be gripped by the unshakeable conviction, characteristic of the age, that the father's authority in the family is an extension of God's authority in the world, and that the words of paternal wisdom and command are an extension of the law and Word of God. Within this world-view, Defoe's hero can move confidently into a patriarchal role towards Friday and the growing colony he establishes and governs. His mother's role in the novel is simply to insist on the wisdom of the father's counsel, and Defoe's text never presents any significant maternal-feminine force to challenge the authority of the patriarchal order and discourse which characterise the earlier novel throughout.

For Tournier's Robinson, however, the father is 'cet homme effacé'(39) - 'effacé' not only in the sense of humble or modest but also *erased*, disqualified as a possible role-model from Robinson's consciousness. In contrast his mother is spoken of, on the same page, as 'une maîtresse femme', an object of admiration. This counterpoint of paternal weakness and maternal strength is reinforced: his voice is a 'fausset toujours plaintif', hers a 'voix ferme et bien timbrée'(49).

Later, in another moment of 'repliement sur lui-même' deep in the underground cave, at a level where he is keenly aware of Speranza's maternal attributes, he is obsessed by the memories of his mother, and of her selfless devotion to her children. Her imperturbable fortitude in adversity (like that of the *Virginie*) is enshrined in the memory of the day the draper's shop caught fire, and in the vision of her walking calmly out of the smoke and flames with all her children about her. In the presence of this heroic gesture, the father is no more than a spectator, kneeling in the street and praying to God (108). This paean to a paragon of motherhood is however compromised by a significant reservation: she is so undemonstrative that he can never remember her embracing himself or any of his siblings (107). This affective deprivation is signalled as a potentially important element in Robinson's make-up,[17] and underlies Robinson's difficulty in accepting his own body and its needs. Robinson(-child) wishes to remain within the maternal security he has known, while Robinson(-man) simultaneously seeks adult carnal satisfaction. It is the problem of Oedipal desire, reflected in the contradictory feminine roles he projects onto Speranza and in his fear of incestuous insemination of her in the womb-like cave.

On the paternal side, after the regressive anality of the mud-pool, Robinson launches energetically on the construction of the 'île administrée', a project building on his father's legacy of mercantilism, capital accumulation and obsessive accounting. On the fractured foundation of his evidently poor regard for his own father, he builds a precarious edifice of totalitarian patriarchy, including elaborate provisions for punishing himself whenever he falls short of the requirements of the authoritarian order to which he seeks to subject every element of the island. Reliance on such a rigid value-system implies inherent weakness (the paternal legacy), as Robinson often recognises, and the 'penal code' implies an associated deep-seated guilt, for the Oedipal crime of disqualifying the weak father in favour of the strong mother, the guilt of admitting patriarchal failure. He strives to realise the project, scripted by Defoe, to construct an absolute patriarchal order in which he casts himself as 'à la fois le maître et le père de Vendredi'(191). In the absence of a strong and humane role-model, however, this enterprise is doomed to contradiction and failure. The sojourn in the maternal depths of the underground cave prepares the metamorphosis which will shatter this order of crude patriarchy, and the rest of the text enacts the dismantling of its code of values.

A series of incidents points explicitly to the assault on the inherited paternal code. The plants in the cactus-garden which Robinson has planted in memory of his father are dressed up by Vendredi in clothes from Robinson's chest, literally *travestied*: from being meticulously labelled specimens assembled as a tribute to the past, they become monstrous variations on the human body, gaudy 'mannequins végétaux' (159) mockingly sporting the uniforms of the patriarchal order. Later, Vendredi will fabricate another 'mannequin', this time representing Robinson himself in his role as governor (210), from which they will progress to re-enactments of past events in their lives, each dressing up as and playing the role of the other. In this way Robinson is emancipated from his commitment to paternalism as his only paradigm, and discovers a *polyvalence* in his relations with Vendredi ('mon fils et mon père, mon frère et mon voisin' (224)), just as in learning to walk on his hands, he moves towards an ideal *'polyvalence* de ses membres'(192).

This shift from a restrictive, patriarchal code to a polyvalent mode of sexuality is wholly characteristic. Tournier's fiction explores a variety of sexualities which transgress more or less radically the frontiers of the restricted zone of social acceptability to savour forbidden fruits of eroticism.

In Chapter 5, Robinson reflects in his logbook on how, in the absence of any human companion, his sexual desire has evolved. The social mechanism which normally channels desire towards the propagation of the species has been removed, and his libido is thus liberated from any prescription; after a while, he can no longer rely on memories and fantasies of the female body to excite him. Yet desire remains, an unchannelled 'fontaine de vie [...] totalement disponible'(119) overflowing in all directions, seeking a new focus. This passage of self-analysis significantly follows on his descent into the grotto at the centre of Speranza, and it is in the shifting ways in which he constitutes the island as female - and thus as a potential object of erotic attraction - that one can trace this delocalisation of desire. He chooses the name Speranza both because, as the Italian word for 'hope', it stands for one of the three theological virtues (Faith, Hope and Charity) and because it recalls 'une ardente Italienne' he had once known (45). When he maps the island, its form recalls for him the profile of a headless female body, 'dans une attitude [...] de soumission, de peur ou de simple abandon'(46). When he discovers the imprint of his foot in the rock, he asserts that 'Speranza [...] portait désormais le sceau de son Seigneur et Maître'(57). In this first phase, therefore, the governing codes of religious dogma and administrative control do not conceal an underlying (sadist-colonialist) fantasy of sexual domination of an enslaved and submissive exotic female.

As the text proceeds, this fantasy role within a heterosexual dominant-submissive relationship is progressively eroded and challenged. A variant of it is manifest in a memory from his youth. Each morning on his way to school, he would watch, through a barred window, a baker kneading his dough. 'Or je ne concevais rien de plus onctueux ni de plus accueillant que ce grand corps sans tête, tiède et lascif, qui s'abandonnait au fond du pétrin aux étreintes d'un homme à demi nu'(81). This erotically charged vision from his childhood suggests a source for his domination fantasy, with specific echoes of the shape he attributes to Speranza as the 'corps sans tête' in a posture of 'abandon'. There are however two important shifts. One is from the visual (the map outline) to the tactile (kneading the dough): the surfacing of this childhood memory is a significant indication of a desire to step outside the 'glass cage' of sensory deprivation discussed in Chapter 2 above.[18] Robinson, like Tournier, sets the 'contact' senses of touch and smell above the more distanced senses of sight and hearing: 'Palper et humer sont pour moi des modes d'appréhension plus émouvants et plus pénétrants que voir et entendre'(81). Following this penchant he will graduate to direct physical and erotic contact with Speranza, in the grotto and the grassy meadow. The second significant feature of the vision of the baker is its context - the unhappy schoolchild is shut out in the muddy street, in the 'noirceur humide du petit-jour'(81). It is the warm scent, the 'haleine chaude, maternelle et comme charnelle'(81), which attracts and grips him, and in this desolate exile can be seen a child's desire for the warmth of the mother's body and the maternal bed from which he has been expelled. Alongside (and inseparable from) the dream of manipulating a compliant female body is the opposite hunger for refuge in a tender and protective embrace.[19]

The principle of heterosexual dominance is further compromised, later in the same chapter, in the account of the 'moment d'innocence'(94), the sense of blessed release which Robinson experiences when his water-clock stops. He first interprets this as an extension of his (sexual) power: 'Ainsi donc la toute-puissance de Robinson sur l'île - fille de son absolue solitude - allait jusqu'à une maîtrise du temps!'(93).[20] He soon perceives, however, that this moment of plenitude emanates from Speranza, not from himself, and for one ecstatic moment 'Robinson crut découvrir une *autre île* derrière celle où il peinait solitairement, [...] plus chaude, plus fraternelle...'(94). Again we see the notion of 'toute-puissance' being displaced by one of comfort and refuge from solitude and arduous routine, implying a sexuality of surrender and acceptance rather than of power and imposition. In this new dispensation the 'abandon' is on his part, rather than his partner's. A significant further shift is from the '[haleine] chaude, maternelle' of the alluring bakehouse to the beatific glimpse of the 'autre île... plus chaude, plus fraternelle' - the shift from maternal to fraternal signifies a realignment of gender and role which is to characterise Robinson's whole subsequent development. The 'fraternal' space of the other island anticipates Vendredi's arrival, whose name and role is associated with Venus, and this ambivalence of gender is already foreseen in Van Deyssel's prophecy: 'Vénus [...] est devenue votre frère jumeau', the twins being placed at the feet of 'l'Ange bisexué'(10).

The episode in the grotto also re-enacts the bakehouse scenario: its entrance resembles 'un gigantesque soupirail'(101) and Robinson, having descended into the crypt-like lower cavity, dwells on the memory of his mother kneading dough for the Epiphany cake. This lower chamber represents maternal space, and in particular the womb, 'douces ténèbres matricielles'(112), and the experience will lead him to recognise that this Oedipal regression is dangerously at odds with his sexual maturity. While Speranza's feminine gender is beyond doubt, ambivalence in other respects persists. Robinson's initial uncertainty as to which orifice of her body the grotto constitutes is developed in the text. The upper chamber is variously characterised as cortex, eye, and stomach (103-4), and the passage he then slides down headfirst is likened to an oesophagus, though the need to strip and lubricate his body before entering might suggest penile penetration. The apertures and chambers seem poised between animal and vegetable (forms) and mineral (substance): 'parois [...] polies comme de la chair', 'des tétons lapidifiés, des verrues calcaires, des champignons marmoréens, des éponges pétrifiées' (105). Ambiguities of sexual politics, of gender and even between the different realms of nature proliferate in this play of erotic contact.

The central identification in this sexual nexus, that between island and woman, undergoes a most significant change. The island-as-woman metaphor began inconspicuously with the conferring of a name, but thereafter these linked terms shift and merge. To start with, Robinson had simply used the island as a substitute for the absent female form (as in his ill-fated embraces with a fallen tree-trunk), but gradually Speranza comes alive for him as an individual in her own right, 'une *personne*, de nature indiscutablement féminine'(101-2). He revels in the imagery of the 'femme-paysage', the woman's body as landscape which he finds in the *Song of Solomon* - 'la Bible débordante d'images qui identifient la terre à une femme ou l'épouse à un jardin'(136). (In *Le Roi des aulnes* Abel also ironically describes Rachel as a 'femme-paysage'(*RA* 32).) In fact, however, Robinson has reversed the direction of the metaphor. While borrowing a discourse in which the erotic attributes of a female body are celebrated through the poetic conceit of a landscape, he is making love to a landscape, while using the poetic conceit of the female form. The 'femme-paysage' has been inverted to become a 'paysage-femme'.[21] It is an island he loves, who will bear him 'children' (the mandragora flowers) and draw him so far from the human into the vegetable realm that his hair will take root in the earth, like the 'homme-plante' of Vendredi's games. Robinson thus undergoes a fantastic 'dehumanisation', and it is this radical reorientation of his desire towards the non-human natural world, his 'sexualité [...] devenue *élémentaire*' (229), which explains his lack of homosexual desire for Vendredi. Vendredi's function in his sexual evolution is not, he explains finally, to make him revert to love for a human being, but to push him on one last stage: it is to emancipate Robinson from his fixation on Speranza-earth, and reorient him towards Uranus, the god of the sky. Thereby the gender-bound model of sexuality is finally set aside. Robinson's relations with Speranza had evolved from the woman-island metaphor - 'En somme, je fécondais cette terre comme j'aurais fait une épouse'(229) - and remained genital in character.[22] In this new stage of evolution, attained just before Vendredi's departure, he feels that he has transcended gender, and that, if human terms are any longer appropriate, his sexuality is feminine in nature: he is 'l'épouse du ciel'(230). In Greek mythology the spouse (and mother) of the sky-god Uranus was the earth-goddess Gaia. Usually depicted as a woman of immense stature, this fertility goddess is evoked in Robinson's description of Speranza as 'cette gigantesque et brûlante femelle'(175), as he unites with her.

In becoming himself 'l'épouse du ciel', he has in effect annexed Speranza-Gaia's role, and aspires to a quasi-divine status worthy of the spouse of the sun-god. A feminine and maternal model is thus incorporated, in place of the dominant and flawed heritage of patriarchy.

As regards the theme of sexuality, therefore, what Tournier offers us in *Vendredi* is an idealised, and ultimately fantastic, prototype of an ordinary man's emancipation from what Tournier regards as an oppressively restrictive model of socialised sexuality to one which has expanded across every conceivable frontier of gender, object and mode of expression to become a total mode of living and feeling. Once the initial impasse is recognised, his sexual growth is characterised by three schematic phases of activity and development. The first takes place beneath the earth, in the grotto, and relates to birth and to his roots in the mother's body. The second is enacted on the earth, in his sexual rapport with Speranza and corresponds to his adult, but still conventionally based, human sexuality. The final stage is, as it were, supra-terrestrial. It is, Robinson suggests in his logbook, scarcely expressible in human language ('S'il fallait nécessairement traduire en termes humains ce coït solaire [...]'(230)). This upward movement is an image of organic growth, from seed to plant to flowering, and it is the first (underground) stage which provides the foundation for the final aspiration skyward. Writing after the grotto episode, Robinson recognises that this revisiting of the origins of his sexuality in childhood has established his identity on a new and fruitful footing: 'Ma vie repose désormais sur un socle d'une admirable solidité, ancré au coeur même de la roche et en prise directe avec les énergies qui y sommeillent'(111). To compensate his previous sense of precariousness, he had long dreamt of a solidly built house, 'massive, inébranlable, assumée par des fondations formidables'(112). Now the dream, he says, is no longer required. On the final page of the novel, as Robinson-Gaia, 'épouse du ciel', stands beside his new child and communes with the sun, these same images of solidity and foundation recur: 'Ses jambes prenaient appui sur le roc, massives et inébranlables'(254). As a parable of sexual liberation the text is immensely optimistic: as a first novel it is both a dramatic, idealistic credo and an exorcism of the failures and deprivations which Tournier diagnoses at the heart of our culture. It is of course for the reader to choose whether to subscribe to this euphoric vision of an ungendered and diffuse sexuality, or whether to regard it as an ultimate fantasy of male sexuality absorbing all other models into itself.

In each of Tournier's first three major novels, the model of the heterosexual couple will be seen as an impasse, which has to be transcended before more fruitful and diverse paths of desire open up. Each new path explored by a fictional hero will throw into question one or more of the prescriptions of the dominant code which requires that sexual activity be heterosexual, genital, adult, non-promiscuous, between two people only and in accordance with pre-defined gender roles. In fact the very first novel, *Vendredi*, throws into question the even more fundamental assumption that the object of desire is necessarily the human body. Tournier rightly describes *Vendredi* as the most 'aggressive' of his novels in this sense: 'L'éclatement de la sexualité y est plus délibéré que dans *Le Roi des aulnes* ou *Les Météores*. [...] Le maximum d'ouverture à la sexualité et d'invention possible était dans *Vendredi*.'[23]

Le Roi des aulnes: Alpha and Omega, Oral and Anal

The 'heterosexual impasse' as the starting point of the narrative is even more dramatically marked in *Le Roi des aulnes*. The opening of the novel records the breakdown of Tiffauges's relationship with Rachel, an outcome on which his whole subsequent evolution will be founded. These pages are a requiem not just for one particular love affair, but for any attempt on his part to meet the demands of an intimate adult heterosexual relationship. The episode is narrated in retrospect, in his newly commenced diary, and thus relegated to a period before the start of the *récit*, i.e. outside the frontiers of the time of narration. The heterosexual impasse is thus inscribed as a premise of the writing of the text. This displacement out of the heterosexual majority is linked to another displacement, apparently more trivial, out of the majority of right-handers, as he discovers his power to write left-handed. These twin displacements are clearly to be seen as complementary, even symbiotic - the new 'sinister' writing is perceived as the expression of a supernatural, pre-ordained self, hitherto concealed, whose desire and sexuality will be resolutely not heterosexual. (The association of these displacements serves also, perhaps, to suggest that the insistence on heterosexual genital sexuality as a norm is as arbitrary as our culture's traditional prejudice in favour of right-handedness, which is itself sustained by a whole substructure of myths and superstitions.)[24] Tiffauges's story will be one of an increasingly dramatic divergence from the 'norm', one in which the concept of normality is attacked as a tyranny of the established majority. Against this imposed norm, he will write a paean to the 'monster' or freak who, he suggests, is characteristically exhibited, mocked, reviled and persecuted. His 'sinister' writing is thus already proposed as a 'monstrous' activity, and the liberation it affords for self-expression and for exemplary verbal revenge on the society of his adversaries is associated with the liberation from any exclusively heterosexual channelling of libido. Like Robinson's logbook, Abel's writings will plot the emergence of an alternative self, with priorities radically divergent from those dominant in his own society. Hence the final fulfilling partnership towards which the whole novel will tend is not between man and woman, but between man and boy-child.

In Abel's account of the Rachel fiasco, the imagery deployed in dialogue and description sharply underlines the lovers' incompatibility. Rachel complains of his lack of concern with her sexual needs, of his haste in sating his 'faim de chair fraîche': 'Tu me ravales au niveau du bifteck'(*RA* 21). While these observations reinforce her refrain of 'Tu es un ogre' noted in the opening line of the novel, other textual elements make Rachel the predator of the two. Her 'tête au profil aquilin' (18) characterises her as a bird of prey, and is supported by other references to air and flight: she is a 'comptable volant'(19) by profession, first seen (pun intended, surely) 'au volant d'une quadrillette Peugeot'(18) who arrives 'en coup de vent'(19) but who has, he suspects, already spotted another love-nest than his to visit, 'une autre couche où elle irait se poser'(21). When she slightingly compares his lovemaking to a canary's, it is with all the disdain of the eagle for a tiny songbird which is its natural prey, and the implicit threat is made explicit: 'Il serait bon en effet, a conclu Rachel, que tu croies que je te dévorerai dès que tu t'arrêteras'(20). These words conjure up for Abel a second predatory image of Rachel as the wolf, intent on devouring the little goat as in Daudet's story 'La Chèvre de M. Seguin'.

This emblematic use of birds and animals to characterise the (sexual and other) warfare between human beings initiates a rich bestiary in the remainder of the text. The eagle vs. canary opposition prepares for the later reference to the (predatory) heraldic eagle adopted by the Nazis, as opposed to the pigeons (inoffensive prey) cherished by Abel and which foreshadow the three boys in their immolation. In part the eagle-pigeon opposition can be taken to stand for the opposition between adult sexual assertiveness (represented initially by Rachel) and a pre-sexual craving for warmth and tenderness. The Mobilgas symbol of the winged horse displayed on Tiffauges's garage is a third, 'phoric' image which in turn anticipates the symbolic significance which he will attribute to the horse as 'Ange anal', image of the non-genital sexuality which he will cultivate. Set against the 'Ange anal' is the stag, the 'Ange phallophore', whose antlers are, as Goering will remind Abel, an exact and spectacular manifestation of its genital power. In the hunting park, however, this proud beast is cast in the passive and pathetic role of prey to the huntsman, so that the hunt becomes a symbolic revenge of the (now predatory) adversaries of genital sexuality.[25] This in turn culminates in the Behemoth role which Ephraim will confer on Abel, that of a beast of immense strength, but wholly non-predatory in nature.

The Abel-Rachel relationship sketched in the opening pages is thus mutually predatory, almost mutually cannibalistic ('Tu es un ogre'/'Je te dévorerai'), and Abel explains this antagonism in terms of a fundamental incompatibility between male and female needs. In his sardonic analysis of Rachel, Abel sees the opposition we have already noted above between the procreative and the erotic. Rachel's body, with its broad hips and ample proportions, seems to him designed for maternity, a vocation she seeks to deny by her self-image as a 'garçonne'(18), adopting the masculine, Don Juan role of seducer and sexual adventurer. Her preferred scenario thus seeks to reduce the role of the male partner to that of instrument of erotic pleasure, the bearer of a permanently tumescent phallus who is liable to be disqualified (devoured) as soon as he fails in this function. This female fantasy of male potency is, however, at odds with the urgent and rapidly satisfied nature of male desire, which seems designed to meet the needs of fertilisation rather than of the woman's erotic satisfaction. Abel, obese and genitally under-endowed ('microgénitomorphe'(110)), is particularly ill-suited to Rachel's demands. In his preferred scenario of a pre-adult non-genital sexuality, her body is there, like the baker's dough of Robinson's memory, to be manipulated and consumed, and the real mark of the feminine gender is not the vulva but the breasts, 'cornes d'abondance'(33) with their promise of oral satisfaction. He in his turn will found his scenario of desire in a (mis)reading of the Creation story in Genesis, in which he imagines Adam first created as a hermaphrodite, 'porte-femme et porte-enfant, perpétuellement en proie à une transe érotique - possédant-possédé - dont nos amours ordinaires ne sont que l'ombre pâle' (132). The 'Fall' occurs when Adam's female sexual parts are amputated to become Eve, a version which disqualifies the opposite sex, reducing woman to nothing more than sexual function. This disqualification of woman is reinforced by Tiffauges's desire to appropriate the maternal role, to be a bearer of children like the original Adam.[26] This fantasy-myth goes beyond the oral desire to enjoy and consume the substance of the female body: in the hermaphroditic Adam, the whole physical vocation and experience of the female body is absorbed into the male. In terms of sexuality, therefore, the project of the narrative is to explore a sexuality which transgresses the norm in two ways: it is oral-anal rather than genital, and it extends the masculine to appropriate a maternal role.

The intense gratification that Abel can derive from oral sexuality is graphically described in his sado-masochistic relationship with a fellow-pupil, Pelsenaire. Pelsenaire enslaves Abel, forcing him to hand over half of his food, to clean his boots and to eat grass every day (in ironic anticipation of Abel's role as the herbivorous Behemoth at the end of the novel). This tyranny reaches its culmination when Pelsenaire, having fallen and cut his knee, obliges Abel to lick the wound clean. The description which follows (31) of the wound, and of the way Abel licks it and then presses his lips to it, is meticulously detailed, conveying Abel's rapt attention and his sense of time being suspended. This transcendent experience, which leaves him in a state of nervous collapse, is deliberately ambiguous in its status. It partakes of vampirism and of cunnilingus: the wound is described in terms reminiscent of a vagina oozing menstrual blood. This analogy between the wound and the female genitalia acts as a transsexual displacement of a female sexual marker on to a male body, and hence a further dispossession of woman. In his essay on the Tristan legend (*VV* 28) Tournier sketches the primary image of Tristan engraved on his mind, that of a young boy bearing a grievous wound, and adds: 'On ne s'étonnera pas de l'absence d'Iseut dans ce frontispice, car *sa blessure tient lieu de femme* au chevalier sans nom' (my italics).

The vampirism[27] implicit in Abel's gesture runs against the context of his (masochistic) enslavement - Abel has already said that being made to clean Pelsenaire's boots gave him secret pleasure, so who is here the exploiter and who the exploited? The ambivalence is further underlined when we recall that Pelsenaire's cruelty started as revenge for the wording of the tattoo ('A.T. pour la vie') which Tiffauges tricked him into accepting on his thigh: by substituting his own initials (A.T.) for the vague 'A toi' Pelsenaire had expected, Abel is making a scandalous claim on his fellow pupil's love and fidelity. He follows it up, when taxed with his deceit, with an unambiguous embrace of his idol. The relationship thus starts with Abel's claim on Pelsenaire inscribed on Pelsenaire's flesh and ends with his sealing this claim with a kiss in his blood. The sexual politics are devious here. Pelsenaire, whose bullying manner and taste for the paraphernalia of virile force (hobnail boots and heavy-buckled belt) cast him as the prototype of the young Nazi thug, may appear to be the master, but the relationship is manipulated by Abel, who, within his apparent humiliation, is pursuing with some success his own agenda of gratification. This vivid early episode is, as so often in this novel, an anticipation in microcosm of the way Tiffauges, the apparently powerless prisoner of the Nazi regime, will subvert the visible power structure to act out his own script, a script which includes the exploration of an alternative sexuality.

This fetishisation of the wounded body of a boy is associated from the start with Tiffauges's 'phoric' vocation: Pelsenaire has already been 'carried', sitting astride Abel as he is made to eat grass on all fours. The first chapter presents three further episodes in which Tiffauges derives intense joy from carrying an (actually or imaginarily) injured child. In the first, he gathers up in his arms his garage apprentice Jeannot, who has been struck on the head by a broken fan-blade (130). In the second, the injury is imaginary: he befriends the young Etienne in the Louvre, and they amuse themselves mimicking the statues of strong men carrying children: in the last of these *tableaux vivants*, they imitate Hector carrying off his wounded little brother, Troilus, slung unceremoniously over his shoulder (143). In the third of these incidents, Abel sees a young roller-skater fall and cut his knee. As with Pelsenaire, he contemplates the wound with delectation - 'la plaie est d'une netteté magnifique'(172) - and this fetishising description of the wound relates this moment closely to that earlier passage. On the level of sexual politics, however, there is a significant shift in Tiffauges's role, from (devious) masochist to sadist: he slaps the injured boy to make him stand upright, so that he can take a reel of photographs of him.[28] The wound this time is described not as a sexual organ but as a ruptured Cyclopean eye, and the reference to the Cyclops, the bloodthirsty ogre blinded by Odysseus in Book IX of Homer's *Odyssey*, suggests the extent to which the erotic has been subsumed into the predatory. The metaphor is again *displaced*: the blinded eye, mark of the defeated ogre, is grafted on to the child, here the victim of the ogre triumphant. (Elsewhere, the 'oeil de Cyclope', intact this time, is Tiffauges's camera lens, capturing its prey (167).) In this phoric sequence (Jeannot - Etienne - the boy skater), Abel's treatment of the child has become increasingly brutal. In the incident with the skater his cruelty to the boy is to serve the needs of his camera, and in the pages immediately preceding, Abel defines the practice of photography as the 'possession mi-amoureuse, mi-meurtrière du photographié par le photographe'(168). This formula, 'possession mi-amoureuse, mi-meurtrière' links photography, by association, with sexual murder, cannibalism or vampirism, and Tournier has himself remarked, in the preface to a volume of photographs of children, that 'le photographe est un ogre qui s'ignore. Si on pouvait manger les enfants, gageons qu'on les photographierait moins souvent'.[29] Even when he has no camera, Tiffauges's text enacts this photographic function, recording and reproducing the wounds in exact, unflinching detail. The disturbing combination in these passages of visual objectivity and morbid delectation makes it possible to speak of a sadism of the seeing eye. 'Regarde! [...] il saigne!', says Tiffauges's assistant Ben Ahmed to his employer holding Jeannot's inert body, words followed by 'un long silence frémissant de bonheur'(131). This sadistic 'regard' deindividualises its object, reducing it to the status of anonymous flesh: the bodies, and the children, are interchangeable. Under the eye of the master observer, as under the eye of the camera, each is generalised, to become a symbolic representative of the whole category: '[...] [U]n enfant photographié, c'est X - mille, dix mille - enfants possédés...'(169).

In the final chapters of the novel, set in Kaltenborn, the male child as object of desire will be almost infinitely multiplied and deindividualised, and the association of 'phorie' with injury and bloodshed grows ever stronger. This link is made when he captures the young Lothar to carry him back to the Napola: 'Au moment où l'enfant bascula dans ses bras, sa joie était si véhémente qu'il ne sentit pas les dents de sa jeune proie s'enfoncer dans sa main jusqu'au sang'(468-9). When he awakes in the middle of the night amidst all the cadets who have fallen asleep hither and thither in the 'hypnodrome' he has constructed for them, they conjure up the image of slaughtered bodies on a battlefield, and he lifts up the twins Haïo and Haro and savours their dead weight with 'une joie grave' (520). Both Lothar and the twins will be the objects of the sadistic 'regard' as their naked bodies are meticulously measured and inspected by Tiffauges in the laboratory of the Centre Raciologique which he has inherited from Professor Blättchen. The seeing eye lays claim to a scientific objectivity in its observation, but the lingering inspection of the docile and unprotected bodies is also a coded discourse of desire: his first tour of the twins' bodies ends on 'la face interne des cuisses'(450), while that of Lothar concludes with a careful description of the boy's genitals. Raising his eyes from his notes, Tiffauges is met by Lothar's smile (whether trusting or coquettish we are left to imagine), in a suggestion of unstated sexual complicity (485).

For Lothar and the twins, the bloody fate which awaits those who, captured and contemplated, are the objects of an ogre's desire, is delayed until the dénouement of the novel. In the meantime that climax is prepared for by the fate of two other cadets, Hellmut von Bibersee and Arnim the Swabian. Hellmut's head is blown off in a military exercise: 'J'ai soulevé le petit gisant dans mes bras, en fixant les yeux sur l'horrible plaie qui couvre l'emplacement du cou'(539). Again, the gesture of 'phorie', the fetishised wound and the 'regard' of delectation come together in an 'extase phorique'(539). In a careful crescendo, the injury, while accidental like that of Pelsenaire or the skater, is a result of war, not children's games. It is mortal, not trivial, but Tiffauges finds in this very fact a dark fascination: 'le goût d'une chair plus grave, plus marmoréenne'(540).

The text thus charts the growth of an oral sexuality which Tournier sees as one dimension of all sexual desire: 'Car le désir sexuel est une faim de l'autre, et ressemble par bien des côtés à une pulsion cannibalesque. Le goût violent de la chair d'autrui, de son odeur, des humeurs qu'elle sécrète a un aspect évidemment anthropophage. Et quand le sexe en reste à ce niveau, il n'est pas loin de basculer dans le sadisme'(*MI* 131). In *Le Roi des aulnes,* from the founding Pelsenaire experience onwards, this oral sexuality has been inextricably enmeshed with a sinister fascination with blood and a relationship of dominance-submission. As Tournier writes in a short article significantly entitled 'Eloge de la chair dolente': 'Le corps humain, blessé, soigné, tué et mis en linceul, grand thème qui remue en chacun de nous des vertiges métaphysiques et des ivresses sado-masochistes'(*CS* 79). We have already seen in *Vendredi* how the patterns of domination originally associated with the heterosexual impasse have to be set aside before a positive alternative can emerge. In *Le Roi des aulnes,* as in *Vendredi,* this turning point is marked by an explosion. The blast in this case kills Arnim the Swabian, who accidentally detonates a mine he is carrying a few yards in front of Abel, who is drenched in the child's blood and pulverised flesh. This cataclysmic event pursues to its end the logical sequence of the destruction of children's bodies, from wounding to decapitation to total annihilation. It frustrates Abel's desire by offering no occasion for phoric or visual delectation - there is no marmoreal body left to lift or to gaze at. The (literal) bloodbath marks Abel's inescapable involvement in the child's death and in the rationale which has led to it. It is however interpreted by Abel not as a condemnation, but as a consecration, a rite of passage to a new and higher status. 'In seinen Armen das Kind war tot' (in his arms the child was dead) - the last line of Goethe's 'Erlking' ballad had already been realised with the death of Helmut, and with this fresh and still more destructive extension of its infernal logic comes a recognition of the pattern which enables Abel to assume fully the role of an Erlking redefined.[30] It is significant that in the section immediately following the explosion Abel recalls the Pelsenaire episode which initiated this pattern and is now able to perceive its determining significance. With the closure of this pattern, the way is clear for the imminent arrival of Ephraim and the reorientation which he will bring about. Seen in this perspective, the death by impalement of the three boys, where the undercurrent of sexual violence is manifest in its simulacrum of homosexual rape,[31] is the epilogue to a pattern which Abel has already disowned, even if the seeing eye is as implacable as ever in recording the postures of their suffering.

In counterpoint to this increasingly sanguinary pattern of predatory desire stand two other recurrent motifs. One counterweight to the figure of the ogre, the devourer of children, is that of the *pater nutritor*, the feeder of children, which represents Abel's attempt to appropriate the maternal vocation of woman. There is much play on the ambiguity of 'porter un enfant', which can refer either to the simple act of carrying a child, or to childbearing, giving birth. Through this equivocation the act of 'phorie' is given a maternal prestige. Likewise the actions characteristic of maternal tenderness - feeding, cleaning and tending - are enthusiastically undertaken by Tiffauges for his cadets (in emulation of Frau Netta, the *Heimmutter*), but like 'phorie' itself they never escape the ambivalence of tenderness/predatory desire which Tournier has summed up in the opposition 'servir/asservir l'enfant'.[32] It is only when the logic of 'asservissement' has been exhausted that the vocation to single-minded 'service' can come into its own.

The second element which stands in opposition to the orality of the ogre is the anal, or excremental, and the text uses the terms Alpha and Omega to refer (among other possible meanings) to the mouth and the fundament respectively. The conventional valorisation of the face as noble and of the buttocks as ignoble is wholly subverted. In passages which snipe mischievously at the taboo which divides one from the other, Tiffauges reverses this hierarchy. Looking at his face in the mirror, he finds it so disagreeable that he puts it under the toilet-flush for a 'shampooing-caca'(73). Elsewhere he is struck with wonder at the 'expression en quelque sorte morale'(94) of Nestor's buttocks, bespeaking naivety and goodness, or of the 'fesses des enfants [...] souriantes et naïvement optimistes, expressives comme des visages'(523-4). For Abel to wipe Nestor's bottom is thus for him a reverential gesture, equal or superior in dignity to wiping the face of a child. The potential malignity of face, eyes and mouth are thus counterbalanced by an opposite, 'fundamental' generosity. Tiffauges learns from Nestor a cult of defecation; what is a 'throne' for Nestor's defecatory ritual becomes for Abel an altar (265, 270). The religious overtones are sustained in his exaltation of the horse as 'Ange Anal', by virtue of its 'perfection dans l'acte défécatoire'(353), and in the notion of 'béatitude fécale' (263). The scatological brings together a number of other thematic strands. It carries a suggestion of an alternative, non-genital sexual pleasure ('un glissement régulier de l'étron dans le fourreau lubrifié des muqueuses'(264)), and there are resonant associations in moments of excremental contemplation such as the following: 'Je regarde attendri ce beau poupon dodu de limon vivant que je viens d'enfanter [...]'(144). 'Poupon' and 'enfanter' relate excretion to a giving-birth, and thus to Abel's desire to appropriate the maternal function, to 'porter l'enfant'. 'Limon vivant' suggests the affinity of faeces with earth, and with the clay from which (according to Genesis) man was made. This association is reinforced later in the novel when Abel describes his ritual of defecation in the fields surrounding the detention camp as the consummation of his 'union intime et féconde avec la terre prussienne' (265).

This quasi-religious theme of a ritual 'union with the earth' reaches its apotheosis in the final paragraph of the novel, as Abel is gradually swallowed up by the swamp. This suggests another possible interpretation of the final page, whereby Tiffauges becomes the 'limon vivant', the glorified excrement beneath the child perched on his shoulders, the 'poupon dodu' of a pseudo-birth. This reading, outlandish though it may seem, accords with the radical revalorisation and veneration of the excremental proposed in the text. At the same time this final metaphor of the self as excrement is a mark of the dispossession of the self in favour of an Other, whose service is freedom. Robinson, in his logbook at the end of Chapter 4 of *Vendredi*, divests the self of the power to confer meaning through perception: reversing the notion of the supremacy of the perceiving subject over the passive object, he has a vision of the subject reduced to a shimmering halo of awareness around the real locus of the fertile, harmonious island. He sums up this necessary dispossession of the self in the phrase 'Robinson est l'excrément personnel de Speranza', words in which he sees revealed 'la voie [...] du salut, d'un certain salut en tout cas'(*VLP* 100). As between Robinson and Speranza, so between Abel and the Child: the Object, once dominated, is now venerated, and the Subject, dispossessed, becomes excrement, possessed of a new dignity in its disqualification. Tournier has even, revealingly, used this figure of the excrementalisation of the self in speaking of his own experience of novel-writing. As a major novel grows in the process of creation, 'il échappe à ma maîtrise. J'en deviens alors le jardinier, le serviteur, pire encore, le sous-produit, ce que l'oeuvre fait sous elle en se faisant'(*VPar* 184).[33]

To sum up, in its thematics of desire, *Le Roi des aulnes* can be read as a triumph of the anal over the oral. In its sexual politics it inverts conventional hierarchies, finding value and enrichment in unconventional and taboo eroticisms, while at the same time showing the lethal consequences of linking desire to absolute power over others.

Les Météores: Mapping the Sexualities

With a wider cast of characters and a less unilinear structure than its two predecessors, *Les Météores* is able to explore and juxtapose a number of different sexualities, and this it does in a relatively schematic fashion. A useful starting point is Alexandre's exposition, derived from Tournier's anthropological studies,[34] of the two contradictory principles by which a heterosexual society seeks to govern the choice of mate (*Mét* 331-2). Endogamy forbids looking beyond your tribe or your caste, while exogamy places an interdict on close family members. Between these two taboo areas, the one too distant and the other too near, lies an acceptable constituency of partners for the socially conditioned heterosexual. Each of these three areas is represented in the novel. The inner area covered by the incest taboo (called zone A in Alexandre's schema) is represented by the twins, Jean-Paul. The outer taboo area ('zone C') is frequented by Alexandre, in his pursuit of partners at or beyond the margins of 'respectability' - immigrant workers, vagrants and criminals. Both the twins and Alexandre add an extra dimension of transgression to their orientation by their homosexuality. The character who conforms to the dominant heterosexual code and whose activity is centred within the intermediate 'zone B' of social acceptability is the twins' father and Alexandre's brother, Edouard.

It is the story of Edouard which illustrates the heterosexual impasse in this novel, a story which reaches its sorry conclusion by the end of Chapter 12. A successful businessman who has married well and presides over a large family, Edouard is conventional even in his extramarital adventures, with his cabaret-singer mistress in Paris and with a shop assistant while on military service: such affairs, conducted firmly at a distance from hearth and home, do nothing to undermine his profile as the stereotypically successful 'homme du monde' - rather the reverse.[35] In the eyes of Alexandre this 'ajustement merveilleux de l'hétérosexuel et de la société où il est né'(231) contrasts with the thorny desert which the young homosexual must traverse, and Alexandre finds himself envying the heterosexual's effortless conformity to all that society offers and requires. Edouard's decline in later life suggests however, as Alexandre sees it, that this total adaptation to social milieu is in the end an obstacle to happiness. With no need to struggle against disapproval or to construct a self *against* the tide of social pressure, Edouard (in the view of Alexandre) is never required to develop the resilience needed by the homosexual. The narrative illustrates and endorses Alexandre's judgment of his brother, and by extension of the whole race of 'well-adjusted' heterosexuals. War and the occupation deprive Edouard of all three women in his life: Angelica is killed by a German bomb, Florence is seized in the round-up of Jews and Maria-Barbara is arrested as a member of the Resistance. While Edouard could flourish in peacetime, these hammer-blows of war destroy the sense and structure of his life, and each would-be heroic gesture, each attempt to sacrifice his life in a way that could restore that sense and that structure is cruelly undercut. Edouard's decline and dissolution is in strong contrast to Alexandre's vitality and control over life. Precisely because he does not feel part of the imperilled social fabric of France, Alexandre is able to pursue his own game-plan on the margins of the war, moving towards a flamboyantly stage-managed death at the time of his own choosing. Despite the affectionate terms in which both principal narrators, Paul and Alexandre, often speak of Edouard, an organic link is suggested in this figure between heterosexuality and weakness, and the narrative is constructed to discredit this dominant sexual preference by comparison with the hardier strains of élite minorities.

None of the heterosexual relationships in the text is shown as happy. In Chapter 16, 'L'île des Lotophages', the bubble in which the 'lotus-eaters' Ralph and Deborah live out their marriage is fragile, and Ralph collapses under the impact of Deborah's death. He sits grieving in the lovingly constructed house and garden now ravaged by the desert storm-winds, and this image of desolation echoes Edouard's plight. Edouard too has inhabited an oasis of complacency and of ignorance (he does not see the peril to Florence, and knows nothing of Maria-Barbara's Resistance involvement) which is likewise devastated by the irruption of external forces. The Frenchman Olivier whom Paul meets in Iceland in Chapter 17 is caught in the time warp of an eleven-year engagement, and has lost all sense of purpose, bewitched by his fiancée Selma and by the arctic nights and days. In Chapter 18 the painter Urs Kraus abandons his Japanese girlfriend Kumiko to return to Europe. Nowhere in this novel, or in any Tournier fiction at least until *Le Médianoche amoureux*, is there a substantial portrait of a satisfactory heterosexual relationship.

Alexandre functions as the antithesis to Edouard, and not simply in his sexual preference: he is nomadic, unencumbered by family and disdainful of class barriers, and exhibits his difference by his dandified clothes. His sexuality, like Abel's, was substantially fixed by his experiences at boarding-school, where he was initiated into a homosexual group of pupils calling themselves 'les Fleurets'. Two members of this group particularly impressed him, Thomas Koussek and Raphaël Ganeça. The two elements of each name (like those of Abel Tiffauges)[36] refer to divergent elements. While Thomas is associated in the text with the Biblical figure of Thomas Didymus, and with the apocryphal Gospel according to Thomas, Koussek ('son pseudo-patronyme' (44)) refers to Thomas's particular erotic innovation, orgasm without ejaculation ('coup sec'). Raphaël's name links that of an archangel to that of a Hindu deity, Ganesa, represented in the form of an elephant, whose trunk is seen as a phallic symbol. (The god Ganesa is also, incidentally, a patron of literature.) The names of both these mentors thus link male genitality with religious tradition, implying a spiritual dimension to their homosexuality. Within this common link, they are strongly contrasted. The containment of the 'coup sec' links Thomas closely to the self-sufficiency of the twin cell Jean-Paul, and beyond that to that 'érotique close sur elle-même, sans perte ni bavure' of which Van Deyssel spoke in his commentary on the sign of Gemini (*VLP* 12). This connection between Thomas and twinship is further reinforced by the appellation of his Biblical namesake, Thomas Didymus, Didymus meaning twin (*Mét* 151). In contrast, Raphael's burning desire to pay homage to the phallic god enshrined in the clothing of each boy (51) aligns him closely with Alexandre and his promiscuous hunt for new partners. While Thomas will move progressively away from a fixation on the body and towards a particular Christian spirituality, Raphaël stands for an idolatry of the physical. Alexandre is fascinated and moved by the account Thomas gives in Chapter 5 of his spiritual itinerary, but his own predilection is more akin to Raphaël's, in his worship of the 'idole à trompe'[37] of penis and testicles as a physical 'sainte trinité' (123). In the structure of the narrative, Thomas's theology is pertinent not to Alexandre's mentality, which remains fixedly focussed on this world and its rewards, but rather to Paul's initiation and apotheosis, in which the physical partner is transcended and the self expands to contain the whole world.

Another contrast between these two guiding spirits is in their relative mix of seriousness and humour. Thomas, in relating his sexuality to the body of the crucified Christ and to the Holy Spirit, confers on it a solemn mysticism, whereas Ganesa is by comparison a grotesque deity. This grotesquery yields a strain of bawdy humour which runs through Alexandre's narrative. This surfaces notably in his comic vision of a rugby scrum (125, 251) and in his delighted discovery of a sodomising dog (224-5), which he adopts and calls Sam. The element of obscene *double entendre* is at its most elaborate in passages concerning his triangular relationship with two young men, Eustache and Daniel, whom he recruits to work in an area of his refuse dump known as the 'Trou du Diable', with the remark: 'L'essentiel est que je les tienne ensemble dans mon trou du Diable, ma proie et la proie de ma proie'(203-4). Shortly after, he sees both men emerging from the same cubicle in the communal baths and is jealous at being excluded. By coincidence there is at that moment some confusion over the customers' ticket numbers arising from the recurrence of the figures 969, which in context clearly suggests a group-sex elaboration of the 'tête-beche' posture favoured by the twins, and generally known as '69'. This undercurrent of often abrasive bawdry stemming from Alexandre helps to lighten a novel which carries a fairly heavy weight of mysticism and metaphysics in its pages.

Underpinning Alexandre's constant vituperation and mockery of heterosexual society there lies a conviction that homosexuals are an élite, in that they represent the full flowering of pure eroticism, devoid of any servitude to procreation, and thus an ideal to which heterosexuals can only aspire. Thomas points out that a disproportionate number of the world's geniuses are homosexual, and dubs them, in a Biblical reference, the 'salt of the earth' (145).[38] Thomas's declaration of superiority is categorical: '[...] [N]ous sommes aux hétérosexuels ce qu'ils sont eux-mêmes aux femmes. [...] Car l'amour avec un hétérosexuel possède une saveur incomparable, tu le sais. Les hétérosexuels sont nos femmes'(145-6). (This 'saveur incomparable' will be illustrated in the crudely comic exploit of the dog Sam, sodomising an already mating dog (224-5)). Thus a definite - and clearly misogynist - hierarchy is established, in which (male) eroticism is the positive factor and the vocation to procreate the negative one.

Alexandre thus defines himself as constitutionally superior to his brother, and to all heterosexuals, and his ability to impose a defiant, cavalier mould on his life and death serves to bear out this claim. He is, however, a character incapable of metamorphosis; as we have seen, it is Paul, not he, who will follow the path of spiritualisation announced by Thomas, and this in turn suggests that, over and above the hierarchy 'homosexual male - heterosexual male - heterosexual female' implied by Thomas, there is a further, transcendent category to which Thomas and Alexandre both aspire, that of twin.

Before going further, this survey should include the one remaining category omitted from the above hierarchy - lesbianism. A rather slight sub-plot is developed in Chapter 7, 'Les perles philippines', centring on the lesbian Fabienne de Ribeauvillé. The inclusion of this episode would seem to have more to do with Tournier's desire for an exhaustive coverage of all possible combinations of male/female heterosexual/ homosexual than with any more intrinsic *raison d'être*. Fabienne is included as a kind of female partner to Alexandre, a counterweight to Maria-Barbara's role vis-à-vis Edouard, and she does of course represent the opposite pole of female sexuality from the mother-figure of Les Pierres Sonnantes. The link between her and Alexandre is however an ironic mixture of anti-heterosexual solidarity and absolute sexual incompatibility. She is shown as less self-assured than he is, since she is prepared to compromise her lesbianism by marrying a wealthy aristocratic nonentity in order to secure the family fortunes, until a scandalous incident at the wedding reception scuppers this plan. At this point her status as homosexual outsider is reasserted when Alexandre replaces her husband as her dancing partner. This attempt by Fabienne to cross, through marriage, from one category (lesbian) to another (heterosexual) anticipates Jean's effort to escape the homosexual twin-cell to marry Sophie. In both cases the fugitive is less than whole-hearted: Jean sneaks back to Paul's bed, and Fabienne dances with Alexandre. Their attempt to deny a fundamental orientation (twinship or homosexuality) founders with the intervention of its most robust guardian (Paul or Alexandre respectively). To underline the similarity, both Fabienne and Jean react to the havoc by leaving alone on their respective planned honeymoon journeys to Venice. While the whole luridly romanesque episode surrounding Fabienne and her twin pearls is attached to the rest of the novel by certain structural balances and parallels, she is (like Edouard) never accorded a narrative voice in the story, and her portrait remains pale and stereotyped beside that of the charismatic Alexandre.

When Alexandre first meets Fabienne in her horse-riding attire, he mistakes both her and the 'groom' whom she whips across the face for men. This similarity between the two lesbians is a faint echo of the theme of pseudo-twinship in human couples which sounds more strongly elsewhere. Alexandre dresses his lover Daniel in dandified clothes identical to his own, as a 'copie conforme'(247), seeing in him a 'frère jumeau'(249). Thomas Koussek, wishing to shed his own identity in favour of that of the Biblical Christ-twin Didymus, strives to look like Christ, in a 'mimétisme blasphématoire'(152). In each case they seek to deny difference and promote identity with the loved one by manipulating external appearances. For the real twins, the position is diametrically different: Paul and Jean are already identical in appearance, to the point at which Jean feels his very identity is threatened when he looks in a mirror. His aim, therefore, is to reduce identity and promote difference within the twin couple. In each case one member of the couple is striving to deny or compromise what is given, be it identity or difference, and this dynamic is an unstable element in the equilibrium of the relationship, which can tend either to an imprisoning (endogamous) isolation from the world, or to a dispersive (exogamous) openness to it.

Les Météores is in this sense Tournier's fullest exploration yet of the chemistry of the couple. His couples characteristically undergo a process of extension and explosion. Fabienne tries to extend her life to include heterosexual marriage alongside her lesbian attachment, and this leads to the explosion of her whole project. Alexandre tries to extend his relationship with Eustache to include *his* lover Daniel, and this will lead finally to Daniel's death. Jean tries to extend the twin relationship to allow for a second relationship with Sophie, and this leads to the explosion which sends Sophie away, and both twins separately round the world. (The force of the explosion is, it appears, in proportion to the strength of the bond being broken.) In Thomas the process acquires an abstract, mystical dimension, where the extension of his loyalty beyond the person of Christ to include the Holy Spirit leads to a liberating explosion in his spiritual life. As contained in the dense recapitulation of his spiritual pilgrimage in Chapter 5, Thomas's story represents a Christian variant on the cosmic integration which Paul achieves only in the final pages.

Gaspard, Melchior & Balthazar: Sexual Tastes

The equations of desire enter too into Tournier's novel of the Magi. Gaspard is obsessively attracted to a blonde, fair-skinned slave, Biltine. She is accompanied by a man of her own race whom she claims to be her brother, but who turns out to be her lover. This situation recalls the Robinson-Speranza-Vendredi triangle: in both cases, the slave-owner is jealous of a successful rival of another race, and yearns to be loved for his own sake, and not simply out of deference to his power. Gaspard's worship of Biltine as a golden image of blondness corresponds to a deep-seated sense of his own racial inferiority. This is embodied in his opening declaration, 'Je suis noir, mais je suis roi', itself a paraphrase on the 'Nigra sum, sed formosa' ('I am black, but comely') of the *Song of Solomon* (1:4), statements which imply some general incompatibility between blackness and male prestige or female beauty. Gaspard's heterosexual desire is thus fatally complicated by both master-slave and racial politics, and reaches the familiar impasse; he is only released from his obsession by the vision of a black Christ-child, embodiment of a love in which all pretensions to power have been set aside.

Balthazar, the 'iconophile'(74), also seeks to base heterosexual union on an image, a woman's portrait with which he falls in love. When, on the strength of this, he marries Malvina, the woman in the portrait, he realises that it is the representation, not the reality, that excites his emotion, and the marriage bond is without substance. Following this fresh variant on the heterosexual impasse, Balthazar, inspired by the example of Greek culture, establishes an élite group of young men, the 'Narcisses'.[39] He is very content to observe that they adopt the Greeks' homosexual mores also, since these afford, he says, 'une diversion légère, gratuite et inoffensive à la pesante et coercitive hétérosexualité conjugale'(78). Such a phrase could have come from Alexandre in *Les Météores*, and this ideological consonance is reinforced by a reference to the presence in Balthazar's art collection of 'des idoles indiennes à trompe d'éléphant'(79), a discreet echo of Raphaël Ganeça.

Melchior, the third of the Magi, comes under Balthazar's protection and associates with the Narcisses. Balthazar, in his experience with Malvina, implicitly exorcises the obsession with an image of female beauty which afflicts Gaspard, and moves beyond it to advocate homosexuality. Melchior, in his turn, casts a sceptical eye on the Narcisses, and on Balthazar's dreams of making them a bridgehead for Greek representational culture against the Judaic hostility to images. Only Assour, a young artist protégé of Balthazar, perceives the possibility of some more fundamental revolution, of the incarnation of eternity and grace which his master will find at Bethlehem.

The sequence of the three Magi stories move in this way from heterosexuality through homosexuality, without finding in either a wholly creative channel for desire, and no kind of resolution is found in this respect until the story of Taor. Taor's story recapitulates the movement which runs through the earlier sequence. It is subdivided into two sections, headed 'L'Age du sucre' and 'L'Enfer du sel'. Taor's craving for sweet things is placed firmly under the sign of the feminine. His mother, the Maharani, wishes to exclude her son from power for as long as possible, and so places by his side a slave companion whose mission is to distract Taor with every possible frivolity, and especially to indulge his appetite for sweetmeats. Sugar is thus the instrument of subjection to the female-maternal. When Taor decides to set out on his apparently frivolous quest for the ultimate in confectionery, he insists against all better judgment that the young female elephant Yasmina must be part of the elephant train. The portrait of Yasmina is that of a winsome childhood sweetheart: 'une jeune éléphante blanche aux yeux bleus, douce, fragile et délicate'(185), 'la petite pachyderme au regard languide, qui avait une façon de passer sa trompe autour de son cou quand il lui avait donné un chou à la crème de coco, à vous tirer des larmes d'attendrissement'(186). As they encounter the sea-storms which the delicate Yasmina is ill-equipped to face, Taor both regrets his decision to bring her and begins to realise the limits of the childhood world within which his mother sought to imprison him. He can finally take his leave of Yasmina when she is lured away by a local tribe who regard her as a matriarchal goddess, 'la mère des arbres sacrés et la grand-mère des hommes'(209), to be lavishly fed on dates and honey. Of all the (invariably unsatisfactory) male-female relationships in the book - Gaspard-Biltine, Balthazar-Malvina, Herod-Mariamme - this is the most caricatural and infantile, and Taor's growth towards selfhood depends on his shedding it.

In the second half of the text, 'l'enfer du sel' is represented by the salt-mines of Sodom in which Taor will work for thirty-three years. The novel here deliberately subverts the Old Testament condemnation of Sodom and the dogmatic sexual taboos which justify it. The scorn of the Sodomites for the 'procréationnisme à tout-va'(261) of their fellow Jews and their belief in the infinite superiority of their own sexual practice reproduce Balthazar's views in more acerbic form. The link between sodomy and salt is already firmly present in Thomas Koussek's claim in *Les Météores* that homosexuals are 'the salt of the earth', and the personality characteristics of the Sodomites - their arrogance, analytic intelligence and cynicism - reflect one side of Alexandre's nature. In their lower depths, however, they are 'le sel du sel' rather than 'le sel de la terre', there being no earth but only salt in their realm. It is consistent with this subterranean, sterile, crystalline existence that Taor, while attracted by the Sodomites' pride and brilliance of mind, is repelled by their lack of any human warmth or generosity of spirit. Despite its more positive presentation, this kind of cerebral homosexuality is as clearly caricatured here as is the infantile heterosexuality of the 'sugar' section. The novel's resolution of these unsatisfactory sexual alternatives will be to move away from the debilitating self-indulgence of the sugar-lover and from the aggressive self-assertion of the salt-dweller towards the sacrifice of self for the Other, where the notion of desire itself can be subsumed in an act of total communion.

Gilles & Jeanne: The Ambiguities of Desire

The Folio edition of *Gilles & Jeanne* bears on its cover the reproduction of a painting by Carpaccio of a slim, long-haired figure in knight's armour. The picture is not of Joan of Arc, as one might at first glance assume, but is entitled simply 'Jeune chevalier dans un paysage'. The reader's surprise at being thus misled mirrors that of the Dauphin's court, who at the start of the story are awaiting the arrival of 'une jeune fille de seize ans', but see instead a 'petit page' (10). Tournier underlines the point in a comment in *Le Vagabond immobile*: 'Beauté incomparable de la fille-garçon et du garçon-fille. Le rire que provoque chez lui, chez elle, la perplexité qu'il-elle fait naître. Jeanne d'Arc, petit page vêtu de gris et de noir, bouleversant Gilles de Rais lors de sa survenue à la cour de Chinon'(*VI* 45). Jeanne's androgyny is stressed throughout: the physical inspection to which she has to submit reveals 'le ventre de vierge et les cuisses de cavalier du petit page'(13). Gilles, in speaking of her, hesitates between the terms 'maître' and 'maîtresse'. In the mystery play in her honour which he stages after her death, her role is taken by an adolescent boy, and Gilles is struck, when he first sees Prelati, at the Florentine's resemblance to her.

Gilles finds this equivocal sexuality deeply attractive, especially by contrast with his unrewarding marriage to Catherine de Thouars, 'grosse fille paresseuse et obèse' (19), and who represents the motif of the heterosexual impasse in this text. Jeanne's other guardian, the Duke of Alençon, comments that no-one could find her attractive 'à moins d'aimer les garçons'(15), thus indicating the channel of desire which Gilles will favour after Jeanne's death. Gilles's greatest moment of intimacy with Jeanne is when he kisses a wound on her knee. This moment is a shorthand recapitulation of Abel's similar embrace of Pelsenaire's wounded knee in *Le Roi des aulnes*, discussed earlier; it is another example of the fetishisation of the wound, poised between vampirism and pious adoration. As in the earlier novel, it leads on to a comparable amorous-sadistic obsession with young boys, in the castle called Tiffauges.

Before this pathological tendency reaches its dénouement, however, the novel touches on the other main sexual option present in *Les Météores* and *Gaspard*, that of adult homosexuality, when Prelati witnesses a rustic ball held in the castle, in which all the participants are male, some dressed as women. The disconcerted Italian also feels that the revellers are half-animal, bred out of the primitive forest, an impression he finds 'à la fois séduisante et repoussante'(98). The episode is scarcely central to the plot - Gilles does not figure in it - but it suggests that transgression of boundaries and extension of sexual desire beyond the bounds of the human which is already suggested in Tournier's earlier fictions.

While Gilles's paedophilia may appear to recapitulate that of Abel in *Le Roi des aulnes*, it is of course far more directly and massively violent and murderous. It does, however, have a similarly double aspect. 'La phorie', for Abel, could signify loving service or brutal abduction. In Gilles's passion too, adoration and brutality co-exist: the children are both prized for beauty of body or voice, and abused and murdered. The ambiguity implicit in kissing the wound is here writ large. Salvation from this cycle of sexual violence can only come with recognition of guilt, in the trial, just as Abel accepted his guilt after listening to Éphraïm's accounts of Auschwitz.

The sexualities in this *récit* are all characterised by this double aspect: Jeanne's 'fille-garçon' nature, the part-transvestite and half-animal dancers, and Gilles's own schizoid division between spiritual and aesthetic sensitivity and the utmost physical brutality. Here as in earlier texts, the issues of sexuality are not resolved in their own terms, but rather subsumed into those of metaphysics and salvation. In an *oeuvre* preoccupied with 'monsters', Gilles remains the most intractable, and some readers may feel, in consequence, that for all its cool brevity this work is among the most disturbing of Tournier's fictions.

La Goutte d'or: Breaking the Glass Cage

La Goutte d'or is among other things the account of Idriss's sexual initiation. When Idriss has his photograph taken by the blonde woman in the Land Rover, he falls prey simultaneously to the power of the image and that of the siren-figure of the provocatively dressed blonde. The theme of enslavement to the image is closely linked to that of servitude to sexual desire. His dream of recovering his photograph is also that of renewing his acquaintance with the woman, and as if in response to this fantasy the figure of the blonde woman recurs in Idriss's life. As soon as he sets foot in France he meets in Marseilles a platinum blonde prostitute, who spots his gold droplet talisman and sees it as a payment worth securing for her services. Just as the first blonde 'steals' his image and as a result lures him to France, the second appropriates his jewel, symbol of his innocence, his childhood and his cultural identity, and lures him off to a hotel. This icon of the predatory blonde becomes for Idriss an expression of what he finds threatening in Western urban civilisation: when a young French fellow-passenger, Philippe, shows him a photo of his blonde girlfriend, this is itself evidence enough for Idriss that Philippe is on the side of the exploiters, and that (as he rightly discerns) he, Idriss, has nothing to hope for from his companion's hitherto friendly attitude. This threatening motif culminates in the fable of 'La Reine blonde', where the theme of erotic subjugation by a blonde woman and the theme of the power of the image are once more conjoined.

This recurrent myth of the siren luring men to destruction is not however simply a figural representation of a threatening female sexuality. Once Riad has decoded the blonde queen's portrait, it becomes a poem, 'la complainte de la reine blonde victime de sa propre beauté'(215). She has suffered cruelly both for the social conflicts and taboos surrounding the love affair of her parents from rival dynasties, and for the murderous passion she has excited in her brother-in-law. She is thus a two-faced figure, at once tyrant and victim of sexual power. Riad notices that her face is unsymmetrical and that the epigrams constituting her portrait are full of paradoxes and contradictions. One side of her hair reads 'Blonde (est) l'innocence' while on the other is inscribed 'Cheveux clairs, femme légère' (214) -

the inscriptions deem her at once innocent and fickle. (This ambivalence recalls the double aspect, saint and witch, of 'Jeanne bifrons' in *Gilles*.) This double-sided icon of the siren-victim has already been manifested twice in the text. The 'femme-lionne' in the peep-show is, superficially, a powerful figure of predatory erotic power - but the lioness is caged, and writhes and snarls to the accompaniment of whiplash sounds on the soundtrack, a animal performing to order in an erotic circus. In the following section, Idriss is in a café, simultaneously reading a book of strip cartoons and half-listening to the conversations around him. The cartoon book seems to be recounting the story of his first meeting with the blonde in the Land Rover, but the conversation continues between her and her male companion, as she complains of having become a commodity in his sexual trade - 'l'esclave blonde vendue sur photographie'(168). Looking up, Idriss thinks he sees the couple in question sitting at the bar and tries to intervene on the woman's side, with humiliating consequences. In this version of the heterosexual impasse, the villain of the piece is not the blonde - not female sexuality itself - but the play of domination, exploitation and distortion of desire prevalent in a repressed and dehumanised society.[40] The counter-image, of a woman who can restore to a man the dignity lost through taboo, is that of the Scandinavian artist Kerstine in 'Barberousse' - herself a 'blonde aux yeux bleus'(43).

Sexual exploitation is not confined to heterosexuals. The succession of young immigrant rent-boys who visit Achille Mage are procured by the street-thug Zob, and Idriss, by virtue of what his friend Achour calls his undoubted 'charm', comes close to falling prey both to the pimp and his client. Mage is cynically amused by the commercial nature of his sexual relationships: the narrative does not however disguise the violence used against the children to ensure their compliance, even if the young commodities in this particular trade are not given a voice in the text as is the blonde model in the café.

Idriss's one positive sexual experience is the night he spends with the young jeweller in the ferry cabin crossing to France. Poised between the two cultures, with a companion who appears at ease in both, he enjoys a moment of physical tenderness, devoid of any sense of exploitation. The other harmless if eccentric passion depicted is that of Etienne Milan for his dummy children, and the real ones he mixes with them, a more innocent and narcissistic version of Tiffauges's non-genital sexuality.

A certain symmetry is apparent in the handling of the theme of desire in *La Goutte d'or*. Section 1 of the book recounts two episodes: that of the woman with the camera, and that of Ibrahim's death down a well. The thematics of the image which is founded on the camera incident is resolved at the end by its opposite, the thematics of the sign in calligraphy. As for the second episode, Ibrahim falls to his death because he jumps up and down on a rotten beam: at this precise moment he is holding his (circumcised) penis and boasting of his 'queue pointue', as opposed to Idriss's 'queue ronde', characteristic of the despised oasis-dwellers. This mockery too is redeemed at the very end of the text, when Idriss, an oasis-dweller no longer, is wielding his pneumatic drill in the Place Vendôme. As Achour tells him, the drill is a giant penis, the instrument of his sexual self-assertion against the French capital: 'un zob de géant'(218). Idriss has earned his right to the 'queue pointue' of the nomad he so much admired, as a sign of his new-found self-respect and freedom from cultural and sexual intimidation. This recovery of dignity and cultural identity is associated with the reappearance of the golden droplet, and the memories it brings of the dancer Zett Zobeida which pervade the final pages. The belly-dancer and her jewel are the cultural counterpoise to the iconic blonde and the image, and especially to the writhing 'femme-lionne', and her flaunting of breasts and pubis. When Idriss returns to the peep-show the following morning to look for the peep-show model, he finds only a cleaner who complains of the semen stains in the cubicles she has to clean, and most notably of the fact that 'il y en a même qui éclaboussent la fenêtre!'(164). There the force of desire is impotent against the wall of the glass cage. On the final page, by contrast, the jeweller's window will shatter as Idriss wields his powerful pseudo-phallus, in a symbolic breach of the barriers by which society seeks to contain the potency of desire.

In Tournier, desire properly overflows its initial, limited channel, and floods into unforeseen territory. The fulfilling metamorphosis which it can undergo is to transcend the glass cage of compartmentalisation within a single relationship or mode or gender, and to inform interaction with the world at every level. His characters can be divided into an élite of initiatic heroes who are capable of sustaining this metamorphosis - Robinson, Abel, Thomas, Paul, Taor, Idriss - and others, such as Edouard and even Alexandre, who do not succeed in departing from their initial path. The name Vendredi, we recall, signified both 'the day of Venus' (the epiphany of desire) and the death of Christ. The dynamic of desire, for Tournier, leads beyond the body to the Spirit, uniting the two. In the Eucharist, Taor will find both the ultimate gratification of his oral desire - the nourishment that will still all hunger and thirst - and the fruit of sacrifice in a double sense: the death of Christ and his own imitation of Christ in giving his body for others.

Tournier's approach to desire and sexuality takes its place in a substantial tradition of post-Enlightenment libertarian thought and polemic.[41] In the eighteenth century, utopian writers used the tales of South Seas mores brought back by travellers to attack the repressive regime of their own civilisation and to envisage an ideal liberation of erotic gratification. Diderot, in his *Supplément au voyage de Bougainville*, inveighs against monogamous marriage as being contrary to the whole order of nature. For Sade, the positive shift from 'passions simples' to 'passions compliquées' (i.e. perversions) follows from the division of sexuality into its constituent parts, the pleasure principle and the procreative instinct: passions become 'complex' when the quest for pleasure seeks new objects of desire to replace the procreative function. By this token, sodomy is for Sade the anticonceptive gesture par excellence.[42] This rhetoric of libidinal liberation finds lavish expression in the early nineteenth century in the writings of Charles Fourier. Despite his fame throughout that century as a utopian social visionary, Fourier's main work on sexual liberation, *Le Nouveau Monde amoureux*, was not published until 1967. His views anticipate those of Tournier in a number of respects. Fourier gives a high status to homosexual eroticism because of its non-productive aspect,[43] and he inveighs against social codes of constraint in sexual relations, and the idea of a prescriptive 'norm'. One critic summarises his attitude thus: 'Codes et règlements n'ont qu'un objet: censurer la jouissance, contrecarrer les poussées du désir, entraver les richesses encore insoupçonnées de la polymorphie passionnelle.'[44] This critique of institutionalised puritanism and of its concomitant insistence on monogamous heterosexuality anticipates Tournier's own views, as summed up for instance in the observation: 'Il est possible que si la société ne harcelait pas sans cesse l'individu, [...] sa sexualité, libérée du moule hétérosexuel et reproductif, s'engagerait dans des voies inédites et aberrantes.'[45]

Tournier's characters, at variance precisely with this social code, thereby qualify for the label of 'monster' which society attaches to deviants in behaviour, physique or status: far from shunning the label, however, they wear it willingly, even proudly. Abel gratefully seizes on the epithet of ogre, 'monstre féerique' (*RA* 13), while Lucien in 'Le Nain rouge' lives up to his appearance as a 'monstre sacré' (*CB* 107). Gilles proclaims himself 'l'homme le plus exécrable qui fût jamais' with an arrogance which takes his judges aback (*GJ* 132-3),[46] while Paul recognises that the truth of the 'monstrosity' of his twinship has passed from being a cause for shame to being one of pride, before becoming a mere fact of life (*Mét* 163). As Pierre Klossowski observes, Sade, and later Nietzsche, saw in humankind a mere raw material, which only found its true justification in exceptional creations: these, the monsters, transcend the status of the ordinary individual by virtue of the phantasms which find full expression in them. For Fourier, however, this 'monstrosity' need not be the privilege of a few: through the untapped richness of so-called deviant eroticism, it is a potential for all, the mark of a wholly new social order.[47] Fourier's utopia, where every taste from the most innocent to the most lascivious is prized, is an 'Utopie des marginalités'[48] in which no-one, therefore, will be marginal; those whom he saw as rejected or underprivileged in civilisation - women, children, the old, the eccentric, the 'perverted' - would find their place.[49] For Fourier, as for Tournier, it is on the experience of the 'deviant' that a tolerant and humane social order must be based: while Tournier's critique implies such a shift without defining it in any detail, Fourier provided a fantastic blueprint for the whole enterprise.

'Le bonheur sur lequel on a tant raisonné (ou plutôt tant déraisonné),' writes Fourier, 'consiste à avoir le plus de passions possibles, et les plus ardentes et les plus excessives, et à pouvoir les satisfaire toutes. [...] Le bonheur se compose de la jouissance alternative de tous les genres et non pas d'un seul.'[50] Tournier, as we have seen, shares his predecessor's appetite for enlarging to the maximum the scope and diversity of pleasure in life, and accords a lower status to those of his characters whose happiness is based on 'la jouissance [...] d'un seul [genre]' than to those initiatic heroes whose quest is for a total, unrestrictive openness to the world. Fourier anticipates the 'delocalisation' of desire experienced by Robinson, in which genital penetration and orgasm ('le coup de volupté brutale') is no longer the dominant model, giving way to a more lasting and more diffused 'jubilation douce' (*VLP* 229).[51] Fourier, like Tournier, sees this undifferentiation of eroticism as extending even to the non-human and the cosmos, to 'des relations amoureuses avec toutes sortes d'espèces et de catégories, hommes, femmes, enfants, vieillards, mais aussi végétaux, animaux, étoiles, climatures, pouvoir donné à chacun d'entre nous d'être branché de manière amoureuse sur le plus grand nombre de flux possibles, flux génitaux, anaux, érotiques, planétaires, aromaux, culinaires, flux marins, cosmiques'.[52] From Vendredi's union with plants to the anality of Tiffauges, from Paul's ecstatic communion with wind and weather to the seafood banquet of *Le Médianoche amoureux*, Tournier's fiction celebrates this power in all its abundance and diversity.

A more recent thinker, Herbert Marcuse, describes this process as the transformation of sexuality into Eros. The 'self-sublimation of sexuality [...] means regression from sexuality in the service of reproduction to sexuality in the "function of obtaining pleasure from zones of the body." With this restoration of the primary structure of sexuality, the primacy of the genital function is broken - as is the desexualisation of the body which accompanied this primacy. [...] Thus enlarged, the field and objective of the instinct becomes the life of the organism itself.'[53] The regression envisaged in Marcuse's commentary on Freudian theory is a positive one, 'a resurgence of pregenital polymorphous sexuality'. 'This change in the value and scope of libidinal relations would lead to a disintegration of the institutions in which the private interpersonal relations have been organized, particularly the monogamic and patriarchal family.'[54] Marcuse goes on to trace in Plato the celebration of the sexual origin and substance of culture and spirituality, Agape as sublimated Eros. He was to become one of the gurus much quoted in the 'sexual revolution' of the 1960s, when Tournier's major novels were in gestation and when Fourier was revived as a fashionable voice of socialist idealism. *Vendredi* in particular reflects strongly the ethos of libertarian utopianism which was prevalent at the time, albeit mostly among those twenty years younger than Tournier himself.

Tournier shares with these predecessors a critique of society as repressive, a celebration of the deviant seen as subversive of this inhumane order, and an immense optimism in the revitalisation of humanity through erotic liberation, extending to a renewal of the self, of culture and of spirituality. Like them he is careless, or ambiguous, regarding many of the ethical issues which such a libertarian approach might bring in practice. His fictions lend support to the notion that, in Fourier's words, 'il n'y a pas de vices mais seulement de vicieux développements', and that 'vices', properly understood, can become the foundations of happiness and fulfilment.[55] It is a philosophy which can serve as a basis for an individual's priorities in life, but hardly as the basis of a social system, and in this too Tournier is rigorously counter-utopian. In his refusal of the practical and the politically realisable, he is true to the spirit of Fourier: while Fourier may be loosely called a utopian, his massive and whimsical elaboration of the structures of his ideal community are often so preposterous and parodical that they subvert systematisation even while mimicking it. In both writers, a fantasy of total self-realisation gives rise, not to a plausible new world order, but more preciously to an unfettered release of the imagination through the enterprise of writing, in projects for an alternative ego which press through and beyond the restrictions of the real.

Notes to Chapter Three

¹ Simone de Beauvoir, *Le Deuxième Sexe* (Paris, Gallimard (Folio/Essais), 2 vols, 1986), I,64-5; II,330; I,62.

² See below, n.26.

³ The same idea, using the same image, is expressed by Thomas Koussek in *Les Météores*: 'Le fardeau de la procréation écrase totalement des femmes, à moitié les hommes hétérosexuels. [...] Le prolétaire, c'est le prolifique, attelé au lourd chariot de la perpétuation de l'espèce' (*Mét* 145).

⁴ This is a rapid summary of views Tournier has expressed consistently and frequently in interviews and writings. A characteristically forceful exposition of them can be found, for instance, in an interview with Brigitte le Péchon (published in *Recherches sur l'imaginaire dans la littérature française contemporaine depuis 1945*, Vol.5 (1978-9), Angers, 1979, 6-29): 'Si vous prenez un homme moyen. Il fait l'amour: disons qu'il a, en gros, entre 5 000 et 10 000 éjaculations dans sa vie et il a en moyenne de deux à trois enfants. Voyez le rapport mathématique que cela suppose tout de même! Alors moi, je suis tout à fait partisan de la procréation, mais le reste? [...] La procréation, c'est une partie infime de la sexualité, absolument infime. Il y a de la part de la morale victorienne qui s'acharne à n'admettre la sexualité que dans les limites de la procréation, il y a un pari, un défi, et à la limite une imposture absolument intenable, il me semble' (12). Tournier's hostility to the socio-political regulation of sexuality finds a strong echo in the writings of the philosopher Michel Foucault, as Mairi Maclean points out. See Maclean, 'Human Relations in the novels of Tournier: polarity and transcendance', *Forum for Modern Language Studies*, Vol.XXIII, no.3 (July, 1987), 241-52 (245).

⁵ As Milne has noted (*L'Évangile selon Michel*, 184), Tournier's definition closely follows that of Georges Bataille in *L'Érotisme*: 'L'érotisme se définit par l'indépendance de la jouissance érotique et de la reproduction comme fin.'

⁶ At another point in the interview with B. Le Péchon referred to in note 2 above, he makes light of the taboo on incest: incest is probably widespread, he suggests, and 'on ne s'en porte pas plus mal. C'est comme toutes les prétendues déviations sexuelles, finalement, ça ne fait de mal à personne et je ne vois pas pourquoi un homme n'aurait pas un enfant de sa fille. [...] Parce que, finalement, les malédictions biologiques qui reposent sur l'inceste, à mon avis, sont infimes, en comparaison de la peur que l'inceste inspire. [...] Je crois que c'est un tabou qui sera dissipé comme les autres, peut-être'(8-9). (See also his comments in 'La Logosphère et les taciturnes', *Sud* (hors série, 1980), 167-77 (175-6).) One somewhat surprising element within this ultra-liberal stance on sexuality is his condemnation of abortion and even contraception as 'subterfuges

dangereux et criminels' (*CS* 103/*PP* 152); they are, in his view, direct and negative consequences of the exclusive insistence on genital heterosexuality.

[7] Interview with A. Poirson, 'Une logique contre vents et marées', 48. See also *VPar* 24-8, where he again speaks of this 'traversée d'un immense et terrible désert'(25).

[8] Tournier's descriptions of inner metamorphosis appear to owe something to André Gide if one considers, for instance, this note in *Les Nourritures terrestres*: 'Obscures opérations de l'être; travail latent, genèses d'inconnu, parturitions laborieuses; somnolences, attentes; comme les chrysalides et les nymphes, je dormais; je laissais se former en moi le nouvel être que je serais, qui ne me ressemblait déjà plus.' See Gide, *Romans*, 159.

[9] For Marthe Robert, even in Defoe's narrative this shipwreck has a double aspect, of both a punishment for Robinson's revolt against paternal authority and 'une renaissance dans laquelle l'angoisse de l'abandon est sans cesse balancée par l'ivresse du recommencement'. See Robert, *Roman des origines et origines du roman* (Paris, Gallimard (Tel), 1981), 136.

[10] The Slough of Despond episode also occurs early in Christian's journey, after he has left his home and his wife and children in the City of Destruction, and just before his spiritual rebirth as he passes through the wicket-gate to start his pilgrimage. See John Bunyan, *The Pilgrim's Progress* (London, Constable, 1926), 15.

[11] When Vendredi flees from the witchdoctor's condemnation into Robinson's keeping, he is convinced that he is dead; his soul is in the Englishman's hands, while he is merely a body, subject to his master's every command (*VLP* 148). The moment of the explosion is arguably the point of rebirth for Vendredi also, when he claims his soul back.

[12] This notion of the boat as maternal space has been touched on by Merllié (*Michel Tournier*) 65, and by Mireille Rosello, *L'In-différence chez Michel Tournier* (Paris, Corti, 1990), 156.

[13] This reading adds an extra resonance to Robinson's later discussion of this misperception: was the 'souche' he saw disqualified when it 'became' a goat? (99)

[14] Van Deyssel's Dutch nationality recalls at once Spinoza, whom Tournier admires as the last great proponent of 'la sagesse antique' (*VPar* 285) and the plump Epicurean figure of 'le royal et rayonnant Mynheer Peeperkorn' (*VV* 294), mentor to the young Hans Castorp in Thomas Mann's *Der Zauberberg* (*The Magic Mountain*).

[15] Paul, in *Les Météores*, recalls a similarly cosy refuge he had as a boy, the 'salle d'ourdissage', like a 'manchon duveteux grand comme une église' (*Mét* 266,268), whose presiding genius is the imperturbable Isabelle Daoudal.

[16] Defoe, *Robinson Crusoe* (Harmondsworth, Penguin, 1965), 198. Similar sentiments are expressed on pp. 31, 103.

[17] In *Le Roi des aulnes*, Tiffauges's emotional legacy is not dissimilar. His father is described as cold, taciturn, unshakeably indifferent towards his son (*RA* 100,107), while his mother is not mentioned. Tiffauges's subsequent development, like Robinson's, could be seen as an effort to fill this emotional and physical void.

[18] Gaston Bachelard, in a chapter on 'La pâte', suggests that there is in all of us 'l'image matérielle d'une *pâte idéale*' which can found a tactile mode of knowledge, a '*cogito* pétrisseur'. See *La Terre et les rêveries de la volonté* (Paris, Corti, 1948), 78-9.

[19] This passage could be read psychoanalytically as a representation of the 'primal scene', the child's view of sexual relations between his parents, and thus as having an Oedipal dimension. This would link it to the theme of patriarchy and of father-substitutes. The episode is in any case strongly reminiscent of Rimbaud's poem 'Les Effarés' (*Poésies*) in which five children, 'noirs dans la neige et dans la brume', peer through a 'soupirail' to watch a baker kneading dough. See Rimbaud, *Oeuvres*, ed. S. Bernard and A. Guyaux, rev. ed. (Paris, Garnier, 1987), 69-70. Tournier's 'haleine chaude, maternelle' finds a pre-echo in Rimbaud's 'souffle du soupirail rouge/ Chaud comme un sein' which suggested a psychoanalytic interpretation to C.A.Hackett in *Rimbaud l'Enfant* (Paris, Corti, 1948), 82-3. A further instance of this motif can be found in Gide's *Les Nourritures terrestres*: 'On voyait, par les soupiraux des caves, des hommes à moitié nus faire le pain' (see *Romans*, 225), while yet another example occurs in Vallès's *L'Enfant* (Paris, Gallimard (Folio), 1973), 42. Entry into the warm bakehouse and the baking and sharing of bread forms a joyful conclusion to Tournier's story 'Pierrot ou Les secrets de la nuit' (*MA*), which thus provides a symbolic resolution of this figure of emotional deprivation.

[20] While 'fille' is in presumably in apposition to 'toute-puissance' rather than 'île', the juxtaposition nonetheless echoes the motif of the subservience of the female island to male 'mastery'.

[21] See Mairi Maclean, 'Michel Tournier as misogynist (or not?): an assessment of the author's view of femininity', *Modern Language Review*, Vol. 83, no. 2 (April 1988), 322-31.

[22] An antecedent for this genital worship of the earth is to be found in Maurice Sachs: 'C'est à cette époque (vers ma treizième année) que je commençai à sentir le caractère sacré de la nature. Et brûlant de me consacrer à elle, par ce qui me semblait le plus sacré en moi, je fis plus d'une fois l'amour avec la terre, seul, les bras en croix, le sexe profondément enfoui dans la fraîcheur de la terre foulée, merveilleusement perdu.' See Sachs, *Le Sabbat* (Paris, Gallimard (L'Imaginaire), 1979), 41 [first published 1960].

[23] Ezine, *Les Ecrivains sur la sellette*, 224.

[24] Tournier touches on the primacy of right over left in the Bible, in *VPar* 136.

[25] Goering, with his huge frame and appetite, is clearly to be categorised as 'anal' in his propensity: he tracks the deer by his expertise in identifying their droppings.

[26] Elsewhere Tournier links this (mis)reading of *Genesis* to a similar myth attributed to Aristophanes in Plato's *Symposium*. See 'Des éclairs dans la nuit du coeur', *Nouvelles littéraires* 2,253 (26.11.1970), pp. 1, 6. This text was also published in a volume containing four engravings of Atlas and Orion by Trémois, entitled *Mythologie* ([s.l.], Pamela Verlag, 1971). On this theme of the original hermaphrodite, see Bouloumié, *Michel Tournier*, 157-63, and Davis, *Michel Tournier*, 193.

[27] In the opening essay of *Le Vol du vampire*, his collection of literary articles, Tournier compares his books to vampires, sent forth to seek out readers who will nourish and vitalise them by contributing the life-blood of their own experience and imagination in the act of reading. In this characteristically half-humorous, half-serious analogy, the author-reader relationship is analysed in similarly ambiguous terms of mutual gratification and exploitation, and the operation of the writer as Dracula, perverse seducer of his prey the reader, is nowhere more apparent than in *Le Roi des aulnes*. See Michael Worton, 'Use

and abuse of metaphor in Tournier's *Le Vol du vampire'*, *Paragraph* 10 (October 1987), 13-28.

[28] As one critic puts it, 'cette prédation photographique est décrite comme un viol accompli selon une mise en scène précise dictée par le désir (érotisation de la plaie [...] et le rolleï comparé à un sexe gigantesque)'. See Liesbeth Korthals Altes, *Le Salut par la fiction? Sens, valeurs et narrativité dans* Le Roi des aulnes *de Michel Tournier* (Amsterdam, Rodopi, 1992), 51. As the term *mise en scène* rightly implies, the scenario of desire is translated (displaced) from the physical, genital level to one of symbolic representation, in which the camera becomes the instrument of abduction and anthropophagy, devouring and taking away the child in image, to feast on later. Idriss is the victim of a similar act of predation at the start of *La Goutte d'or*.

[29] See preface to Mason, Jerry (ed.), *La Famille des enfants* (Paris, Flammarion, 1977), 3.

[30] In Chapter 7, it will be suggested that there are two distinct images of the Erlking in the text: the 'rite of passage' celebrated by the litany marking Arnim's death is arguably from the first definition (predator) to the second (earth-deity).

[31] For Merllié, it is the last in a series of scenes which function as 'transpositions d'une sodomie meurtrière'. See her *Michel Tournier*, 90.

[32] 'Le fond de la phorie est équivoque et rejoint le drame de la *possession*. Car si elle est service rendu humblement, elle est aussi enlèvement, rapt. [...] Saint Christophe *porte*, tel une bête de somme, l'enfant-Dieu. Le roi des Aulnes *emporte*, tel un oiseau de proie, l'enfant vers la mort. Plus généralement, *servir* c'est *asservir*: on *serre* toujours ce que l'on *sert*.' See 'Petit lexique d'un Prix Goncourt: treize clefs pour un ogre', *Figaro littéraire* 1,280 (30.11.70), 20-2 (22).

[33] The same image is used for the thinker creating a new philosophical system: '[L]e philosophe [...] n'est que le déchet que laisse tomber dans le monde empirique le système qui se forme'(*VPar* 157).

[34] See the note on 'Endogamie et exogamie' in *MI* 39-42, and its reference to Claude Lévi-Strauss, *Essai sur les structures élémentaires de la parenté*.

[35] In the title-story of his collection *Le Coq de bruyère*, Tournier offers in his portrait of Baron Guillaume de Saint-Fursy another variant on the successful 'homme du monde' and ladies' man, and his life too, like Edouard's, slumps to an ignominious end.

[36] While Abel explicitly refers back to the Cain and Abel myth in Genesis, Tiffauges was the name of one of the castles belonging to Gilles de Rais. This pairing of names sets the pattern of Christian first name and dissonant second name followed in Thomas Koussek and Raphaël Ganeça, as well Raphaël Bidoche in 'Que ma joie demeure'(*CB*).

[37] There exist fragments of an early, uncompleted work by André Malraux called 'Ecrit pour une idole à trompe', in whose title one critic finds a Baudelairean echo, from a line in 'Le Voyage' (*Fleurs du mal*, cxxvi): 'Nous avons salué des idoles à trompe.' See André Vandegans, *La Jeunesse littéraire d'André Malraux* (Paris, Pauvert, 1964), 194; and Baudelaire, *Oeuvres complètes*, ed. C. Pichois, 2 vols (Paris, Gallimard (Pléiade, 1975), I:129-34 (132)).

[38] See Matthew 5:13.

[39] The Narcisses are, their name suggests, equally obsessed by an image - that of themselves in a mirror. The attraction of like to like provides a link to homoeroticism.

[40] The photographer Mustapha touches skilfully on this chord of sexual

domination when he urges his client to imagine he is a sheikh, a 'grand mâle dominateur', with a flock of naked women languishing at his feet (82). This cultural myth of course bears no relationship to the sexual and family politics of Idriss's village, any more than Idriss can hope to realise in France the tempting Western myth of a marriage deriving from love, as opposed to the arranged marriage which will be his fate at home.

[41]   On this tradition, see Sarane Alexandrian, *Les Libérateurs de l'amour* (Paris, Seuil, 1977).

[42]   See Pierre Klossowski, 'Sade et Fourier', in *Les Derniers Travaux de Gulliver, suivi de Sade et Fourier* (Montpellier, Fata Morgana, 1974), 35. Tournier develops exactly this line of thought, as we have seen, in his essay on 'L'image érotique' (*CS* 103-8; *PP* 151-4).

[43]   See M.C. Spencer, *Charles Fourier* (Boston, Twayne, 1981), 70.

[44]   Pascal Bruckner, *Fourier* (Paris, Seuil, 1975), 38.

[45]   Tournier, *Journal de voyage au Canada* (Paris, Laffont, 1984), 129.

[46]   The paratext on the back cover of the Folio edition refers twice to Gilles's monstrous nature. Having been himself a publisher's editor, Tournier drafts all such texts for his own works.

[47]   Klossowski, 'Sade et Fourier', 49-50.

[48]   The expression is Bruckner's (*Fourier*, 40).

[49]   Spencer, *Charles Fourier*, 76-7.

[50]   Fourier, *Le Nouveau Monde amoureux*, quoted in Bruckner, *Fourier*, 9.

[51]   Bruckner's summary (*Fourier*, 85-6) of this notion of 'indeterminacy' of sexual pleasure in Fourier is full of echoes for the reader of Tournier: 'En laissant volontiers indéterminé l'instant sexuel, l'instant de l'engagement, l'Utopie fouriériste apparaît comme une approche caressante de l'univers [...]; [...] elle n'a pas la fixité de l'étreinte mais le versatilisme de la perversion. Dans le langage de la caractérologie alchimique, l'Harmonie correspondrait aux côtés du clown agile au type mercuriel: euphorique et léger, tandis que notre monde, à l'égal du balourd, figurerait le type terrien: pesant, froid et carcéral.'

[52]   Bruckner, *Fourier*, 87-8.

[53]   Herbert Marcuse, *Eros and Civilisation*, 2nd edn (Boston, Beacon Press, 1966), 204-5. Marcuse notes Freud's emphasis on perversions as a rejection of the procreative sex act and an expression of 'rebellion against the subjugation of sexuality under the order of procreation, and against the institutions which guarantee this order'(49).

[54]   Marcuse, *Eros and Civilisation*, 201.

[55]   Bruckner, *Fourier*, 39.

4

(Mis)Reading the Bible

Je suis un grand lecteur de Bible, aussi bien l'Ancien que le Nouveau Testament. Je trouve que c'est un immense grenier où il y a vraiment tout ce que l'on veut et on peut y puiser une inspiration indéfiniment.

(Interview with Brigitte le Péchon)

To the reader of Tournier's most substantial works - *Vendredi, Le Roi des aulnes, Les Météores, Gaspard* - it is indeed evident that the writer is (as he once described himself in an interview) 'plongé jusqu'au cou dans la Bible',[1] since woven into each of them are reflections on Biblical texts and episodes.[2] Tournier uses the Bible as a constant sounding board to his ideas, by making his characters look to it for a commentary on or an illuminating parallel to their own situation. Moreover, this intertext becomes a narrative generator in its own right, when the Biblical analogy is at the root of the construction of a character, as indicated by the symbolic nomenclature (Abel, Thomas etc.), or central to the conception of an event (the fall of the Third Reich as Apocalypse). In *Gaspard*, of course, a Biblical episode becomes itself the generative framework of the novel.

As a postscript to *Gaspard*, Tournier takes the trouble to reproduce the sixteen verses from St Matthew's Gospel which contain all the Bible tells us about the Three Kings. To this quotation he adds a note emphasising how slender is the information given, and how much of the myth as we know it has accrued later. 'L'auteur avait donc toute liberté pour inventer [...] le destin et la personnalité de ses héros'(*GMB* 277). This invention extends not only to the detail of the lives and preoccupations of the Three Kings, but to the elaboration of the story of a fourth king, who has figured in some earlier legends. Tournier's story does not, therefore, content itself with timidly amplifying known details but transcends and transforms the structure of the whole story. This procedure, in the most explicitly Biblical of all his novels, is enough to indicate to his readers that his interpretations and rewritings of Biblical material will never be respectful in this sense. Impatient with conventionally pious glosses, which are too often likely to support the puritanical status quo which he deplores, he reads the Bible against the grain, with and through his characters, seeking other and more surprising meanings. Further than this, he will recast a story completely, to change its meaning, like a composer who writes variations on a well-known musical theme. If the variations are memorable, they may for ever affect the way we react to the original melody.

This (mis)reading of the Bible is thus central to the production of meaning in Tournier's texts and in particular to the ethical and metaphysical reflections they develop. In each text the selection of episodes or passages referred to is different, as is the interpretative grid applied to them. In *Vendredi*, the Biblical dimension is of course already given in Defoe's text: his Robinson also turns to the Bible for consolation and guidance, and instructs Friday in its interpretation. As Tournier has pointed out, this interface with the Bible is thus part of the 'rules of the game' he has inherited from his predecessor.[3] The author of *Vendredi* is, however, more acutely conscious than his predecessor of the complexity and ambivalence of the process of reading and interpreting, and Tournier's version will, as we shall see, thoroughly subvert the relatively simple function it had in Defoe of inspiring in the castaway reconciliation to his condition, repentance of his past life and humble acceptance of a patriarchal divine order.

The Bible in Vendredi: Patriarchal Readings[4]

When Robinson undertakes the construction of *L'Evasion* at the beginning of Chapter 2, it is not the legacy of prediction from Van Deyssel which preoccupies him, despite the obvious relevance of the first tarot card depicting 'Le Bateleur', struggling to impose order 'avec des moyens de fortune' (7).

Rather than Van Deyssel's discourse, it is the fortuitous inheritance of the Second Officer's Bible retrieved from the wreck which furnishes him with his guiding text. We are told that 'il n'avait jamais été un grand lecteur des textes sacrés'(26), but now that these are the only text he has, his 'seul viatique spirituel'(26), he peruses it regularly. Later, in times of trouble, he will adopt the practice of opening the Bible at random when in situations of perplexity in the hope of finding appropriate guidance. (This procedure is of course curiously analogous, in its reliance on a supernatural guiding force, to the random drawing of tarot cards.) From Chapter 2 on, the significant clusters of quotations from and references to Biblical passages as well as a periodically Biblical tone in Robinson's discourse bear witness to the impact of this reading.

It is significant that such intertextual references to the Bible virtually cease after the end of Chapter 8, with the explosion: there is just one quotation from Scripture in the last four chapters. This is an indication that the dialogue with the Bible was part and parcel of the order of European values which Robinson has sought to reconstruct: the only Bible he possesses is in any case lost in the debris of his shattered 'oratoire'.

One of his main needs in reading the Bible is to find authoritative models for his role as one chosen by God for a special destiny. The narrative mimics the Creation in that the new island world emerges in Chapter 1 from the primal chaos (matrix of all that is to come) of the prologue. When Robinson finds his own footprint already mysteriously imprinted on the rock, he speaks of it as the mark of 'Adam prenant possession du Jardin' (57), the word 'possession' underlining the ethos of property and dominion. This echoes the assurance given by God first to Adam, then to Noah, of their power over the earth and all its creatures: '...Replenish the earth, and subdue it: and have dominion over the fish of the sea, and over the fowl of the air, and over every living thing that moveth upon the earth.'[5] In Defoe's novel, Crusoe rejoices in being 'king and lord of all this country indefeasibly'.[6] William Cowper, writing later in the eighteenth century, no doubt had such passages in mind when composing his *Verses supposed to be written by Alexander Selkirk*: 'I am monarch of all I survey,/ My right there is none to dispute;/ From the centre all round to the sea/ I am lord of the fowl and the brute.' These lines establish a similar link between the Genesis text and the origins of the Robinson Crusoe myth.

In another episode which Tournier borrows from Defoe, Robinson constructs a boat in which to escape, but finds too late that it is too heavy, and built too far from the shore, for him to launch. Unlike Defoe, however, Tournier stresses that in this enterprise Robinson's model is Noah,[7] and in his version it is this prestigious prototype, not mere lack of foresight, which is in the end catastrophically misleading, seducing Robinson into building his boat on a high cliff from which a flood would be needed to launch it. Despite this debacle, Robinson remains literalistic in regard to Biblical authority as when, for instance, he refuses to weed his corn because of the injunction in one of the parables to let wheat and tares grow together until the harvest (57).[8] On another occasion after a rainstorm, 'semblable au premier homme sous l'Arbre de la Connaissance [...] après le retrait des eaux'(31),[9] he asks for a literal manifestation of God's presence with him, whereupon a brilliant rainbow appears. The obvious reference here is to Genesis 9:13-16, where, after the flood has abated, a rainbow appears as a token of the covenant between God and Noah, setting a seal upon the promise just made to Noah of dominion over all created things. In the first instance, therefore, Robinson sees around him what he takes to be the signs of divine corroboration of his authority and status, although the outcome of the Noah episode already suggests the illusory aspect of the Bateleur's project predicted by Van Deyssel.

In Chapter 4, Robinson, pausing while drafting his penal code, feels the moment to be auspicious for another such sign that the Holy Spirit is working through him: 'Une langue de feu dansant au-dessus de ma tête ou une colonne de fumée montant toute droite vers le zénith ne devraient-elles pas attester que je suis le temple de Dieu?' (74). The 'tongue of fire' would equate Robinson with the apostles on whom flames descended, inspiring them with the Word of God.[10] The column of smoke might recall the 'pillar of cloud' which was one of the manifestations of God to His chosen people,[11] or more plausibly the smoke which was supposed to rise vertically from sacrifices which were pleasing to the deity. He is struck by wonder and gratitude when a column of smoke does indeed begin to rise from the shoreline he has called the 'Baie du Salut' - but this turns out to signal the first visit of the Araucanian tribespeople and their grisly human sacrifice.

On each occasion, Robinson's biblical reading of the 'signs' around him is subverted by doubt or contradiction. The Noah's Ark scenario is a mirage (as much as the galleon he is to see in the bay): the island itself, populated with many species, is *already* the ark of his salvation when all his fellows have been destroyed. The footprint in the rock is not the brand mark of his ownership of the island, 'le sceau de son Seigneur et Maître'(57). Rather it anticipates the 'bodyprint', the hollow into which he will fit exactly, curled up like a foetus, in the underground cave: it is Robinson's *matrix*, a mark of Speranza's formative, not subservient, role towards him. The rainbow is a natural phenomenon after rain, and this attempt to translate a glorious spectacle of nature into a sign from God suggests a potential pantheistic confusion between God and Nature. This confusion will become still more explicit when Robinson resolves to regard the success or failure of his first harvest as 'un jugement porté par la nature - c'est-à-dire par Dieu - sur le travail de ses mains'(46). 'C'est-à-dire' begs a host of questions, and this conventional view of fertility as a mark of divine favour (a view characteristic of the Old Testament, and of primitive mythology) threatens to confuse God and Speranza, Jehovah and the

Earth Goddess. As for the rainbow, a creation of sunlight, it could more appropriately be seen as an anticipation of the solar apotheosis of Jovian splendour in the final pages of the text. The column of smoke, in its turn, is no euphoric sign of the rightness of things, but a brutal reminder of what superstitious beliefs in wrathful deities can lead to. No tongues of fire endorse the Penal Code flowing from Robinson's pen. Rather, the ironic contradiction between the real purpose of the fire on the shore and Robinson's initial interpretation of it as a sign suggests if anything a negative judgment: that the primitive codes of punishment which make up his rule of law are of a piece with the practices of the tribesmen on the beach.

Robinson's application of the Biblical code in interpreting his life continues to yield disconcertingly contrary conclusions for him. When he seeks vindication for the self-righteous anger he feels when he discovers Vendredi emulating his own copulation with the island, the Biblical texts he reads (177-8) speak only of Speranza as whore, not of Vendredi's guilt - the terrible retribution he dreams of finds no scriptural support. He thinks to find an authentic image of his own jealous rage in verses from Isaiah 30 which speak of Jehovah's wrath: 'Son souffle [...] comme un torrent débordant', 'la majesté de sa voix', 'la flamme d'un feu dévorant' (175) - but the destruction threatened in these texts is destined to fall not on Vendredi, but on the whole order of 'civilisation' which Robinson has laboured to construct, when it is blasted away by the explosion just a few pages later. 'C'est alors que les quarante tonneaux de poudre noire parlent en même temps. Un torrent de flammes rouges jaillit de la grotte' (183-4). The textual echoes - 'torrent', 'flamme(s)', and the notion of voice ('voix', 'parlent') - establish the link between 'prophecy' and event. If the explosion is the manifestation of divine wrath, then the object of that anger is not what Robinson imagined it to be.

The authority of Robinson's readings of Scripture, and by extension his implied pretensions to be the apostle or representative of God, are thus consistently negated, and the images of patriarchal authority become more discredited. As he mulls over his rage at his subordinate's sexual relations with Speranza, he comes across the story of Joseph, sold in slavery to the Egyptian captain Potiphar (178-9).[12] Potiphar's wife tries unsuccessfully to seduce the young Israelite, and then takes her revenge by denouncing him to her husband for making sexual advances to her. If this story is applied to Robinson's own situation, it places him in the unattractive role of Potiphar himself, who will unfairly punish the innocent slave. As early as Chapter 4 there is the first sign of Robinson taking a more critical view of this self-image as Old Testament authority figure, when he looks in the mirror: 'Ah, certes, cette barbe carrée [...] n'avait rien de la douceur floue et soyeuse de celle du Nazaréen! C'était bien à l'Ancien Testament et à sa justice sommaire qu'elle ressortissait, ainsi d'ailleurs que ce regard trop franc dont la violence mosaïque effrayait' (90). As has been seen, violence and summary justice are indeed to be the negative features of this patriarchal image. After the explosion, and the dramatic reorientation which it brings about, this critical view of the Moses prototype is strongly reinforced. The visual icon of the stern, bearded prophet is caricatured in Andoar, the goat which Vendredi combats and kills, and Robinson recognises the ironic personification of himself, in his patriarchal mode: 'Andoar, c'était moi. Ce vieux mâle solitaire et têtu avec sa barbe de patriarche [...] c'était moi' (227).[13] Vendredi's defeat of Andoar in single combat, and his subsequent transformation of the goat's remains, thus acquire the value of a symbolic triumph over Robinson's previous persona as would-be Old Testament prophet. It is a ritual sacrifice of a proxy *scapegoat* ('bouc émissaire'), and thus a more humane variant of the Araucanian tribesmen's ritual on the beach; it is also a therapeutic displacement of Vendredi's need to destroy the oppressive patriarch figure, comparable to the symbolic games in which the two men create models of each other on which to vent their aggression and resentment (210-11). Finally it is a coded lesson about the sense of what has happened, which the perplexed Robinson gradually deciphers.

The only Biblical quotation to feature hereafter comes near the beginning of the final chapter (250), at the one moment of renewed desolation and despair after Robinson's discovery that Vendredi has left, and before the emergence of the runaway cabin-boy. 'Le Roi David était vieux, avancé en âge. On le couvrait de vêtements sans qu'il pût se réchauffer [...]'(I Kings 1:1-2). The patriarchal figure is now pathetically moribund, dependent on the arrival of a new young companion to give him any solace. Like the quotation from Isaiah about Jehovah's anger, this text will turn out to be predictive of an imminent and far-reaching change in Robinson's life, in which the boy Jaan will confer the rejuvenation which King David's servants hope for from the young virgin which they bring to their ailing master.

To sum up, the Biblical code functions in the text in a number of different ways. It is closely linked to the project of patriarchal authority for which Robinson seeks endorsement from Scripture, and it consequently fades away when that project is discredited. References are overwhelmingly to the Old Testament, which is a much more fertile source of the rhetoric of authority, law and vengeance than the New Testament. Interestingly, of the two quotations exceptionally taken from the New Testament, one is the terrifying injunction: 'And if thy right eye offend thee, pluck it out, and cast it from thee [...] And if thy right hand offend thee, cut it off [...]' (Matthew 5:29-30), which Robinson finds disturbingly close to the logic of the barbarous sacrifice of the tribesmen on the beach (77). The other quotation, in sharp contrast, is of Jesus' words: 'Whosoever shall not receive the kingdom of God as a little child, he shall not enter therein' (Mark 10:15; Luke 18:17). This utterance sounds confusingly in Robinson's ears both as an invitation and a warning in regard to his sojourn in the womb-like cave (112, 114). It can be seen however as predictive, on a more far-reaching level, of the notion of salvation through an *alter ego* as child at the end of the narrative, a motif discussed more fully in Chapter 6.

In one sense, therefore, the text functions as an anti-Bible, or rather as an assault on those aspects of the Bible which sustain a patriarchal world-view. More interestingly, however, it is the process of reading and decoding the Biblical texts which is scrutinised. The Biblical intertexts confuse, betray and undermine Robinson's efforts to sustain and justify a paternalistic order: the advocacy of mutilation as necessary to spiritual health, in the passage from Matthew quoted above, is unacceptable to Robinson's sense of human decency and of economy of resources. By contrast, he will discover and savour, in passages from Ecclesiastes (168), Isaiah (134), the Song of Solomon (135-6) and in the final quotation mentioned above concerning King David, words of passion and desire, in praise of companionship and erotic tenderness, forces subversive of the order of patriarchal authority.

The Bible thus emerges as a multiple text: the single-minded reader, such as Robinson, will be more often confused and frustrated than satisfied in consulting it. Like Speranza and Vendredi, it is a source of messages to be interpreted in open dialogue, not a faithful mirror of a single model of reality. As with the tarot, the truth lies not in cards or in text but in inspired reading of the symbols. This emphasis on reading rather than on text is made explicit in the reference to Robinson's mother's Quaker beliefs:

> Très attachée, comme le père, à la secte des Quakers, elle rejetait l'autorité des textes sacrés aussi bien que celle de l'Église papiste. Au grand scandale de ses voisins, elle considérait la Bible comme un livre dicté par Dieu certes, mais écrit de main humaine et grandement défiguré par les vicissitudes de

l'histoire et les injures du temps. Combien plus pure et plus vivante que ces grimoires venus du fond des siècles était la source de sagesse qu'elle sentait jaillir au fond d'elle-même! Là, Dieu parlait directement à sa créature. Là, l'Esprit Saint lui dispensait sa lumière surnaturelle. Or sa vocation de mère se confondait pour elle avec cette foi paisible. (107-8)[14]

The text is seen here as a corrupt code, whose true sense can only be restored by the reading of the individual attentive to the inner voice which is that of the Holy Spirit. This furnishes the pattern followed by Robinson every Sunday: 'Debout devant le lutrin, il psalmodie des versets de la Bible. Cette lecture est coupée de longs silences méditatifs que suivent des commentaires inspirés par l'Esprit Saint' (150). Clearly, however, as all Robinson's 'readings' of the Biblical texts suggest, this faith in the infallibility of the inner voice, and the assumption that it carries divine authority deriving from the Godhead, may be seen by the reader as perilous.[15] The equation of God with Nature has already been identified as one possible source of confusion: that of the voice of human nature with the Holy Spirit is certainly another.

It is significant that this attack on the authority of the text and the assertion of the supremacy of the inspired individual as interpreter should derive from the mother (while both parents are Quakers, it is her views which are emphasised). The assault on the patriarchal authority of the Word as Law comes from the maternal, female inheritance (as has already been seen in Chapter 3), and it will be continued in the dialogue Robinson maintains with Speranza, with Vendredi/Venus and with the feminine aspects of his own being.

Le Roi des aulnes: Origins and Tribulations

While Tiffauges's reading of his life is much affected by the non-Biblical intertexts which Nestor in particular infiltrates into his consciousness and into the narrative, these are complemented by Biblical references which, while not as explicit or as fully quoted as in *Vendredi*, are nevertheless insistently present and influential. They can be considered broadly under two headings: origins and tribulations.

Two references to Genesis convey Tiffauges's preoccupation with what he calls 'l'antiquité vertigineuse de mes origines' (13). Early in the novel Tiffauges reflects on the Biblical account of the creation of Adam and Eve (33-4). He subverts the text of Genesis 1:27 to read 'Male and female created he *him*', thereby radically revising the creation myth in order to suggest that the original Adam was androgynous. The subsequent creation of Eve from Adam's 'rib' (Genesis 2:21-2), which seems superfluous if male and female had already been separately created,[16] can then logically be understood as the amputation of Adam's female nature and the partition of gender: the real Fall of Man (35).[17] Tournier's work is, as we have seen in the previous chapter, shot through with nostalgia for this pre-lapsarian state of total integration. Tiffauges is, in this Biblical misreading, seeking authority for a vision of erotic fulfilment very different from the monogamous heterosexuality posited as the ideal by Judaeo-Christian tradition, and it is not surprising that the passage conjuring up this vision follows on from the account of the failure of his liaison with Rachel and the memory of his erotically charged masochistic subjection to his classmate Pelsenaire, which precipitates a nervous breakdown. This mismatch between his own sexuality and social-heterosexual expectations generates a theory, and a myth, which can console him and revalue his own experiences of pleasure: the second evocation of this myth of the bi-gendered Adam follows the Jeannot episode (the euphoria he experiences when he gathers up his wounded apprentice boy after an accident in the garage), and it thus validates his adoption of the conventionally female role of 'porte-enfant' by founding it on this myth of origin.

The second Genesis myth of origin referred to is that of Cain and Abel. Just as the creation of Eve represents the catastrophic scission of male and female, and thus of man and maternity, so the murder of Abel represents the cleavage between settler and nomad, the established and the marginal. By virtue of his first name, Abel seems predestined to be the victim of persecution, and the first part of his story appears to corroborate this course: bullied at school, he avoids an intolerable life thanks only to Nestor's powerful protection. Later, the unjust accusation of rape is given credibility by the police investigation of his eccentric obsessions which fixes him within the caricatural mask of the child-molester. From being a garageman, concerned with the instruments of travel, he himself becomes a prisoner-nomad, moving from point to point eastward until he reaches Kaltenborn. From this point on, his life takes its cue, not from his first name Abel, but rather from his sinister surname, Tiffauges, the name of a castle owned by the infamous child-murderer Gilles de Retz, condemned and executed in 1440. The name Tiffauges thus evokes the oppressive power of the *sédentaire* (Cain), in contrast to the nomad-victim Abel, and thus represents the temptation to which Tiffauges succumbs to fill the power-vacuum at the fortress of Kaltenborn and exert authority himself. His first name, nevertheless, continues to mark him as an interloper in this power-structure, a mere prisoner of war, freakishly promoted to a position with no legitimacy. From here on, the story can be read as the revenge of Abel and the fulfilling of the curse on Cain. Tiffauges listens to Blättchen ranting about *Blut und Boden* (Blood and Earth), that is, the necessity fearlessly to shed the blood of inferior races to fertilise the soil of the Reich, and he reflects that he is himself of the race of Abel, of the chosen victims. He recalls God's curse on Cain (433): 'And now art thou cursed from the earth, which hath opened her mouth to receive thy brother's blood from thy hand' (Genesis 4:11). This image of the blood-soaked earth is most vividly realised when he sees a human corpse so crushed and flattened by the passage of tanks, vehicles and people that it has become incorporated into the road surface (529-30).[18] Cain's punishment is that his worst fear will be realised: he, the *sédentaire*, will become a nomad, an outcast like the brother he has killed, 'a fugitive and a vagabond shalt thou be in the earth' (Genesis 4:12). On the road from Arys to Lyck in December 1944, where Tiffauges sees the crushed corpse, he also watches German refugees streaming past fleeing the Soviet advance. The population of the Reich is now itself forced to take to the road as nomads, in an 'exode' which mirrors, with a savage poetic justice, the exodus of the French in the face of the *blitzkrieg* in 1940. They are like Cain 'cursed from the earth', whereas he, with Ephraïm on his shoulders, will be received into the earth on the final page.

Each of these myths of origin leads into exile and hardship: Adam's expulsion from the paradise of androgyny, and God's retribution against the fratricidal Cain. This brings us naturally to the second motif of Biblical reference, that of tribulation. The final chapter, 'L'Astrophore', is prefaced (526) by a quotation from (appropriately) Exodus (12:29) about the Lord smiting the first born of Egypt. Reinforcing this reference, when the Soviet troops attack Kaltenborn, Ephraïm is celebrating the Seder, or ritual feast commemorating the Passover, the miraculous crossing of the Red Sea by the Israelites. The link is thus forged between this chronicle of the Eastern Front and the Old Testament story, and the element common to both is the Jews' escape from bondage, together with the punishment visited on their captors, and especially on their male children. This is another component of the 'mécanique des symboles'(473) which determines that the three Jungmannen must be smitten, in some clearly spectacular and exemplary manner, 'that the prophecy might be fulfilled' and the author's intertextual analogy made manifest. Their death is, in terms of poetic or divine justice, Ephraïm's revenge: the children of the oppressor must atone with their blood for the suffering of the children of Israel.[19]

The execution of Stefan Raufeisen by Soviet soldiers might likewise be seen as part of a complex pattern of retribution. Tiffauges has uttered what sounds at once like a prediction and a curse against Raufeisen for trampling on the bodies of the Jungmannen whom he has ordered to lie down on parade ('Stefan de Kiel, je t'annonce une mort cruelle et imminente!'), and thereby anticipates Raufeisen's brutal end (549). Raufeisen deserves attention as a character, since Tournier halts the chronological narrative in order to give us a biographical account of Raufeisen's life, in his own words (416-21), the only point in the entire novel where the voice of any character other than Tiffauges assumes the narrative. One effect of this insertion of what one might call the 'Raufeisen dossier' is to answer the question (to misquote Montesquieu) 'Comment peut-on être nazi?': it gives some human and social depth to a character who might otherwise seem merely brutish, as well as some insight into the experience of a whole generation between the wars. More profoundly, though, Raufeisen is a part-reflection of Tiffauges himself. His revolt against the stuffiness of the Weimar Republic led him to join the 'Wandervögel' ('Migrant birds') - like Abel, then, he had been on the side of the nomads. From there he joined the Nazi-oriented 'Bund der Geusen' (League of Beggars). Despite its nomadic title, the order of the day at the great rallies is not wandering, but 'Marschieren, marschieren, marschieren!' (420). The one-time free-flying *Wandervögel* are now proud of their 'muscles de bronze' and of their 'jambes devenues dures [...] comme des roues, comme des bielles', and they joyfully dedicate their lives and deaths to the Führer. It is, in miniature, the story of the transformation of a man from nomad to tyrant, from Abel to Cain. While this in part reflects the shift noted above in the central character from the Abel aspect to the Tiffauges aspect, Raufeisen represents an unequivocal Nazi conviction and instinctive brutality which acts as a foil to Tiffauges's much more equivocal role and consequently casts him in a less damning light. Raufeisen's death is the symbolic, atoning, vicarious death of all in Tiffauges that resembles him, the purging that precedes redemption. Its function in this respect is comparable to that of the Andoar episode in *Vendredi*.

References to the tribulations visited on the Egyptians in the Old

Testament are counterpointed by more general allusions to the Massacre of the Innocents in the New Testament. Tiffauges notes the detail of a summer solstice ritual at the Napola, in which the Jungmannen gather round a fire to remember the dead, to commit themselves to future sacrifice, and finally to leap one by one through the flames. For Tiffauges this is 'l'évocation en clair et l'invocation diabolique du massacre des innocents vers lequel nous marchons en chantant'(444). This notion of the young Nazi as Paschal lamb destined for sacrifice had already struck him when he saw the film *Hitlerjunge Quex*, in which the youthful Nazi hero is portrayed, contrary to expectation, as a fragile, vulnerable figure, a 'vision [...] d'une enfance allemande [...] vouée de tout temps à un massacre d'innocents' (414-15). In this novel, therefore, the final massacre is foreseen, and again we are in the realm of the 'mécanique des symboles' which 'overdetermines' the outcome. It is noteworthy that in St Matthew's Gospel, the original Massacre is also seen as the fulfilment of a prophecy: 'Then was fulfilled that which was spoken by Jeremy the prophet, saying, In Rama was there a voice heard, [...] Rachel weeping for her children, and would not be comforted, because they are not.'[20] The name Rachel sends us back to Tiffauges's Jewish mistress, and provides yet another link between this text and the Bible, as well as between the opening and closing of the novel.[21]

Just as the smiting of the first-born of Egypt is indivisibly linked with the liberation of the chosen people, the Biblical Massacre of the Innocents (which will feature in the plot of *Gaspard*) centres on the rescue from peril of the Chosen One, the Christ-child, in the ensuing flight into Egypt. This intertext thereby provides a second, related reading of the final pages, in which Ephraïm is cast as the Christ-child being borne to safety out of the place where his contemporaries are being slaughtered by soldiers. In this scenario, Tiffauges's role is that of the donkey (Ephraïm calls him 'Cheval d'Israël' (567)), a role which Tournier will more fully and amusingly develop in 'Le Dit de l'Ane' in *Gaspard*. This indirect evocation of the Nativity which mysteriously accompanies and counterbalances the massacre is present too in the description of the 'Julfest', the pagan midwinter ritual, in which the Jungmannen are reminded of their calling as bearers and wielders of the sword. This parody of Christmas ceremonial, celebrating the opposite of peace and goodwill towards men, is interrupted when the window is blown in by 'une bourrasque de fin du monde'(413) to reveal, in the thick, roaring darkness, a single star 'comme un oeil jaune' shining in the East. This rich image refers outward not just to the Magi's star (which will be variously interpreted in *Gaspard*), but to the yellow star compulsorily worn by Jews in Germany, and finally the 'étoile d'or à six branches' (likewise the Star of David) which Abel sees as he looks up for the last time, in the final sentence of the novel. As for the comparison of the star to an eye, this can be read in relation to Hugo's well-known poem 'La Conscience', in which the guilt-ridden Cain is haunted by the accusing eye of conscience, an intertextual link back to the Cain and Abel story through the common theme of the shedding of innocent blood, of guilt and the need for atonement.[22]

Following the bondage of the Israelites and the Massacre of the Innocents, the third and greatest Biblical tribulation evoked in the text is the Apocalypse. In *Le Pied de la lettre* (29), Tournier gives two definitions of the word *apocalypse*: '1. Révélation, dévoilement de la vérité. 2. Cataclysme, catastrophe, fin du monde.' Tiffauges refers to 'la Grande Tribulation' which will make manifest 'le secret le plus intime et le plus noir de ma vie' (117), and in the diary entry (3 July 1939) which recounts his arrest for the rape of Martine the same prophesy is sounded, in Nestorian tones: 'Tu sais bien maintenant que la grande tribulation se prépare, et que ton modeste destin est pris en charge par le Destin!'(194). In the immediate context, the Great Tribulation can obviously be seen as referring to the imminent World War, which will overtake individual destinies and allow Tiffauges's deepest and most secret impulses to find expression. In the Bible, however, these words are used in Christ's prophecy of the Apocalypse and the Second Coming: 'For then shall be great tribulation, such as was not since the beginning of the world to this time, no, nor ever shall be' (Matthew 24:21). The verse immediately preceding this one in Matthew's Gospel ('Pray ye that your flight be not in the winter') is quoted by Tiffauges as he watches the refugees on the road to Arys (529). Indeed, the whole final section, leading up to the description of the attack on the Napola by invading Soviet forces, is increasingly charged with the constituents of apocalyptic vision. These constituents are, characteristically, 'fire mingled with blood' (Revelation 8:7), and 'lightnings, and voices, and thunderings, and an earthquake, and great hail' (Revelation 11:19). Accordingly, Tiffauges feels as though drawn up into a thunderous sky, 'un ciel noir qu'ébranlait [...] la pulsation des canons de l'Apocalypse' (539); later, under bombardment, 'un tremblement de terre secoua le plancher sous ses pieds, et une grêle de plâtras tomba du plafond' (573). His final journey is through a landscape of fire and bloodshed.

What finally underlines the importance of this intertextual

relationship to the Apocalypse is that the last words of Tiffauges reported in the narrative (578) are an explicit quotation from Revelation, 1:14-16: 'Éphraïm, est-ce qu'il n'est pas dit dans les livres saints que sa tête et ses cheveux étaient blancs comme neige, ses yeux comme une flamme de feu, ses pieds semblables à de l'airain rougi dans une fournaise, et qu'une épée à deux tranchants sortait de sa bouche?' In the Biblical context this is the description of the 'one like unto the Son of man' (1:13) who speaks with the voice of Christ: 'I am Alpha and Omega' (1:11). In the context of the novel, the quotation is clearly associated with the immediately preceding spectacle of the pseudo-crucifixion of the three impaled boys, and in particular with the middle one of the three, the white-haired Lothar, who is impaled in such a way that the sword's tip protrudes from his mouth. Tournier has, in characteristic fashion, taken this rhetorical metaphor of the mouth and the sword and, horrifically, literalised it. The biblical metaphor of the protruding sword-point is presumably an attribute of power, and in particular verbal power, and like the bronze feet and the eyes of flame, contributes to a formidable evocation of supernatural might. Transferred to Lothar in a literal realisation, it is on the contrary an attribute of the sacrificial victim. True to the notion of linking Alpha and Omega, there is here a confusion and conjunction of opposites - the suffering of the victim, and the apotheosis of power: the Crucified and the Glorified. This conjunction was already present in the cry which Tiffauges heard, and which is presumably to be linked to the moment of the boys' death, a cry combining 'une étrange allégresse' and 'la plus intolérable douleur' (574). It is immediately after the sight of the boys - described in hyperrealistic detail - that Tiffauges complains that without his spectacles he can scarcely see. It is as though the vision of this parody crucifixion has almost blinded him, or was already being seen more with the mind's eye than with real vision. He asks Ephraïm to guide him from now on, and his speech and his vision become, like Ephraïm's, those of prophecy: he interprets a shower of tracer bullets in the sky as a clenched fist spurting blood, a literal manifestation of God's words to Cain (433 - see above) about 'receiving thy brother's blood from thy hand'. This apocalyptic reading of the grisly detail of war is continued in his quotation of the passage quoted above from Revelation which speaks of a figure with four attributes, of which two, the snow-white hair, and the sword-in-mouth, can be linked to Lothar. The other two, the eyes as of flaming fire, and the feet as of forged bronze, have nothing to do with the adolescent victim figure. The notion of a body of metallic power may recall the final transfiguration of Robinson in *Vendredi*, discussed in the next chapter, but in this text it immediately recalls the nickname of Behemoth by which Ephraïm calls Tiffauges, his 'cheval d'Israël', and the description of Behemoth quoted from the book of Job (40:15-22) a few pages earlier: 'Ses os sont des tubes d'airain, / Ses côtes sont des barres de fer' (567). As for the eyes as of fire, these are arguably realised at the very end. Ephraïm becomes the eyes of Tiffauges, guiding him when he cannot see, and in the last sentence of the text, as Tiffauges looks up for the last time, the child has become a star, and the guiding eyes a guiding star, celestial fire.[23] While many elements of the Apocalypse are present, they have been reshuffled and redistributed. The Biblical code has been scrambled, and opened to new meanings.

One further implication of this intertext deserves comment. The figure 'like unto the Son of man' who is so described in the first chapter of Revelation goes on to command St John to 'write the things which thou hast seen, and the things which are, and the things which shall be hereafter' (1:19). Here the prophet is giving an account of the genesis of his own writing, just as Tiffauges did at the start of his *Écrits sinistres*, and in so doing both authors claim supernatural authority. Tiffauges's narrative likewise comprises the past (reminiscence of schooldays), the present, and the future, in that it is constantly shot through with a strain of prophecy, of 'the things which shall be hereafter'. Again, this allusion to the authority and the origins of narrative ties together the beginning and end of the novel, its Alpha and Omega. When we consider that the significant strand of Biblical quotation and reflection in *Le Roi des aulnes* starts with the book of Genesis and ends with the book of Revelation, that is to say, the first and the last books of the Bible respectively, then we can see that the Alpha-Omega idea is ingeniously respected in the intertext also, and we may even suspect that (as with other Tournier texts) the novel is in one of its aspects a shadow, or alternative, Bible.

Les Météores: Variations on a Pentecostal Theme

While *Les Météores* has far fewer specific Biblical references than *Vendredi* or *Le Roi des aulnes*, it nevertheless develops a strain of theological reflection which is an essential part of the ideology of the text.

This reflection is primarily mediated by characters with a religious vocation - notably by Thomas Koussek, but also by the two nuns, Sister Béatrice and Sister Gotama, who look after the handicapped children at Sainte-Brigitte. Béatrice is in charge of children with mental disabilities, whom she regards as spiritually superior beings, exempt from sin, and akin to angels, but simply deprived of the power to communicate. She dreams of a day of divine inspiration, 'une Pentecôte des Innocents, qui descendrait en langues de feu sur leur tête, chassant les ténèbres de leur cerveau et dénouant la paralysie de leur langue'(55). Her unorthodox vision draws support from the findings of a psychopaediatrician which suggest that these children use the full range of sounds on which the world's languages are based, an observation which leads Béatrice to imagine that the language of her children is the one universal original language, the language of Eden, before Babel and the multiplicity of tongues.

Sister Gotama, a taciturn Nepalese nun, takes care of children with gross physical handicaps and deformities. She is concerned to account for the existence of these children, and to give them value. She derives comfort from her reading of Genesis 2:20, in which God seeks a mate for Adam among cattle, beasts and fowl. This, to her, suggests a divine indifference to the frontier between human and non-human forms and justifies the strange hybrid shapes of some of her charges, which she views as exotic prototypes from the experimental beginnings of Creation. '[...] [N]'auraient-ils pas eu leur place dans un univers autrement conçu?'(66).

Both sisters draw sustenance from a heterodox myth of origins to sustain them in their task and in their faith, one on the level of the spiritual and the linguistic, the other on the level of the physiological. Each subverts a hierarchy of human value - the supremacy of the articulate, or the superiority of the 'normal' human form - on behalf of the 'monster', on the periphery of human society, and each looks for a world which would allow of this revaluation, a post-Pentecostal world or an 'univers autrement conçu'. In this they reflect Tournier's ongoing concern with the situation of marginal individuals and the challenge they represent to imperious notions of normality. Clearly they complement each other, in their respective orientation towards spirit and flesh, and establish a context within which the abnormal, 'monstrous' phenomenon of twinhood will be worked through in the narrative, and its status revalued.

The passage dealing with the nuns occurs in Chapter 3, in what we have called sequence A (the twins' sequence). In the preceding chapter, in sequence B (Alexandre's sequence), comes the section concerning two formative figures in his life, which we have already discussed, Thomas Koussek and Raphaël Ganeça (see Chapter 3). Interestingly, these two pairs can be seen as counterbalancing each other. Béatrice finds Gotama's orientalism suspect, imagining a pantheon of Indian 'idoles à trompe' (65). The term 'idole à trompe' recalls, of course, the Hindu god Ganesa (as we noted in the previous chapter), and draws attention to a common strand between Raphaël and Gotama, in their oriental associations, their reverence for the flesh, and their perception of the divine in grotesque forms, be it elephant-god or a real-life 'cyclops' or 'enfant-sirène'(65). Similarly, Béatrice's dream of a 'Pentecost of the Innocent' prepares us for Thomas's Pentecost, his far-reaching conversion to the Holy Spirit.

On one side Ganesa, on the other the Holy Spirit: East and West, Flesh and Spirit. Ganesa's totemic animal is the rat, while the Holy Spirit is depicted as a dove - 'le poil et la plume'. In the chapter which bears this heading (Chapter 9), Alexandre, in the midst of a huge refuse dump near Marseilles, undergoes a kind of parody Pentecost, in which the 'rushing mighty wind' of the Holy Spirit (Acts 2:2) takes the form of the viciously gusting Mistral sweeping round his caravan. The gentle dove of the Holy Ghost, by a similar transposition, becomes the horde of gulls which dominate the dump by day; at night, it is the rats who are masters of the area. When Alexandre discovers the body of his lover Daniel being devoured by rats, he recalls Koussek's words about the Holy Spirit, and ironically underlines in his narrative the caricatural aspect of this experience: 'la Vérité [...] sous un déguisement hideux et grotesque'(304). He watches a white rat clambering slowly out of the crater where the body lies: 'Est-ce pour avoir dévoré le sexe de Daniel qu'il était devenu si lourd?'(304). This genital communion with Daniel's body (a cruel parody of fellatio) links the rat to Alexandre himself, and through him to Raphaël Ganeça, the phallic Indian god and his totem rat. Alexandre watches the courageous but hopeless last stand which the white rat makes against the marauding gulls: this scene anticipates the shape of his own death in the back-streets of Casablanca, outnumbered and cut to pieces. Thus in the opposition between fur and feather, and symbolically between flesh and (Holy) spirit, Alexandre sides with flesh, and remains sequestered within its demands and his own particular sexuality. While it is he who receives Thomas's Pentecostal message of the coming of the Spirit and the transcendence of the body, it is not given to him to follow it, but rather to Paul, at the end of the novel.

It is the account of Thomas's spiritual itinerary that gives the novel its theological dimension. Thomas's initial obsession with the body of Christ is at once mystical and homoerotic, as Alexandre realises when, hearing noises from the crypt of the school chapel, he discovers his fellow-pupil lying naked, in the place of the cross, beneath a life-size carved figure of Christ's body (48). Thomas is thus a 'Christophore' or Christ-bearer, as Abel Tiffauges aspires to be, and the fact that this scandalous episode takes place in the crypt beneath the chapel sanctuary suggests the notion that religious manifestation has, hidden at its foundations, a charge of erotic desire.[24] Thomas finds a similar meaning in the Biblical story of his namesake, 'doubting Thomas', who required to put his finger into the wound in Christ's side before he would believe in his resurrection (John 20:24-9): 'Il lui faut l'expérience mystique d'une communion charnelle, d'une pénétration de son corps dans le corps du Bien-Aimé'(151). There is present here the same heady convergence of a mystic communion of the flesh and the erotic fetishisation of the wound as in the episodes relating to Pelsenaire's knee in *Le Roi des aulnes* and to Jeanne's injury, discussed in the previous chapter: carnal and spiritual passion combine. By the analogy with homosexual phallic penetration, this physical verification of Christ's bodily presence is made even more shocking, and an erotic dimension is conferred on the manifestation of a truth central to Christian belief, the Resurrection.

After a nervous breakdown (comparable to Abel's after the Pelsenaire incident), Thomas, sent to live in the monastery of the Paraclete, comes to understand that he must transcend his fixation on the person of Christ, whose function was essentially to be the precursor of the Holy Spirit. He now transfers his highest devotion to the third Person of the Trinity. This does not mean that all corporality has been left behind: 'L'Esprit-Saint est vent, tempête, souffle, il a un corps météorologique'(158). Pentecost, he explains, was originally a festival of harvest, and the Pentecostal wind is a wind of fertility. Mary, mother of Jesus, is made fertile by the coming of the Holy Spirit, and at Pentecost, the Spirit brings to the Apostles the gift (dreamt of by Sister Béatrice) of a universal language, which allows the propagation of the Word. (In the opposition of 'le poil' and 'la plume', the latter can also be taken to mean the pen, the medium of language.) In this new dispensation of the Paraclete, the elements of flesh and spirit are conjoined and balanced.

Thomas's metamorphosis, described in a few dense pages in Chapter 5, programmes that of Paul through the novel. Thomas seeks to cling to his Christ-twin in mystic and carnal communion, just as Paul seeks to maintain the twin-bond with Jean. As Christ leaves his disciples behind, so Jean abandons Paul, and in each case the bereaved twin finds in the emptiness of his loss the space for a new, all-embracing communion, with the Paraclete wind or the 'corps météorologique'.[25] As in *Vendredi*, the pervading spirit of the ending of *Les Météores* is more to do with engaging with the natural elements rather than with Christian symbolism;[26] this ambivalence within the text, between reading the Bible and reading the world, is a constant feature of Tournier's relationship to Christian belief, which is at once passionate and subversive, seeking to shift the emphasis back from theological abstraction and moral orthodoxies to assert the spiritual status of physical and carnal experience.

Gaspard, Melchior & Balthazar: Beyond the Nativity

The relationship of this fiction to the Bible is necessarily different from that in Tournier's preceding novels. There Biblical reference served, in a variety of complex ways, as a counterpoint to narratives set in the modern era: through quotation, evocation and (mis)reading by characters, it irrigates the narratives of modernity with metaphysics and theology. *Gaspard*, however, explores a quite different strategy. Here, the Bible is no longer a distinct intertext, since the novel takes its starting-point from the Biblical account of the Nativity, quoted in full as an epilogue to the text. This bare outline it then proceeds to amplify, disrupt and transcend. Some aspects of this amplification have been discussed in earlier chapters, centring on patterns of power and of sexuality. The Biblical episode is not only expanded and interpreted in this way: it is also disrupted, notably by the discrete Barbedor chapter, and transcended by the last King's tale, which skirts the Nativity to culminate finally in the legacy of the Last Supper. The disruption places the Nativity in dialogue with a non-Christian narrative, while the conclusion subordinates it to the final Sacrament.

'Barbedor' was published separately as an illustrated children's story, thus emphasising its autonomy from the other parts of the novel. It tells of a king who, grown old, is moved to leave his palace to follow a bird back to its nest, and in the process undergoes a magic rejuvenation, becoming himself the child who will succeed the old King, who has just died as he returns. Standing at the very centre of the loose seven-part structure, this story is an interloper in the sequence of historical narration and Christian myth which surrounds it, and this makes it the most problematic element in this perspective. Its function is perhaps to suggest that the notion of the gift of eternal life, associated in theology with belief in Christ, can be expressed in wholly non-Christian terms, and that the Christian myth is itself nourished by the more ancient fertility rite of passage from the dying Old King to the advent of the young New King.[27]

This bridge-building between a non-Christian, or pre-Christian, point of reference and the Nativity story which encloses it is also a function of the story of the fourth Wise Man. Taor is a King from India, untouched by Judaic or Hellenic thought, and his invented presence thus extends the dialogue with non-European beliefs developed in *Les Météores*, and notably in the thinking of Raphael Ganeça and Sister Gotama. It is Taor who brings to the central sacrament of Christianity a reading rooted not in notions of Love, Beauty or Truth but in a more physical and down-to-earth reflection on hunger and thirst. We have already noted how the story of Taor enacts a closure both in the structure of the book and in the thematics of power and sexuality. In this respect too, by adding the physical to the metaphysical, East to West, the last of the seven sections has a synthesising function, and the essence of a Christian myth is freed from its cultural specificity.

Gilles & Jeanne: The Two Faces of God

The early fifteenth century, in which this story is set, is, Tournier tells us, 'une époque où il était courant d'avoir un commerce quotidien avec Dieu, Jésus, la Vierge et les saints'(17): Gilles, like Jeanne and most of their contemporaries, 'vit aux confins du naturel et du surnaturel'(21) - the preferred domain of Tournier the fiction-maker, we might add. Tournier insists on Gilles's religious belief: he is 'profondément croyant'(17), and is terrified into submission by the threat of excommunication in his trial - it is only within the bosom of the Church that he is confident of avoiding eternal damnation. Not content with ordinary salvation as the prize of a pious and dutiful life, as urged on him by Blanchet, he is inhabited by a Faustian aspiration to the supreme accolade. His cry to Jeanne is 'Fais de moi un saint!'(26), and this overweening ambition never changes.

Tournier also shows how Gilles's Catholic belief is shot through with a primitive spiritism - he speaks to Jeanne of the maleficent sprites who inhabit thickets and caves, casting evil spells, and of demons whispering temptation. Gilles's world is a Manichaean one, in which the forces of good and evil coexist. This dualism pervades his thinking: he gets Jeanne to speak of a patently pre-Christian fertility rite around a magic tree near Domrémy in which she took part. Yet unlike Gilles himself she remains innocent of heart, hearing only holy voices, and like Albuquerque in the Father Superior's sermon in *Le Roi des aulnes* (*RA* 88), Gilles counts on his association with this creature of innocence to assure his own salvation.

When Jeanne is captured, condemned and burnt at the stake, Gilles's dualist view is exacerbated. The Maid of Orleans whom he knew to be chaste and holy is also, by the edict of Mother Church, a witch, a heretic and a blasphemer. Jeanne thus acquires two irreconcilable faces: like the god Janus she is 'Jeanne bifront' (48), whose dying cries of 'Jésus! Jésus!' are counterpointed with the litany of her indictment.[28] Prelati will suggest a reading of the Bible which underpins this dualist view. Lucifer, he recalls, was an angel, and, with his understanding of evil, is now an intercessor between Man and God. Just as the beauty of Renaissance art draws on an intimate familiarity with corruption and death, so the path to salvation can lie through an expertise in evil. God himself can require Abraham to kill his son,[29] and while the final sacrifice is not demanded here, God will in due course have his own child scourged and crucified. In this perspective, the dualism is absolute: the deity himself has two faces, of which Christ and Lucifer are the expressions. This implies in turn two opposite but complementary paths to salvation - the vocation to holiness and to martyrdom (Jeanne, invoking Christ) and the vocation to the knowledge of evil, to the role of sacrificer rather than sacrificed, in the name of Lucifer, Bringer of Light. Seeing that Jeanne is an 'ange'(15), Gilles will become her perfect and necessary complement, an 'ange infernal'(45).[30]

Tournier's purpose is not that of exonerating Gilles's crimes, any more than *Le Roi des aulnes* excuses Nazi atrocities: in both cases the dreadful facts are set out with unvarnished clarity. What he is doing is exploring the logic whereby a fervent if heterodox believer, relating theology and experience, can come to act thus. Gilles's trajectory through depravity to redemption is used to highlight the complex, and even alarming, relationship of salvation to conventional notions of good and evil, in a religion which centres on the scandal of the Crucifixion and which teaches that 'le plus grand pécheur de tous les temps et le pire homme qui fût jamais' (152) is not beyond salvation through faith and repentance.

In *La Goutte d'or*, religion is a minor theme only. On the ferry Idriss's companion, the jeweller, recommends a full observance of Islam as a defence against despair in France. 'Contre le désespoir et la misère, tu n'auras peut-être que le Coran et la mosquée'(99). Idriss indeed finds this defence finally in the study of calligraphy, and the copying of the Koran. He reads a quotation from the Koran placed on the wall in the master calligrapher's workshop: 'Il y a plus de vérité dans l'encre des savants que dans le sang des martyres', a saying which, the narrative voice insists, 'tranche absolument entre la sagesse de l'Islam et le culte de la douleur et de la mort propre au christianisme'(198). This cult of pain and death is symbolised in the crucifix, and is somewhat light-heartedly evoked a few pages earlier in the anecdote of the sculptor who, required to produce a life-size image of Christ on the cross, uses a mould of his own body. This passing reference to the crucified twin-image is perhaps in part a nod from the author, for the benefit of his more devoted readers, in the direction of *Les Météores* and Thomas Koussek, recalling his transcendence of the cult of the Christ's bodily pain and death. While Thomas's (Christian) release comes through the wind of the Spirit, Idriss finds in calligraphy a dialogue with God in the timeless space of the desert. In both cases the power of the image, an image of the mortification of the flesh, is dissipated to make way for a principle that is at once more allusive, open and liberating.

Tournier's work is shot through with his reading of and reflection on the Bible, but it is a reading and a reflection that is always disrespectful. Like Robinson's Quaker mother, he treats the Bible as a corrupt text which needs to be interpreted and even reformulated in the light of the reader's inner conviction. Robinson discovers early on to his cost how treacherous a literalistic reverence for Scripture can be, but will go on to rejoice in the celebration of physical desire in the Song of Solomon which expresses his abandonment of puritanism and his new-found pan-eroticism. Tiffauges's rewriting of Genesis founds his rather different sexual project of annexing the maternal function through 'la phorie'. What Tournier aspires to is a version of the Bible which reinstates the body and physical experience as central, and re-establishes the link between spiritual love (*agape*) and carnal love (*eros*). In *Vendredi*, the spiritual is carnalised, so that the final ecstasy of communion with the universe is presented as a mythic apotheosis of the body, while the Biblical intertexts have become less and less authoritative and authoritarian (the last quotation speaking, significantly, of carnal solace). In subsequent novels, the Biblical dimension is more fully maintained, and the carnal is spiritualised. In *Le Roi des aulnes,* salvation is associated with carrying on your own body that of a child, with all the potential for erotic or sadistic gratification which that implies. In *Gaspard*, the first eucharist is not seen as some merely symbolic act, but as the supreme meal offered to a man who has been obsessed for his whole life with eating and drinking: it is approached by way of a morally undignified and apparently self-indulgent fleshly appetite. In *Les Météores*, Paul enacts with his body, and in relation to his physical twin and the physical universe, the self-transcendence which Thomas has preached on a more purely theological and metaphysical level. Paul is the hero of the text in this sense in that it is he, not Thomas, who most fully achieves the apotheosis of the bodily self. The climactic moments which celebrate the presence of the sacred in Tournier centre on the body - Robinson's body bathed in sunlight, Tiffauges's sinking into the accepting earth, Paul's mutilated body made mystically complete by encompassing the world, Taor's bodily and spiritual hunger finally assuaged.

The moral implications of placing the body back at the centre of religion in this way are far-reaching. All human appetites, even the basest, are open to spiritualisation: it is not just the soul, but the whole person which is saved. This potentially scandalous doctrine of total salvation is tested to the limit in *Gilles & Jeanne*, where we are invited to confront fully the doctrine that even the worst criminal imaginable can be saved, and that a path to God may lie through such barbarity. If Joan of Arc, inspired by her own inner voices, is a saint and not the heretic which the Church decreed her to be, then the door is open to wilder heterodoxies.

For a writer who has described himself as an 'écrivain croyant',[31] Tournier's dialogue with the Bible is a delinquent one. He borrows its authority for his idiosyncratic characters and their destinies, as in the use of Revelation to add epic weight to the culmination of *Le Roi des aulnes*. He also uses the unorthodox priorities of his characters to interrogate the text and the message of the Bible, and to propose surprising and sometimes scandalous rereadings and rewritings. More generally, he brings Christian tradition into dialogue with other beliefs and mythologies: this kind of confrontation is embodied in the names of Vendredi (= death of Christ, day of Venus) and of Raphaël Ganeça, and in the encounter of the young Muslim Idriss with a (supposedly) Christian culture. These dialectics of reading, writing and cultural relativism are so mobile that Tournier's own position is impossible to determine with any exactness from his writing. What is manifest is a simultaneous celebration of the carnal and embracing of the supernatural, and above all the insistence on the coexistence of the two. In the Gospel of Michel Tournier, flesh and spirit are indivisible, not opposed.

Notes on Chapter 4

[1]   Interview with Vera Kornicker, 'Montre-moi ta bibliothèque, je te dirai qui tu es', *Le Figaro* (20.8.79), 18.

[2]   See in general the section on 'La Bible, pré-texte' in Merllié, *Michel Tournier*, 247-50.

[3]   Interview with Le Péchon, 29. For references to Bible-reading in Defoe's *Robinson Crusoe*, see e.g. pp.108, 110, 126, 222-3. It features too in Defoe's own source, the narrative of Alexander Selkirk, who is 'thoroughly reconciled to his Condition' by 'frequent reading of the Scriptures' (*ibid.*, 308).

[4]   For other commentaries on the Bible as intertext in *Vendredi*, see Susan Petit, 'The Bible as inspiration in Tournier's *Vendredi*', *French Forum*, IX (1984), 343-54, and Hutton, *Tournier: Vendredi*, 27-41.

[5]   See Genesis 1:28; God accords a similar authority to Noah (Genesis 9:2). See also Genesis 2:15 : 'And the Lord God took the man, and put him into the garden of Eden to dress it and to keep it' ('dress' here in the Authorised Version meaning order, cultivate).

[6]   See *Robinson Crusoe*, 114; similar sentiments are expressed also on pp.139, 157.

[7]   Genesis Ch.6, not Ch.4, the reference given in the Folio edition.

[8]   Cf. Matthew 13:30. Robinson is reduced to a literal decoding of symbolic discourse; he can no longer cope with metaphor. 'Je ne puis plus parler qu'*à la lettre*' (68 - italics in original).

[9]   The reference to the Tree of Knowledge of course designates Adam as 'le premier homme', but 'le retrait des eaux' could refer either to the 'gathering together of the waters' at the Creation (Genesis 1:10) or to the Flood survived by Noah. The two prototypes of mankind in Genesis here seem to be conflated, suggesting a cycle of birth and rebirth, creation and re-creation which is a fundamental pattern in Tournier's narrative structures.

[10]   See Acts of the Apostles, 2:3.

[11]   See e.g. Exodus 14:21.

[12]   Cf. Genesis 39: 7-15, 19-20.

[13]   Vendredi too, in mid-combat, sees Andoar's face as 'un masque de patriarche sémite [...] à la barbe annelée'(196).

[14]   This Quaker inheritance appears to be an invention of Tournier, not being mentioned in Defoe's novel; it is however in the spirit of Defoe's hero, who feels he needs nothing more than the word of God and the inspiration of his Spirit to understand the fundamentals of faith and communicate them to Vendredi. See e.g. *Robinson Crusoe*, 223.

[15]   Just such a sceptical view is hinted at in Voltaire's account of his conversation with a Quaker: '- Mais comment pouvez-vous discerner, insistai-je, si c'est l'Esprit de Dieu qui vous anime dans vos discours?' See the 'Seconde lettre: Sur les Quakers', in Voltaire's *Lettres philosophiques*, ed. R. Pomeau (Paris, Garnier-Flammarion, 1964), 27.

[16]   Voltaire, in similarly mischievous and subversive vein, draws attention to this incoherence in the article 'Genèse' in his *Dictionnaire philosophique*: 'On ne sait d'ailleurs si l'auteur veut dire que l'homme avait d'abord les deux sexes, ou s'il entend que Dieu fit Adam et Eve le même jour. Le sens le plus naturel est que Dieu forma Adam et Eve en même temps; mais ce sens contredit

absolument la formation de la femme, faite d'une côte de l'homme longtemps après les sept jours.' See Voltaire, Dictionnaire philosophique, ed. R. Pomeau, (Paris, Garnier-Flammarion, 1964), 206-7.

[17] Compare 'La Famille Adam'(*CB*), 'La Mère Noël'(*CB*) and 'Le Sosie de Dieu' (*VI* 65) for other heterodox versions of the creation myth. Bouloumié (*Michel Tournier*, 161) suggests some theological sources.

[18] It is anticipated much earlier, however, when the wounded Jeannot's blood drips on to the earth floor of the garage (131).

[19] There is a further reference to the plagues of Egypt, the turning of the rivers into blood (568 - cf. Exodus 7:20). A rusty discolouration of the water is taken by Tiffauges as a sign of approaching deliverance. It is Éphraïm's voice which imposes this reading of immediate events as a re-enactment of Biblical myth. Tiffauges's frantic report that 'les Soviétiques détruisent le château' is obstinately translated by the young Jew as 'les soldats de l'Éternel frappent de mort les aînés des Égyptiens'(573).

[20] Matthew 2:18; cf. Jeremiah 31:15.

[21] The link between the fictional and the biblical Rachel is not, however, a clear one. In the novel Rachel, despite her 'corps ample, accueillant, maternel' (32), is concerned with erotic satisfaction rather than with maternity. The role of bereaved mother is filled rather by Frau Netta, whose son is lost on the Eastern Front (385), though she receives the news without lamenting, like Brecht's Mother Courage. Furthermore, Tiffauges's reference to his mistress's 'petite tête de berger hébreux' may suggest another biblical Rachel who kept her father's sheep, and became the wife of Jacob (Genesis Ch.29ff.). This latter Rachel's story is visibly one of the sources for 'Les deux soeurs' (*CS* 13-16).

[22] See 'La Conscience', in Victor Hugo, *La Légende des siècles*, ed. A. Dumas (Paris, Garnier, 1964), 26: '[...] [A]u fond des cieux funèbres,/ Il vit un oeil, tout grand ouvert dans les ténèbres,/ Et qui le regardait dans l'ombre fixement.'

[23] On pp. 578-9, Ephraïm is described as the 'Porte-Étoile', by virtue of the yellow star which Jews in the Third Reich were obliged to display on their clothing, while Tiffauges is described as the 'Porte-enfant', as he carries the boy. At the very end, however, when Tiffauges looks up and sees a star in place of the child, he has thereby become himself the 'Porte-étoile' or 'Astrophore' referred to in the title of the final section. This destiny he has long since predicted for himself, in a diary entry reflecting on Atlas, pillar of the heavens, as his personal mythological hero: '[...] [M]a fin triomphale ce sera, si Dieu le veut, de marcher sur la terre avec posée sur ma nuque une étoile plus radieuse et plus dorée que celle des rois mages...'(136).

[24] This simulacrum of an embrace between two male bodies, overladen with a mystical sense of communion with Christ, is a deliberate echo of the extraordinary ending of Flaubert's 'St Julien l'Hospitalier', the second of his *Trois contes*, in which Julien embraces a leper who then changes into Christ, and is carried into heaven. Tournier sees in this episode 'une fantastique inversion de l'acte sexuel, consommé dans un paroxysme de chasteté, l'amour-charité ayant brûlé jusqu'à la cendre l'amour sexuel' (*VV* 170).

[25] When Paul sees Urs Kraus's portraits of his brother, he finds there 'du vent, du vent et encore du vent [...] Ce n'est plus un visage, c'est une rose des vents'(539). This curious observation links Jean to the meteorological, and thence to the wind of the Spirit.

[26] The link between the Holy Spirit and the phenomena of weather is made in Paul's initiation into meteorology by the scientist Giuseppe Colombo.

The surname Colombo suggests the dove of the Holy Spirit, while Giuseppe, the Italian form of Joseph, is that of the earthly father of Christ, and thus the physical counterpart of the Holy Spirit as progenitor.

[27] See section on fertility in Chapter 7 below.

[28] In Gilles's promise to follow Jeanne 'au ciel comme en enfer'(33), one could perceive (as often in Tournier) an echo of Baudelaire, here of the final lines of 'Le Voyage' (*Fleurs du mal*, cxxvi), 'Enfer ou ciel, qu'importe!...', and of the poet's play with the moral ambiguity of audacious spiritual experiments. See Baudelaire, *Oeuvres complètes*, I:134.

[29] Kierkegaard struggles, in *Fear and Trembling*, to come to terms with the outrage to human morality which Abraham's readiness to kill his son at God's behest represents. He develops the concept of a 'teleological suspension of the ethical' - a phrase that could be used to vindicate Gilles's whole enterprise. See S. Kierkegaard, *Fear and Trembling, Repetition,* ed. and trans. H.V. and E.H. Hong (Princeton, Princeton University Press, 1983), 54ff. We have already noted above, in *Vendredi*, an ironic treatment of the notion of a sacrifice acceptable to God.

[30] With regard to Jeanne's function as angel of the Annunciation and intertextual references to the Nativity, see Gascoigne, 'Michel Tournier', in Tilby (ed), *Beyond the Nouveau Roman*, 88-9.

[31] See Milne, *L'Evangile selon Michel*, 1.

5

The Order of the Elements

In *Gaspard*, Melchior recounts that the sanctuary of the temple at Jerusalem is protected by a veil embroidered with the symbols of fire, earth, air and sea and depicting 'une carte du ciel' (105). In the edifice of Tournier's fiction too such symbols are prominently displayed for our contemplation. In *Le Vent Paraclet* (152-4), he speaks warmly of his debt to Gaston Bachelard, whose lectures and writings on the scientific imagination and on the archetypal imagery linked to the four elements greatly stimulated Tournier from his student days on.[1] The function of this chapter is to study the interplay of elements and their significances in Tournier's work, and to establish their role in his 'carte du ciel' - the itinerary toward salvation pursued, in one form or another, by all the heroes of his novels.[2]

Vendredi

In a richly significant entry in his logbook in Chapter 10, Robinson, analysing his evolution so far, defines its guiding principle as follows: 'Ainsi étais-je amené par tâtonnements successifs à chercher mon salut dans la communion avec des éléments, étant devenu moi-même *élémentaire*' (226). Here, as elsewhere, the elements are defined as, on one hand, the fundamental constituents of the natural world and, on the other, forces or affinities within the self.[3]

Classical mythology generally envisaged the universe as being composed of four basic elements: water, earth, air and fire. Ovid's *Metamorphoses*, for example, offer a more or less traditional cosmology in placing the elements in a descending hierarchy, in the order: fire, air, earth, water. The lightest, least tangible elements (fire, air) are higher, while the solid and weightier ones that gravitate downwards (earth, water) are lower.[4] This hierarchical framework is indispensable to a reading of the novel as a progression towards a 'salut [...] élémentaire'.

If we turn once more to the 'prologue' as the seed-bed of the narrative, it can be noted that there all four elements are present. The fatal storm is announced by the 'feux Saint-Elme', the electrical discharges playing around the ship's masts (10). The subsequent maelstrom of wind (air) and sea (water) finally drive the boat on to the rocks (earth). It is the watchman's shout of 'Terre', the advent of the fourth element to complete the mayhem, which marks the moment of cataclysm.

The main narrative thereafter can readily be viewed as a progressive ascent through the classical hierarchy of the elements. In the first two chapters, Robinson is fixated on the sea. 'Tournant le dos obstinément à la terre, il n'avait d'yeux que pour la surface bombée et métallique de la mer [...]' (21). All his energies at this stage are devoted to a marine project: the building of *L'Évasion*. Following the disastrous failure of this undertaking, he rejects the sea as the saving element in favour of the land, and the second chapter closes with the words: 'Tournant le dos au grand large, il s'enfonça dans les éboulis [...] qui menaient vers le centre de l'île' (42).

In Chapters 3 to 8, Robinson's focus is on the island: he cultivates and orders its surface area and natural resources, explores its subterranean depths and constitutes it as the object of his emotion and desire. The gunpowder explosion marks the moment of transition from lower to higher elements, and indicates fire as the essential element of transmutation. In the period of Vendredi's ascendancy until his departure (Chapters 9 to 11), air is the presiding element. With Vendredi gone, and the arrival of Jaan, the final page completes the hierarchical ascent with the celebration of the sun, fire now in its celestial form.[5]

In terms of their affinities to the elements, Robinson and Vendredi are opposite and complementary. Robinson's orientation is towards earth and fire, Vendredi's towards air and (to a lesser extent) water. Each man partakes of one lower, base element and one higher, more ethereal or spiritual element, and in both cases it is finally the attraction of the higher element which is decisive in their destiny.

While Robinson's relationship to the element of earth is shifting and multiform, it is finally the spiritualisation of the influence of fire on his being which is decisive, and Vendredi's vital function in this regard is as the catalyst to this process of refinement and redirection. The best starting-point, then, for a survey of elements and elemental affinities in the text is with the raw energy of fire as it is present in Robinson before the Vendredi effect begins to change its nature.

It is to his father that Robinson owes his red hair (his 'barbe rousse' (8) and later his 'boucles ardentes comme un brasier' (218)), a colouring conventionally seen as the outward sign of a fiery temperament, and sometimes, in earlier centuries, as the mark of the Devil.[6] Van Deyssel points to the potentially destructive effect of such inner fire in interpreting the tarot card of Chaos: 'La bête de la Terre est en lutte avec un monstre de flammes. L'homme que vous voyez, pris entre des forces opposées, est un fou reconnaissable à sa marotte. On le deviendrait à moins' (9).[7] The captain's legacy to Robinson is his cherished porcelain pipe, almost the last thing he mentions (14), and smoking it becomes in turn one of Robinson's special pleasures. For him 'le fourneau brûlant et vivant' is 'l'enveloppe terrestre d'un petit soleil souterrain, une manière de volcan portatif et domestiqué qui rougeoyait paisiblement sous la cendre [...] C'était la chambre nuptiale *possédée*, enfermée dans le creux de sa main, de la terre et du soleil' (182). The attraction to Robinson of this conjunction of earth and fire is self-evident, given his temperamental affinity with both elements. Significantly, too, the emphasis is on the containment of the fire within its 'enveloppe terrestre', so that the 'volcano' is kept within safe and harmless limits ('domestiqué', 'paisiblement'), and this containment of the elements ('possédée', 'enfermée') is a symbol of human mastery. The reference to the 'chambre nuptiale' suggests also an erotic dimension, and recalls the 'douceur nuptiale' (164) of his liaison with Speranza and the 'couche nuptiale' (176) of the valley where it is celebrated. The analogy between these two sources of gratification is underlined by such textual echoes: just as, in the pipe, the fire is contained in an 'enveloppe terrestre', so the earth of Speranza envelops and warms him. 'La présence presque charnelle de l'île contre lui le réchauffait, l'émouvait. Elle était nue, cette terre qui l'enveloppait. Il se mit nu lui-même' (126). His fire is contained by the earthly receptacle of the island.[8] The convergence of these two narrative elements comes when Robinson's exclusive 'droit de seigneur' in respect both of Speranza as sexual partner and of the pipe as a source of pleasure is challenged by Vendredi. His burning rage, which will lead directly to the explosion, is expressed as the unleashing of the fire within him: '[...] [L]e feu qu'il sentait couver en lui paraissait d'une essence plus pure [...] qu'une simple passion humaine. [...] Sa fureur avait quelque chose de cosmique.' He feels himself to be 'une force originelle, issue des entrailles de la terre et balayant tout d'un souffle ardent. Un volcan' (174). Containment is at an end, the 'volcan' is no longer 'domestiqué', and its explosive 'force originelle' will sweep away both the physical buildings of his administration and the painstakingly elaborated construction of his old self. The forty barrels of gunpowder which are detonated present a similar narrative configuration.[9] They come from the cargo of the *Virginie*, details of which Van Deyssel had never revealed (24-5) and are stored in the grotto - safely contained, for the moment, by the rocks of the earth. The ship's captain is thus the source of the two things which cause the physical explosion, pipe and gunpowder: the narrative logic thus makes him the architect of the central event symbolic of the releasing of inner fire, and of the whole transition from 'le petit soleil souterrain' of the pipe-bowl to the 'explosions de cymbales' of the 'astre-dieu' of the final page.[10]

It will be useful here to consider the elements in turn, in ascending hierarchical order, starting with water, and concluding with fire in its higher manifestation. The sea 'd'où viendrait [...] le salut'(21), or rather 'd'où pouvait venir le salut'(26), does not fulfil Robinson's hopes of rescue. Its surface, 'bombée et métallique'(21), 'miroitante et glauque'(22), is a negative reflector. Robinson's mesmerised perceptions of it as the back of some fabulous beast whose head is beyond the horizon, and then as a great blue eye staring upwards (22-3) suggest a cosmic scale which dwarfs his own being into insignificance. The looked-for rescue boat it provides will be a mirage galleon, image of a long-dead past. This phantom ship is inhabited by the ghost of Robinson's dead sister, Lucy, whose 'sourire [...] abandonné' (41) evokes the buried guilt of Robinson's disloyalty towards the family he has, in Van Deyssel's belatedly tactful words, 'abandonné... euh... laissé à York'(8). The deceptive fantasy of escape from his situation on the island, images of death and madness, the dark weight of past guilt and pain - these are the poisonous gifts of the sea. Water has nothing positive to offer to the man of earth and fire.

When discouraged by the eventually fruitless labours on *L'Évasion*, he lapses into 'la douceur [...] des vases' (38) of the mud wallow - a regression textually reinforced by the sound-association *évasion/des vases*. Immersed in the mud, in which his own element of earth is vitiated by the negativity of water, 'libéré de toutes ses attaches terrestres', he is prey to fragmentary memories of his childhood and a 'démission en face du monde extérieur' (38-9).

When, much later, he descends into the underground cave (which is perfectly dry, untainted by the negativity of water), he recognises the affinity of this new experience with that of the 'souille', in the 'rêverie rétrospective' which it induces, distracting him from his essential programme of everyday tasks. This time, however, he is convinced that the contact with earth is beneficial, anchoring his being in an essential foundation of untapped vitality: 'Ma vie repose désormais sur un socle d'une admirable solidité, ancré au coeur même de la roche et en prise directe avec les énergies qui y sommeillent'.(111)[11] While the 'souille' invoked the ghost of Lucy, a negative image of weakness, guilt and death, the cave experience, rooted in the rock, is presided over by the memory of his mother, a commanding figure of austere strength. These 'ténèbres matricielles'(112) of the earth's depths are thus (as was seen in Chapter 3) a necessary counterpoise to the patriarchal order Robinson struggles to maintain on the surface.

Robinson resolves that when the time comes to die he will return to the cave as his final resting-place. Its status is thus simultaneously that of womb and tomb: 'Elle réunit miraculeusement la paix des douces ténèbres matricielles et la paix sépulcrale, l'en deçà et l'au-delà de la vie'(112).[12] The surrounding rock delimits the space of the cave, just as birth and death define the span of a life. While a coming to terms with the before and after of life is indeed a good spiritual foundation, Robinson realises that to inhabit for too long the darkness of the earth, the womb-tomb of pre- and post-existence, is to undermine identity in the present, in the sunlight of the here and now.

In due course Speranza's feminine persona shifts from that of mother to that of bride and lover, waiting to be embraced and made fertile, and in this new phase of Robinson's relationship to the earth, this coexistence of life and death is again emphasised.

> Et la terre répondit, elle lui renvoya au visage une bouffée surchargée d'odeurs qui mariait l'âme des plantes trépassées et le remugle poisseux des semences, des bourgeons en gestation. Comme la vie et la mort étaient étroitement mêlées, sagement confondues à ce niveau élémentaire! Son sexe creusa le sol comme un soc et s'y épancha dans une immense pitié pour toutes choses créées. Étranges semailles [...]! Ci-gît maintenant, assommé, celui qui épousa la terre [...] (126).[13]

Once more the parentheses of the natural cycle of life, womb (*semences, gestation, semailles*) and tomb (*âme, trépassées, ci-gît*) are conjoined, in a powerful reminder of mortality and transitoriness. Robinson will go on to develop a theory of sexuality which sees it as a process in which parents beget the generation which will displace them: the sexual act anticipates the death of the participants, and betokens their involvement in the ongoing life of the species which places no value on their existence as individuals. The procreative instinct is 'un instinct de mort'(131).[14] The mandrake plants which seemingly result from his congress with Speranza are traditionally associated not only with female fertility (as, for example, in Genesis 30:14-17) but with death, reputedly springing up from the seed of an executed murderer, and only uprooted at risk of one's life.

Earth thus incorporates 'l'en deçà et l'au-delà de la vie' (112: quoted above) as expressed in particular through the forces of fertility and procreative sexuality, with their twin faces of birth and death. It can give Robinson a frame or foundation for his being, but not the vital spark of fulfilment in the present. He has looked outward to the sea, and inward to the island, and he has faced downward to clasp Speranza's body. From now on, his gaze will be directed by Vendredi upwards, into the air.

Vendredi's lesser element, it has already been noted, is water, and his greater element air. In Van Deyssel's tarot code he arrives in the guise of Venus, arising from the waves, a scene whose re-enactment is recorded in a tone of wonderment in the logbook: 'Sur le miroir mouillé de la lagune, je vois Vendredi venir à moi [...]'(221). This identification is reinforced by the name he receives from Robinson (Vendredi = *dies Veneris*, day of Venus) (228) and the 'beauté évidente, brutale' (221) of his 'corps de triton'(216), tritons being the mythological attendants of Poseidon, the sea-god. To that grace which Robinson comes to worship in him he gives the name of 'la vénusté' (228).

In his triton/marine Venus aspect, then, Vendredi is of the sea. The Venus tarot card is, however, quickly superseded by the next card to be drawn, which is Sagittarius: 'Vénus transformée en ange ailé envoie des flèches vers le soleil'(9).[15] Vendredi is invariably attracted to pastimes 'dont le sens [...] avait presque toujours quelque rapport aux choses aériennes' (207), and the Sagittarius sign is literally realised when he spends much time and effort in the confection and firing aloft of huge feathered arrows. He is not satisfied until one of his arrows, reaching a prodigious height, does not then fall but is swept out of sight by the wind. This can be read as an image of Vendredi's own 'salut élémentaire', and anticipates how the wind in the sails of the *Whitebird* will carry him in his turn over the horizon.

Vendredi's feat also represents an exemplary triumph over gravity, and connects to a rhetorical play in the text around the notions of 'gravité' and 'légèreté', both literal and metaphorical.[16] After Robinson's very first night on the island, his awareness of solitude makes him 'plus grave - c'est-à-dire plus lourd, plus triste'(19). In the mud-pool 'il [...] se délivrait de sa pesanteur'(38), but Vendredi (Vent-dredi?), his 'compagnon éolien'(217), will teach him that this liberation is to be found in the heavens, not in earth and water: 'Son visage brillait de plaisir aussi longtemps que la force vive l'emportait sur [...] la pesanteur'(193). Robinson, re-educated, formulates a new litany: 'Soleil, délivre-moi de la gravité. [...] Apprends-moi la légèreté [...]'(217). This play on 'gravity' and 'lightness' is enriched by its alignment with the progression from the heavier, base elements (earth, water) to the lighter, more ethereal ones (air, fire).

The image of the plumed arrow returns, slightly incongruously, in the description of Andoar charging Vendredi: '...Elle [la bête] vola vers la poitrine de Vendredi comme une grosse flèche empennée de fourrure' (196). This signals Andoar as the object of Vendredi's next aeolian project, the kite to be made from his pelt, and as we have already seen, Andoar is a symbolic substitute for Robinson himself. When Vendredi and Andoar, still struggling, fall over the precipice, the anxious Robinson is forced to climb up a cliff to reach them, and has to overcome vertigo, 'l'attraction terrestre', in the process: 'Il y avait la terre et l'air, et entre les deux, collé à la pierre comme un papillon tremblant, Robinson qui luttait douloureusement pour opérer sa conversion de l'une à l'autre' (199).[17] The scapegoat falls to its death, and by a kind of reciprocal magic Robinson is released from the fear of falling and sustained in his 'conversion' to air.

The first of Robinson's new logbook entries, at the opening of Chapter 10, celebrates the sunrise ('l'héliophanie', the revelation of light) in an expansive rhetoric of grandiose religious ritual.

> Le premier rayon qui a jailli s'est posé sur mes cheveux rouges, telle la main tutélaire et bénissante d'un père. Le second rayon a purifié mes lèvres, comme avait fait jadis un charbon ardent celles du prophète Isaïe. Ensuite deux épées de feu ayant touché mes épaules, je me suis relevé, chevalier solaire. Aussitôt une volée de flèches brûlantes ont percé ma face, ma poitrine et mes mains, et la pompe grandiose de mon sacre s'est achevée tandis que mille diadèmes et mille sceptres de lumière couvraient ma statue surhumaine. (216)

Regarding this very resonant passage, suffice it to say for the moment that it records (with no *explicit* irony, at least) the accession to superhuman status. The sequence of images which carry the weight of this ascendancy move through paternal endorsement, initiation to prophecy, and conferral of knighthood to martyrdom and coronation. The self, having discovered its proper element in the light and fire of the sun, is vouchsafed a sense of its own infinite plenitude and prestige.[18] Fire is no longer perilously contained within: it suffuses the cosmos. In the final solar apotheosis of the novel, which this passage anticipates, the image of the 'statue surhumaine' is further developed:

> Sa poitrine bombait comme un bouclier d'airain. Ses jambes prenaient appui sur le roc, massives et inébranlables comme des colonnes. La lumière fauve le revêtait d'une armure de jeunesse inaltérable et lui forgeait un masque de cuivre d'une régularité implacable où étincelaient des yeux de diamant. Enfin l'astre-dieu déploya tout entière sa couronne de cheveux rouges dans des explosions de cymbales et des stridences de trompettes. Des reflets métalliques s'allumèrent sur la tête de l'enfant.(254)[19]

In terms of the play of elements, the notable point here is the massive reintegration of earth elements: stone columns set in rock, diamonds, and the pomp and circumstance of armour, mask, trumpets and cymbals made from bronze or brass which are the elements of earth tempered by fire. This final section is in this sense an alchemical crucible, in which Robinson's two constituent elements, now fully discovered, explored in their properties and accepted, are fused into a compound of ideal strength.

This progression through the elements is a complex reworking of the idea of metempsychosis, the transmigration of souls from one level to another on the ladder of being, which is characteristic of many primitive belief-systems, as well as of Neoplatonism and Buddhism. In more recent French culture, the writer who most spectacularly depicted this vision of the moral and physical order was Victor Hugo:

> [...]
> Car les choses et l'être ont un grand dialogue,
> Tout parle; l'air qui passe et l'alcyon qui vogue,
> Le brin d'herbe, la fleur, le germe, l'élément.[20]

These lines are taken from 'Ce que dit la Bouche d'ombre', the penultimate poem of *Les Contemplations*, which sets out Hugo's belief that while an evil person may be reincarnated as beast or plant or stone ('Le mal, c'est la matière'[21]), a good one may be promoted through an equally elaborate but invisible hierarchy of superhuman and angelic orders. Tournier, unlike Hugo, does not here attempt to link the system of metempsychosis to a Christian moral order, but his emphasis on Robinson's desire to escape weight and 'gravity' and his movement of ascension from mud-pool and rock-cave to a communion with sky and sun partakes of Hugo's metaphysics and sometimes generates a similar rhetoric. Much of the visionary power of the final chapter of the novel is contained in Hugo's lines: 'C'est le feu du vrai jour./ Le sombre univers, froid, glacé, pesant, réclame/ La sublimation de l'être par la flamme...'[22]

'Le Satyre', one of the major poems of Hugo's cycle *La Légende des Siècles*, provides some even more resonant pre-echoes, when for instance the satyr sings to the gods of his vision of man's glorious future:

> Qui sait [...]
> S'il n'arrachera pas de son corps brusquement
> La pesanteur, peau vile, immonde vêtement
> Que la fange hideuse à la pensée inflige?
> De sorte qu'on verra tout à coup, ô prodige,
> Ce ver de terre ouvrir ses ailes dans les cieux.
> [...]
> Transfigure-toi! [...]
> Prends le rayon, saisis l'aube, usurpe le feu;
> Torse ailé, front divin, monte au jour [...]![23]

In Hugo's poem, the satyr himself undergoes a fantastic metamorphosis under the very eyes of the astonished gods, from lascivious faun to the incarnation of the god Pan. Tournier's text, as has been shown, evokes a similar transformation and deploys similar mythic motifs. Van Deyssel is described as 'ce gros silène': Silenus, tutor to Dionysos, was a fat old man, usually drunk, but endowed with wisdom and the power of prophesy, and the *sileni* were akin to satyrs. Marsyas, the faun who challenged Apollo to a musical competition and was subsequently flayed for his audacity, was a silenus. In Hugo's poem, the satyr borrows Phoebus Apollo's lyre when he comes to sing of the evolution of mankind, while in Tournier's text the goat Andoar, 'faune tellurique' (227), 'grand écorché' (200), becomes itself the aeolian harp on which the elements play their music, 'Andoar-chantant' (209).

The comparison with Hugo is suggestive in a number of ways. It underlines the extent to which Tournier draws on a powerful traditional and quasi-allegorical imagery of the earthly and the heavenly, from the mire to the heavenly bodies, from satyrs to angels, while *literalising* them: the mud-pool and Andoar, for instance, are realistically described and yet also function in context as symbolic externalisations and instruments of Robinson's spiritual itinerary. In the light of this concept of the 'ladder of being' (which, in the words of 'Ce que dit la Bouche d'ombre', 'rattache l'astre esprit à l'archange soleil') Robinson's final transformation can be read as a metempsychotic passage to a higher, superhuman status. The process of *déshumanisation* which he initially fears, the transition to an 'elemental' mode of being, is thus finally to be understood in a positive sense. The loaded Hugolian rhetoric of the ending is a solution to the problem of writing at the frontier of the supernatural. It is only later in his *oeuvre* that Tournier will, like Hugo, seek to combine this pagan, Panic vision of human fulfilment with material from the Christian tradition.

Le Roi des aulnes

The play of elements in *Le Roi des aulnes* is neither as central nor as detailed as in *Vendredi*, but a coherent pattern can nevertheless be discerned. The lower elements, earth and water, are early on associated with humiliation and degradation, like the 'souille' in *Vendredi*. One diary entry links Abel's obsessive childhood memories with the ditty which 'la vieille Marie' sang to him on rainy days when his soul was 'transie de chagrin'(61). The accounts of Abel's ordeals at school are pervaded by references to water and mud. 'L'humidité où baignait notre misère d'orphelins' (29) is much in evidence on the day Abel is forced to lick Pelsenaire's mud-covered knee. Later, as he plods off to receive the ritual punishment of the *colaphus*, 'un crépuscule mouillé noyait la cour' (47). As he kneels in the darkness , what arrives is not the expected retribution, but - as light floods into the room from the door of the prefect's office - a formal reprieve. This is the first manifestation of Nestor's benign patronage, which is characterised in terms of a radiant sun. As the 'pluie des punitions' seems to lift from Abel's head, he basks in the 'rayonnement' that emanates from Nestor's person in class, 'le foyer central de toute la classe'(53).

Nestor is the bringer of fire. When Clément, another pupil at Saint-Christophe, proposes to sell him a lighter made out of a First World War hand-grenade, Nestor insists on a demonstration, and provides the necessary petrol, thereby causing a brief conflagration in chapel. Abel, wrongly accused of involvement in the incident, runs away from school, and has dreams of the school burning down. 'Flammes de l'enfer certes, mais aussi flammes libératrices, car si Saint-Christophe brûlait, si le monde entier brûlait, mon malheur serait lui aussi englouti' (101). On his return to school, Abel finds that fire has indeed broken out in the basement, from which Nestor, who was attending to the boiler, is brought out lifeless. 'On se montrait surtout une sorte de cratère charbonneux ouvert dans le plancher à l'opposé de l'emplacement de l'estrade. C'était là que le feu après avoir longtemps couvé dans la cave avait fait éruption comme un volcan'(102). As in *Vendredi*, a vital turning point in the novel is marked by a kind of volcanic explosion, the devastating release of a fiery element hitherto safely contained. In *Vendredi*, it marked the end of the 'administered island', while here it in effect concludes the account of Abel's life in the ordered environment of St Christophe, the rest of his school career being dismissed in a few lines. The memory of this eruption, recalled and recorded in Abel's diary in 1938, becomes in addition a premonitory metaphor for the imminent collapse of the precarious political order of Europe. Nestor's passing is less a death than a transmutation of his spirit into its native element of fire: we note that the crater appears in the classroom 'à l'opposé de l'emplacement de l'estrade' (102), recalling Nestor's position at the back of the class as a powerful and subversive counter-authority. Released from its bodily incarnation, this spirit of fire will continue to express itself as a voice in Abel's consciousness and (in Abel's vision of things) in the eruption of war itself.

Abel's characteristic environment remains one of earth and water. As a milieu it has, as we have seen, an oppressive aspect. One night, afflicted with chronic breathing difficulties, he is 'obsédé de rêves de noyade et d'ensevelissement sous le sable, sous la terre, dans la boue...'(144). When associated with his oral-anal sexuality, however, this mud can become the object of mystical euphoria, as when it is mingled with blood on Pelsenaire's knee (the first example of *Blut und Boden*) or in the act of defecation, the production of the body's own 'limon vivant'(144) which counteracts the memory of the nightmare of drowning and burial.

At the prisoner-of-war camp at Moorhof, whose very name refers to its marshland setting ('Moor' = marsh), Abel experiences, paradoxically, a sense of liberation (253) and, as he defecates on the open ground, an erotico-anal affinity comparable to the erotico-genital bond which Robinson feels towards Speranza. As a trusted supply-lorry driver, he is sent on a trip northwards to the Elchwald region, with its treacherously shifting, sandy soil and its 'dissolution générale de la terre dans l'eau' (288). His return is delayed when his lorry gets bogged down in the mud. This trivial example of the threat of absorption into the earth is immediately followed by a vastly more significant one: the lieutenant tells him that a body has just been extracted from the bog, and that he had wondered if the corpse was that of Abel himself. The body in question, thus gratuitously associated with Abel, turns out, according to Professor Keil's findings, to be a sacrificial victim, perhaps voluntary, of ritual immersion from the first century AD. The bog corpse, fancifully christened the 'Erlking' by the

Professor, thus becomes for Abel an exemplar of one who has lived through his own nightmare of drowning and burial, to attain a kind of posterity. Much later, when Tiffauges is confronted by the horrifying sight of a corpse flattened by the traffic on a frozen road - a body not absorbed into the earth - he is consoled by the abiding counter-image of the 'Roi des Aulnes, immergé dans les marécages, protégé, par une lourde nappe de limon, de toutes les atteintes [...]'(531). The oppressive aspect of the elements of earth and water has been exorcised, and his acceptance of sacrificial immersion on the final page is thus prepared.

The element of air as wind is experienced both positively and negatively by Tiffauges. In its positive aspect, it is part of the figure of desire, in the 'bourrasque chargée de grains de pollen' he experiences in the torrent of schoolchildren (147); in its negative aspect it recurs in the stormwind imagery of Apocalypse, the 'bourrasque de fin du monde' (413) which shatters the great hall window, and the shockwave ('ouragan', 'cyclone') which drenches him with Arnim's blood (544-5).

The sky exercises however a powerful upward attraction on his imagination, implicit in the sequence of animal images, from the Mobilgas symbol of the winged horse (15) to the later characterisation of deer and horse as angels, 'Ange Phallophore' (331) and 'Ange Anal'(353). Earthbound creatures are thus given a celestial vocation, like the homing pigeon which is released by Tiffauges and escapes over the heads of the Germans guns with its message (242). Throughout the last part of the novel, Tiffauges is shown as intensely aware of the vast space of the Prussian sky and migratory birds which traverse it, an orientation in tune with his Atlas-like 'astrophoric' vocation symbolically realised at the end. While it is only occasionally explicit in this text, the element of air will return to full prominence in *Les Météores*.

The Nestorian element of fire undergoes a similar revalorisation to that of earth. Nestor's words on the negative aspect of fire, as symbol and instrument of the demon of 'purification'(125) are borne out in the apocalypse of the war and in particular in the crematoria of Auschwitz. Abel's dream of the destruction of the school was however one, we recall, of 'flammes de l'enfer, certes, mais aussi flammes libératrices' (101). In Abel's˜life, fire is associated with escape from punishment - when the school catches fire, his abscondence is overlooked. When the conflagration of war breaks out, the accusation of rape which hangs over him is set aside. When he falls asleep before the fire in the hut he calls Canada and misses roll-call, his absence from the POW camp goes wholly unnoticed. While the negative power of fire will reach its climax with Éphraïm's account of the death-camp and the apocalypse of the final battle at Kaltenborn, its mysteriously liberating and redemptive function in Abel's life will be symbolised by the distant burning fire of the star he fixes with his last gaze, as he sinks into the marsh. The narrative thus works towards a final encompassing of water and earth, sky and fire, a redemptive fusion similar in function, even if different in its alchemy, to the crucible ending of *Vendredi*.

Les Météores

From the very opening paragraph describing the wind sweeping in from the Atlantic, air is established as the presiding element of this novel, while the others feature only intermittently at best. Alexandre is dismayed at the incineration of refuse at Issy-les-Moulineaux, in which he sees an infernal symbol of the effort by heterosexual society to purge all deviation from a tyrannical norm, and to eliminate difference. In this observation, Tournier is presenting in another guise Nestor's warning in *Le Roi des aulnes* about fire as the hellish instrument of political, religious and racial purification (*RA* 125). Elsewhere, Edouard languishes for health reasons in a mud-bath, a pastime which leads him to conjure up thoughts of his past life and of death. This in its turn is a reprise, in lightly ironic mode, of Robinson and his mud-wallow, and even of the theme of enclosure by the earth treated on a grand scale in the earlier novels. It is the wind, however, which is wholly predominant, active even on the level of the plot. It is an unusually violent storm which causes the death of Gustave beneath a falling crane, and which thus brings about Alexandre's inheritance of the refuse business. It is the Atlantic breeze of the opening which wakes the twins from a slumber in which they are indistinguishable, to assume their separate reactions, expressions and identities (12-13): while purgative fire abolishes difference, air, it seems, provokes it. Thus the wind is inscribed as a generating principle of major constituents of the narrative: Alexandre's self-realisation, the twins' drama of identity and difference.

It is Thomas Koussek who makes the major statement in the novel on the wind, seen in symbolic and theological terms as the manifestation of the Holy Spirit. It is 'semence et parole'(158), principle of fertility and of language. The first heading, 'semence', has been anticipated by the 'brise pollinique' of dried semen shaken from the dormitory sheets of the boarding school, and which so enthuses Thomas (46-7).[24] The second endowment of the wind, that of language, is implicit in the name given to the special private language of the twins, 'cet éolien', 'la langue du vent'(70).

Contemplating his refuse dump, Alexandre will later call to mind this gospel according to Koussek, and the Paraclete's two attributes of 'le Sexe et la Parole' (348). By then he has experienced the ferocious power of the Mistral wind blowing across the Miramas dump, and the grisly death of his lover Daniel which it causes. This is what Thomas called a 'mauvaise ruah'(157), an ill wind, and this echo suggests that Alexandre is subject to the same pattern as Thomas, but in a limited and debased form. The Miramas dump is the site of a constant lethal dispute between the rats and the gulls, 'le poil et la plume' of the title to Chapter 9. The rat, as we noted earlier, is the totemic creature of the phallic god Ganesa, and thus associated with sexual potency, while the 'plume' can also refer to the writer's pen, and linguistic potency. For Alexandre, the wind and its attributes of 'le sexe et la parole' bring on the one hand death to his sexual partner, and, on the other, his own death as the project towards which his autobiographic narrative is finally directed.

Paul comes to experience these attributes in their benign aspect. The Holy Spirit, Koussek tells Alexandre, has 'un corps météorologique' which is the wind (158). Paul, as has been noted earlier, sees in Jean's portrait a face inhabited by the wind from every quarter: 'Ce n'est plus un visage, c'est une rose des vents' (539). In the final chapter, Paul aspires to being a 'corps poreux où la rose des vents viendra respirer' (610), in emulation of the *corps météorologique* of the Spirit itself. To become fully open to this breath of the spirit is, the text suggests, to accept its two gifts: an unconfined and joyous fertility, and the power of the *logos*. The wind, as we have seen, sows the fertile seeds of the narrative at the outset, and the novelist's ambition is doubtless that the power of the author's word will bear witness to its *inspiration*. As every Larousse dictionary proclaims, 'Je sème à tout vent'.

Gaspard, Melchior & Balthazar

The reader familiar with the earlier novels will not find here such an explicit and developed thematics of the elements, but it is noticeable how even a brief paragraph can set resonating a motif already well established in Tournier's *oeuvre*. An example of this is an apparently trivial episode when Gaspard, coming across a well in the desert, cannot resist the temptation to climb down into it and submerge himself up to his eyes in the water.

> Au-dessus de ma tête, je voyais le trou rond de l'orifice, un disque de ciel phosphorescent où clignotait une première étoile. Un souffle de vent passa sur le puits, et j'entendis la colonne d'air qui le remplissait ronfler comme dans le tuyau d'une flûte gigantesque, musique douce et profonde que faisaient ensemble la terre et le vent nocturne [...] (37).

This symphony of the elements orchestrating earth, water, wind and star represents a moment of natural epiphany, with subtle echoes (for the student of Tournier's work) of the music of Vendredi's aeolian harp, of the light-flash which penetrates the grotto where Robinson, likewise naked, is curled up, and, most particularly, of Abel immersed in the marsh yet stargazing at the end of *Le Roi des aulnes*. There the Alpha of the star is linked to its opposite, the Omega of the anal mire, and here similarly a star is viewed through the anal 'trou rond de l'orifice', from within, as it were, the body of the earth. Thus, in a couple of sentences, Tournier can deftly evoke the aspiration to a synthesis of the elements, to a spanning of the highest (fire) and the lowest (water), to the music of earth and air.

On a more general level, Taor, like Robinson and Tiffauges before him, is required to live out a distinctive relationship to the earth. His prolonged enslavement in the salt-mines has affinities with Robinson's sojourn in the grotto, as a period of metamorphosis from which he emerges physically enfeebled but inwardly strengthened. Structurally, it has a similar function to Abel being sucked into the marsh, or to Paul being engulfed in the underground tunnel, in that it represents a final nightmarish bodily entombment which appears as a necessary counterpart to an emancipation of the spirit. The passage from 'l'âge du sucre' to 'l'enfer du sel' is less a change of element - both are earth-related - than a shift from the (earthly) organic to the (infernal) inorganic. A graphic image of this transition from sensual vitality to an inhuman, deathly milieu comes in the description of the life-bearing river Jordan being stifled and poisoned as it enters the Dead Sea (254). The bitter and toxic mineral 'fruits', the 'pommes de Sodome', deposited there are a lifeless parody of organic form like the 'champignons marmoréens' and the 'fleur minérale' of Robinson's grotto (*VLP* 105). This process of mineralisation finds a biblical symbol in Lot's wife, transformed into a pillar of salt; her statue is an object of veneration to the Sodomites, who deck it with mineralised flowers.[25]

When Taor is released from the mines, he returns to the Jordan estuary, the symbolic gateway to the 'salt hell', and thence back, like an Orphic hero, into the world of human and natural vitality. His final tasting of the elements of the first Eucharist precipitates his entry into heaven, in that the bread and wine are not simply the natural fruits of that fertility, but also (in Catholic belief) the very flesh and blood of Christ, at once bodily and spiritual food. Taor's salt-saturated body, absorbing a natural and supernatural food of life, realises a synthesis of all the levels - the infernal regions, earth and heaven - and thus attains consummation.

Gilles & Jeanne

Gilles is dominated by a single element, that of fire. The plot is structured around the literal fire of the autos-da-fé inflicted on Jeanne and then on Gilles, and the second half is dominated by Gilles's double use of fire, in alchemical experiment and to destroy the bodies of his victims. From this stems a reflection on fire as a metaphor of heaven or hell, punishment and purification. Just as Thomas Koussek provides the heterodox theology of air as the wind of the Spirit in *Les Météores*, it is Francesco Prelati who here expounds the heretical theology of fire which informs the text.

Prelati finds in the Breton seascape and landscape a 'vaste plaine liquide [...], pays de lagunes et de marécages' (103), the ambience already evoked in the first part of *Le Roi des aulnes* as a realm of the lower elements, corporal, devoid of spirituality and redolent of abject degradation. Prelati equates it at once with an 'humanité vautrée et humiliée'(103). Fire is the principle antidote he will deploy to restore a sense of the vertical dimension to this flat, two-dimensional world which encompasses Gilles: 'Sauver Gilles par le feu!'(103).

From the beginning, Gilles has more and more perceived Jeanne as a vessel of fire. He is first struck by the light which emanates from her, the light of heavenly innocence (15). Further on, the fire he sees as the source of this light acquires a more ambiguous status: 'Il y a un feu en toi. Je le crois de Dieu, mais il est peut-être d'enfer'(31). She is now seen as a being of untarnished purity - but, as we have seen, purity is for Tournier a suspect quality implying a brutal suppression of 'impure' elements, and as such capable of becoming the malign opposite of innocence.[26] (Gilles's observation on Jeanne's ambiguous attribute of purity is immediately followed by the highly ambivalent gesture of kissing her wound, discussed earlier.) When Jeanne ends her life amid the flames, they are perceived mostly in terms of their basest emanation: not light, but whirls of smoke and 'une affreuse odeur de chair carbonisée' (45). Fire in Jeanne thus manifests itself in modes which descend from the spiritual to the sordidly carnal, moving from the light of the spirit through the ambiguous purity of flame to its most degraded by-products of smoke and stench. Gilles's association with fire is presented as aspiring upward, through the same stages in reverse order. Blanchet is disturbed by the smoke and the 'odeur de chair carbonisée' coming from the castle chimney, and the re-use of the same words to describe the smell links Gilles's crimes implicitly to Jeanne's death, even before Gilles himself makes the connection.[27] Prelati expounds the necessary link between infernal fire and celestial light, symbolised by Lucifer, whose name means 'bearer of light'(89), the angel who, by virtue of his complicity with human evil, is best placed to act as man's intercessor with God. Gilles's destiny, as mapped out for him by Prelati, is to pass through a 'rideau de flammes'(107) to reach an 'au-delà radieux' (106): the highest expression of fire, which is light ('il alla au supplice en chrétien apaisé et *rayonnant*' (125 - my emphasis)), can only be attained by first accepting all its capacity for evil and destruction. This itinerary of salvation is associated with the alchemical experiments in which both men are also engaged: both are concerned with 'les travaux sublimes de la transmutation'(112), a term which recalls *Vendredi* and its extended characterisation of the evolution of the self as an alchemy of the elements.

La Goutte d'or

The elements play a smaller part in *La Goutte d'or* than in any other of Tournier's major fictions. One reason for this is no doubt that its theology, given the cultural background of the principal character, draws on Islamic rather than Christian thought, and thus Tournier is not here working at the rich interface of Christian and biblical (as well as classical) sources on one hand and elemental associations and archetypes on the other, an interface which proved so fertile in previous works.

A further significant reason is that the reflection on the subject of the elements in his earlier fictions rests on the assumption that there exists a spiritual or metaphysical dimension of the material world, whereby the elements encode, in some sense, spiritual or psychological forces. *La Goutte d'or*, however, charts the passage of Idriss into a world devoid of this spiritual or metaphysical dimension, where materialism and its representation through images encode, encapture and thwart human aspiration. Paris in this novel is a kind of hell, devoid of the capacity for higher values. Idriss is the hero who escapes the bonds of this infernal region to the extent that he rediscovers and re-evaluates the spiritual heritage of his upbringing, which he is able to express through the sacred art of calligraphy. Such reflection on the elements as there is in the text occurs, therefore, in the opening pages relating to his life in the desert, and in the pages on his apprenticeship in calligraphy, which represents at once a kind of salvation and a reaffirmation of his roots.

The opening paragraph of the text mentions Idriss's grandmother's tale of how foolish or disobedient children are carried off by the powerful spirits of the desert winds. It is the unease which this tribal lore engenders in him that impels him to seek out his friend Ibrahim. Ibrahim is a kind of wizard of the elements, capable of making the wind change direction, and audaciously defying the accepted taboos against speaking of fire without euphemism, dousing fire with water or drinking without kneeling on the ground. When the well collapses, Ibrahim is swallowed up by the earth, but his nomadic and adventurous spirit inhabits Idriss, whose departure in a sense realises his grandmother's fear that the desert wind will snatch away the errant child.

Once he has traversed the 'anti-desert' which is Paris, Idriss rediscovers the desert's space and timelessness within himself: 'il comprenait maintenant que ces vastes plages de durée étaient un don de son enfance'(199). This gift is recuperable in the exercise of calligraphy, an art which is here firmly associated with wind and air, in two senses. 'La calligraphie a horreur du vide. La blancheur de la page l'attire, comme la dépression atmosphérique attire les vents et fait lever la tempête. Une tempête de signes qui viennent en nuées se poser sur la page comme des oiseaux d'encre [...]' (200). Firstly, then, the dynamic of writing is depicted as the rush of the wind, and the script likened to flocks of birds. Secondly, the master calligrapher instructs the practitioner to exercise a discipline of breathing in harmony with the rhythm of his transcription. The notion of 'inspiration' is thereby given its full etymological sense.

It thus turns out that even though the ideological orientation of this text is Islamic rather than Christian, the access of the hero to spiritual values takes place under the sign of Air and Wind, as in Thomas Koussek's cult of the Holy Spirit. The ritual preparation of the calligrapher's ink is carefully described: in its ingredients - water, salt, gum arabic, gall-nut, iron sulphate, honey and lampblack, all heated over a flame - it can be seen as a compound of the other three elements of Water, Earth and Fire, ready to be placed at the service of the breath of the spirit.

In conclusion, it can be seen that of all Tournier's texts it is *Vendredi* which presents the most systematic exploitation of the thematics of the four elements, and which most clearly reveals the influence of Bachelard on Tournier's reflection and imagination. In later works, the storehouse of the 'elemental' imagination is used more selectively and more diffusely, but it still contributes more or less significantly to all the other major fictions. The novelist is clearly attracted by this ancient mythic patterning which offers a framework for exploring the constituents both of the material universe and of the human psyche, and predicates special affinities between the two. These 'elemental' affinities provide in Tournier's writing a useful bridge between the intellectual/ideological and the sensual/erotic. In terms of the spectrum of the writing, it helps him to span the poles he himself identifies as characterising his fiction - philosophical speculation, and the 'naturalist' reportage of the sense-data of immediate experience. This play of the elements in experience becomes especially fruitful for Tournier's imagination when brought into conjunction with theological metaphors of the wind of the Spirit, of man created from clay or of celestial/infernal fire, and in making these links he goes decisively beyond anything he found in Bachelard. By emphasising the poetics of religious thought and its animistic origins, Tournier can deal confidently with metaphysical issues through physical phenomena which are presented as at once material and symbolic, and he can bring new possibilities of meaning to modern culture and history by placing them in a dialogue with some of the (supposedly more naïve) belief-systems which form the substrata of our cultural consciousness.

Notes to Chapter Five

[1]   Tournier has most recently acknowledged his debt to Bachelard by dedicating *Le Miroir des idées* to his memory. For details of Bachelard's works on the elements, see the Select Bibliography.

[2]   At the time of writing, I have not had an opportunity to consult a recent study by Jonathan F. Krell, *Tournier élémentaire* (West Lafayette, Purdue University Press, 1994).

[3]   Bachelard drew on this idea of elemental affinities, to be found in ancient

and medieval philosophers: while rejecting any physical basis for the link, 'Bachelard admet comme eux une certaine communion du moi et des choses dans tel élément privilégié'. See Michel Mansuy, *Gaston Bachelard et les Elements* (Paris, Corti, 1967), 47.

[4] See lines 26-31 and 52-3 of Book I of Ovid, *Metamorphoses*, ed. G. Lafaye (Paris, Belles Lettres, 1928), 8-9.

[5] Bouloumié (*Michel Tournier*, 170) views this process as one of purification by the four elements, comparable to Masonic ritual.

[6] Tournier notes the tradition of red hair as a mark of bestiality in his discussion of Balzac's descriptions of Vautrin in *Le Père Goriot* (*VV* 148). The trait of red hair, signifying at once a fiery temperament and a kind of curse, recurs in the story 'Barberousse ou le portrait du roi' in *La Goutte d'or*.

[7] Robinson will come to recognise this 'chaos' within himself. 'Il y a en moi un cosmos en gestation. Mais un cosmos en gestation, cela s'appelle un chaos. Contre ce chaos, l'île *administrée* [...] est mon seul refuge [...].' (117) Characteristically, Tournier exploits another, more literal sense of the word: a geological term for a piling-up of certain kinds of rock. The island has such a 'chaos' at its centre, and there is a flagrant semantic irony in Robinson's attempt to impose absolute order on an island which has a 'chaos' as its 'point culminant' (18).

[8] In his chapter on 'Le feu sexualisé', Bachelard refers to the erotic aspect of the alchemist's fire, 'ce feu intime et mâle, objet de méditation de l'homme isolé'. In a note curiously applicable to Robinson, he speaks of alchemy as 'une science d'hommes, de célibataires, d'hommes sans femmes, d'initiés retranchés de la communion humaine. [...] Sa doctrine du feu est donc fortement polarisée par des désirs inassouvis'. See *La Psychanalyse du feu* (Paris, Gallimard, 1968), 90.

[9] In Defoe's novel there were only three barrels, but Tournier needed a bigger bang: in a sense this explosion is the flashpoint of the whole chain reaction of the narrative.

[10] Merllié (*Michel Tournier*, 113) comments on this function of Van Deyssel as a transmitter of fire.

[11] Bachelard records a similar reaction on the part of Goethe. '[...] Goethe écrit: "Les rochers dont la puissance élève mon âme et lui donne la solidité." Il semble que le rocher de granit soit non seulement le piédestal de son être magnifié, mais qu'il lui confère sa solidité intime.' See Bachelard, *La Terre et les rêveries de la volonté*, 202.

[12] Again Bachelard notes, in his chapter on 'La Grotte', this double aspect of the underground cavern: 'La grotte est une demeure. [...] Mais [...] cette demeure est à la fois la première demeure et la dernière demeure. Elle devient une image de la maternité, de la mort.' See *La Terre et les rêveries du repos* (Paris, Corti, 1948), 208.

[13] 'Celui qui épousa la terre' could be taken as a reference to the sky-god Uranus, who in the ancient Creation myth set down by Hesiod, was born of Gaia the earth-goddess, and then coupled with her to beget the first human beings. See *Larousse Dictionary of Mythology* (London, Paul Hamlyn, 1959), 90. 'Ouranos' is mentioned briefly later in the novel (228).

[14] Davis (*Michel Tournier*, 21n) refers to Freud's discussion of the link between the death instinct (*Todestrieb*) and the sexual urge. In *Vendredi* this conjunction gives rise to a rich play of meaning and language. In line with his vision of the island as a woman's body, Robinson is struck by the consonance between

'combe' and 'lombes' (127). The associative series could easily extend to the 'limbes' of the title, or to 'l'appel doucereux des *tombes* en désordre' (199: my emphasis), each implying the same complicity of life and death. There are similarly rich echoes of both sound and sense between his phallic penetration of the 'combe' ('creusa le sol comme un soc') and the 'socle d'une admirable solidité, ancré au coeur même de la roche' with which the grotto experience had provided him (111: passage already quoted).

[15] Vendredi's link to both elements (and their hierarchy) is neatly pictorialised in his technique of fishing, by attaching his line to a kite high in the air, and letting it dangle from there into the water (205-6). This detail was apparently borrowed from Tournier's anthropological studies: see his interview with Jean Prasteau, 'Comme Robinson, Michel Tournier a trouvé son île déserte...', *Figaro Littéraire* 1,127 (20-26.11.67), 24-5. One might even detect Vendredi's symbolic presence at the end of the novel when, at dawn, just as the *Whitebird* bearing him away has disappeared, a seagull swoops down and then soars up, a fish in its beak (253).

[16] Vendredi's successful arrow is flighted with albatross feathers, and the sight of a pair of albatrosses 'planant fraternellement' (199) will comfort Robinson a few pages later as he climbs the cliff. Later he will receive from Vendredi an albatross quill for writing new logbook entries, along with sky-blue ink. The freedom from gravity of the arrow is thus indirectly linked to that of the writer - with perhaps a reminiscence of Baudelaire's famous comparison of the poet to an albatross, monarch of the upper air but confounded at sea-level. See 'L'Albatros' (*Fleurs du Mal*, ii), in Baudelaire, *Oeuvres complètes*, I:9-10. Hitherto, Robinson had always used vulture feathers as quills, and the vulture, whose wings will frame the funereal skull-harp of Andoar, could be seen as the polar opposite of the 'force vive' of the albatross (a point touched on by Milne, *L'Evangile selon Michel*, 233).

The lightness-gravity opposition will be further discussed in the next chapter, as it relates to the figure of the child.

[17] The butterfly image has a double resonance. As a creature of air, it is associated with Vendredi ('Tel un lépidoptère [...]'(207)) and when Robinson is enraged at his companion, butterflies and birds are the substitutes which he lashes (in reality or in fantasy) with his whip (174-5). But in the metaphorical logic of metamorphosis, Robinson's own conversion is that from earthbound larva to airborne butterfly, as he comes to resemble his friend more and more. Here he is 'trembling' on the brink of that conversion. In a chapter headed 'Le rêve de vol', Bachelard speaks of an 'impression intime d'*allégement*'. 'C'est une conquête d'un être jadis lourd et confus qui, par le mouvement imaginaire, en écoutant les leçons de l'imagination aérienne, est devenu léger, clair et vibrant.' See *L'Air et les songes* (Paris, Corti, 1950), 74.

[18] Cf. Bachelard's resonant passage on the importance of the sunrise in Nietzsche's 'psychisme ascensionnel', as a reassumption of the will to power (*L'Air et les songes*, 180). Another antecedent in this cult of the sun can be found in a passage from an eccentric book by John Custance, describing how mental illness evoked in him latent primeval reactions to the universe which form part, in Jungian theory, of the collective unconscious: 'Le soleil en vint à avoir sur moi un effet extraordinaire. Il semblait détenir tout pouvoir et non seulement symboliser Dieu, mais être Dieu. [...] [L]a simple vue du soleil suffisait à intensifier l'exaltation maniaque dont je souffrais. Une force me poussait à m'adresser au soleil et à établir tout un rituel d'adoration du soleil.' (Tournier

translated Jung's preface for the French translation of the book published by Plon, where he was an editor.) See Custance, *Le Livre de la sagesse et de la folie* (Paris, Plon, 1954), 23-4. For the original English text, see Custance, *Wisdom, Madness and Folly* (London, Gollancz, 1951), 18.

[19] The motif of the bronze statue is persistent: it recurs in a work published twenty-seven years later, in a more mundane remark on sun-bathing, whose aim, says Tournier, is to 'transformer le corps en sa propre statue de bronze doré, une statue solaire' (*MI* 200) - a reflection which is perhaps at the origin of this grandiose metaphor of transmutation in *Vendredi*.

[20] See 'Ce que dit la bouche d'ombre', lines 11-13, in Victor Hugo, *Les Contemplations*, ed. L. Cellier (Paris, Garnier, 1969), 433. Hugo is also, according to Michel Mansuy (*Gaston Bachelard et les éléments*, 129), the author most frequently quoted by Bachelard.

[21] 'Ce que dit la bouche d'ombre', line 82 (p.435).

[22] 'Ce que dit la bouche d'ombre', lines 712-13 (p.454).

[23] See section III of 'Le Satyre', in Victor Hugo, *La Légende des Siècles*, ed. A.Dumas (Paris, Garnier, 1964), 461-2. On a mundane level, Hugo has in mind here (as in 'Plein Ciel') the possibility of powered flight, but the pretext is less important than the epic vision of human emancipation it sustains.

[24] This in turn echoes Tiffauges's euphoric image of the inseminating breeze, the 'bourrasque chargée de grains de pollen' (*RA* 147), referred to above.

[25] The mineralised or petrified human form is a recurrent motif in Tournier, from Robinson's 'statue surhumaine' (*VLP* 216) to Tiffauges's 'homme de pierre'(*RA* 150), to the sand-sculptures of Patricio Lagos which recall the 'corps minéralisés' of the victims of Pompeii and Hiroshima (*MA* 27).

[26] See the note on 'La pureté et l'innocence' in *MI* 171-4.

[27] There is a second textual echo, between Jeanne's body as a 'pauvre charogne à demi calcinée'(44) and the 'puanteur de charogne calcinée' (62) emanating from Gilles's castle.

6

At the Dictate of the Child

'En vérité, le petit a toujours raison.'

(*VPar* 56)

Man and Boy

The figure of the child occupies a central and profoundly ambivalent place in Tournier's writing. In seeking to define its significance and function, a useful starting point is the general statement with which he introduced an appreciation of the work of the photographer Lucien Clergue, even if, as we shall see, it is in a sense misleading. 'Les hommes disposent en général à leur naissance d'un capital de bonheur: leur enfance. Ce capital de bonheur, ils le conservent jusqu'à leur mort et ils viennent y puiser régulièrement pour y trouver l'espoir et la lumière.'[1] Childhood, as a general rule, is here seen as providing an abiding store of strength and enlightenment. The statement is misleading because Tournier quickly goes on to add that this general rule did not apply to Clergue, who apparently had a difficult childhood. More importantly, Tournier sees his own case as a similar exception: his various accounts indicate that his own childhood also failed to provide this lifelong source of light and hope. To Theodore Zeldin he declared: 'I had a miserable childhood. I was sickly and a weakling till the age of 12.' It seems that he felt desperately starved of affection: 'I love my mother dearly, but she was not an ideal mother. She is a woman of the 19th century, with its prejudices.'[2] The account of his childhood which he offers in the opening chapter of *Le Vent Paraclet* lists causes for his unhappiness: being sent away at the age of six to school in Switzerland, being victimised there, being constantly kept thirsty, and above all being subjected to a traumatic tonsilectomy at the age of four. This episode he describes in graphically nightmarish terms, designating it as 'l'Agression, l'Attentat, un crime qui a ensanglanté mon enfance et dont je n'ai pas encore surmonté l'horreur'(17).[3] He has, he tells us, ruminated ever since on this 'sanglante mésaventure'(19), deriving questions and ideas from it.[4]

In this way, his own childhood, as he perceives it, has indeed provided a crucial reservoir of experience from which his mature thought flows. 'The child is father of the man', one might say, and in fact Wordsworth's famously paradoxical line is quoted in *La Goutte d'or*, at the culmination of the story of 'La Reine blonde'. For Tournier as for Clergue, however, this wellspring of childhood experience is no 'capital de bonheur'. Rather, he says, 'l'enfance nous est donnée comme un chaos brûlant, et nous n'avons pas trop de tout le reste de notre vie pour tenter de le mettre en ordre et de nous l'expliquer'(*VPar* 19).[5] To the attentive reader of Tournier's fiction, the phrase 'chaos brûlant' evokes significant echoes: of the gunpowder explosion at the end of Chapter 7 of *Vendredi* which erupts from the cavern beneath the 'chaos', or jumble of rocks, at the centre of the island and which marks a kind of rebirth, a completely new beginning in Robinson's life. By the same token it evokes the tarot card of Chaos which figures in the prologue of the novel. Another 'burning chaos' is to be found in Tiffauges's extraordinary assertion at the start of *Le Roi des aulnes* that he was present at the dawn of creation: 'Quand la terre n'était encore qu'une boule de feu tournoyant [...], l'âme qui la faisait flamber, [...] c'était la mienne' (*RA* 13). This private creation myth enshrines the 'childhood', as it were, of his mythical self.

The essentials of Tournier's adult psychology were fixed, he asserts, early on; by the 'age of reason', he had little left to learn of the joys and, especially, the pains of the heart. '...Une maturité monstrueusement précoce s'est muée peu à peu en une immaturité inguérissable' (*VI* 11). That statement is a revealing summary of his self-development as he sees it: a child prematurely thrust into adulthood evolving into an adult incurably locked into childhood. In both cases what is evoked is a 'monstrous' hybrid of child and adult.

One further significant feature of *Le Vent Paraclet*, his most substantial statement so far of autobiography and reflection, deserves to be noted. It opens with an anecdote telling how his grandfather, as a boy of six at the time of the Prussian invasion in 1871, was made to hold up the heavy volume of music for the conductor of the German military band. From this anecdote of family history, Tournier derives a suggestive emblem to place at the head of the whole book: 'un enfant en larmes caché par l'oeuvre qu'il porte'(11). It is possible to infer that not just *Le Vent Paraclet* but the whole of Tournier's *oeuvre* is, explicitly or unobtrusively, sustained by the figure of a suffering child.[6]

Tournier's principal characters are often, as we have already noted, delinquent or marginalised. In three of his most important shorter fictions, 'Amandine ou les deux jardins', 'La fugue du petit Poucet' and 'Tupik', published in the collection *Le Coq de Bruyère*, the principal character is a child, and here the child is also at the margin, at odds with the adult world and its rules, struggling to adapt, potentially subversive of its ordered scheme of things: from an unsympathetic adult point of view, children are 'ces demi-fous que nous tolérons parmi nous' (*CB* 196).[7] One of the child's principal weapons against an oppressive adult world is 'playing the fool', 'faire le clown'(*VPar* 38). Tournier speaks of how a dissident child 'se réfugie [...] dans la grimace et la contorsion' (*VPar* 38), and we recall how Abel Tiffauges adopts this tactic: when the intimidating Professor Blättchen insults him, Tiffauges responds with a horrendous grimace, which at once reduces the scientist to nervous respectfulness (*RA* 407). The fifteen-year-old Vendredi giggles irreverently at the theology Robinson tries to teach him and which he finds incomprehensible or absurd, and later, he will use the weapons of grotesque clowning to teach Robinson a lesson by dressing up as the white man and caricaturing his manner. If Tournier's work is based on a child's suffering, it also employs these counter-weapons of caricatural mimicry of the languages and demeanours of authority, not least in the portrait it offers of Robinson as self-styled Governor of the island.

Before this discussion proceeds further, a caveat is required. In this chapter, 'child' refers, if not solely at least primarily, to the male of the species, because this is implicitly or explicitly the case in most of Tournier's writings or utterances. In *Le Roi des aulnes*, Abel Tiffauges is at one point led to explore what he calls the *'terra incognita'*(163) which the female child represents for him. This relationship ends brutally with Abel being falsely accused of rape, which leads him to opine bitterly that there are no young girls, only precocious young women, or 'manqué' little boys (204). Clearly we are not entitled to assume that such a provocative statement is typical of the views of Tournier himself, who has after all also given us in 'Amandine ou les deux jardins'(CB) a sympathetic study of an adolescent girl.[8] Nevertheless, it remains the fact that girls feature rarely, and never centrally, in the major works, which are overwhelmingly centred on male experience.

Tournier is deeply interested in the relationship of children to the society around them. In two articles in *Le Vol du vampire*,[9] he reflects on the changing status of children in society and literature since the seventeenth century. He asserts, quite uncontroversially, that a crucial turning-point in the history of attitudes to children is marked by Rousseau's *Émile*, which promotes a view of children not as unsocialised pre-adults unworthy of parental attention (as they were generally viewed in aristocratic families up to then), but as precious creatures of natural innocence, as yet untouched by the distortions of adult society. He quotes Rousseau's eulogy of Émile at the age of twelve, an age seen as the zenith of boyhood perfection, which can then only fall away into what Rousseau considers the disgrace of puberty (*VV* 181).[10] He lauds Rousseau's perspicacity in identifying this paradoxical concept of the grown-up child, 'l'enfant adulte', and in admiring this moment of 'childhood maturity'; for his own part, he deplores the modern tendency to negate the special qualities of this stage of youth by describing it merely as 'preadolescence'. Rousseau's revaluation of the child led directly on, Tournier suggests, to the 'angélisme enfantin' (*VV* 179) of Bernardin de Saint-Pierre's *Paul et Virginie* and especially of Victor Hugo. Hugo developed a 'fantastique mythologie pédophile' (*VV* 186) which makes of the child a providential vessel of divine grace and innocence. Tournier refers specifically to Hugo's narrative poem 'L'Aigle du casque' in *La Légende des siècles*,[11] where the murder of the boy Angus by Tiphaine calls forth an exemplary supernatural punishment: the eagle on Tiphaine's helmet comes to life and pecks him to death. This poem so caught Tournier's imagination that he used it as the basis for one of the stories in *Le Médianoche amoureux*.

In effect, in these historical surveys, Tournier is acknowledging the post-Rousseauian tradition of the idealisation of the child which strongly marks his own work. In *Le Roi des aulnes*, Tiffauges concludes from his study of the children in the Napola that both in their physical proportions and in their capacity to learn, children stand higher than adults on the evolutionary ladder, and must be deemed by comparison 'suprahumain, surhumain'(*RA* 484). Even in small matters, like the habit he notices in young children of offering you their left hand (the hand unsoiled by contact with those corrupted by power), Tiffauges finds a kind of instinctive wisdom to note and emulate (*RA* 53-4). Tournier himself avers that a child is for an adult an ideal companion and stimulus to discovery:

> Il est pour l'adulte un alibi, un passeport, une clé, l'initié-initiateur grâce auquel son vieux copain va redécouvrir toutes choses dans leur fraîcheur première. L'enfant est aussi la pierre de touche de nos préoccupations. Comment lui faire entendre l'importance qu'on attache à l'argent, à l'honneur, à une décoration, à la vengeance d'une humiliation? Il est sage de considérer avec méfiance - sinon avec mépris - tout ce à quoi un enfant est censé ne rien comprendre.[12]

For Tournier as for Tiffauges, the child's understanding is a yard-stick against which the values of civilisation are tested, and frequently found wanting: it is a powerful instrument of demystification. A paragraph in his notebook *Le Vagabond immobile* sums up this ideal of the child as 'initié-initiateur: 'Votre idéal de bonheur? Elever un enfant génial. Voir naître et s'épanouir ses dons éclatants. Pour toute oeuvre littéraire, tenir le journal de ses progrès. Fondre en un seul sentiment tendresse et admiration' (*VI* 43). The fantasy here is of a wholly child-centred *oeuvre*, a super-*Émile*. This dream of a dialectic of discovery involving adult and child underlies the concluding scene of *Vendredi*, as man and child enter a new phase of life together.

The final fruition of the adult-child relationship in both *Vendredi* and *Le Roi des aulnes* is only reached by passing through a stage of destructive conflict between child values and adult values. Tournier presents two of the uglier products of civilisation, colonial violence and mechanised warfare, as expressions of child-adult conflict. The young Vendredi is subjected to slavery and gratuitous punishments, until Robinson's brittle authority is blown apart by forces it is unable to contain. In *Le Roi des aulnes*, Tiffauges sees war as providing an opportunity for men to play children's games, with toys - tanks, guns, planes - which are full-size versions of those they played with as boys. This regression to childhood is, however, fatally flawed, for in the absence of the child's instinct for play and make-believe, the toys become in adult hands malignant and flesh-devouring (*RA* 455-6). Later, more diabolically still, these same toys - mines and mortars - are given to the Napola cadets, whom Raufeisen encourages to undertake near-suicidal anti-tank missions which he persuasively describes in terms of an entertaining if rather large-scale boar-hunt (*RA* 536). As Tournier himself points out in *Le Vent Paraclet*, this brutal and reckless waste of young lives is just one consequence of the Nazi cult of youth, in which the youth of 'pure Aryan' stock were just as liable to be massacred as the 'racially inferior', albeit for different reasons and by different means (*VPar* 106).

Tournier's novels have much to say about the coexistence of these contradictory adult attitudes to children - compassion and humility on one hand, and cruelty and demagogy on the other. It underlies the ambiguity of the figure of 'la phorie' in *Le Roi des aulnes*, in its twin aspects of the predatory Erlking and the submissive Saint Christopher; in *Gaspard*, it underpins the simultaneous occurrence of the feast offered to the children by the munificent Prince Taor and the Massacre of the Innocents by the soldiers of Herod. In Robinson, in Tiffauges and even in Gilles these two aspects coexist. In *Vendredi*, there is an incident when Robinson is showing Vendredi how to strip osier, and in doing so makes a vigorous gesture with his hand, where-upon Vendredi cringes away from him in anticipation of a blow. The disconcerted Robinson reflects sadly on the madman he must appear to be in the youngster's eyes: 'Alors je me mets à sa place, et je suis saisi de pitié devant cet enfant livré sans défense sur une île déserte à toutes les fantaisies d'un dément' (*VLP* 155). To be precise, what dis-concerts Robinson in Vendredi's defensive gesture is not that he is seen as capable of violence, but that the child should have failed to grasp the logic behind the use of violence, whereby it is quite appro-priate in contexts of discipline or punishment, and quite out of place in others, e.g. when he is trying to explain something difficult. De-spite this incisive moment of insight, the next paragraph finds him forcing the boy to perform the pointless task given to convicts of digging holes and filling them in again. In the final chapter, however, when the cabin-boy Jaan emerges from the rocks with a similar cring-ing gesture, Robinson's reaction is wholly one of tenderness, not of authority, and this is a small index of Robinson's metamorphosis, and of his re-education by Vendredi.

What sets Tournier's work apart from the sentimentality which hangs over Hugo's 'angélisme' is his strong awareness of sexuality. Hugo, Tournier points out, invariably stresses the virginity of the chil-dren he describes: 'Cependant, à l'heure où Hugo écrit ces vers [L'Aigle du casque], Freud est déjà né qui restituera sa sexualité à l'enfant...'(*VV* 186). Tournier's view is Freudian in its stress on the child's 'polymor-phic perversity', its undiscriminating capacity for deriving sexual pleas-ure in many different ways. This positive but diffuse pre-adult sexual-ity is a challenge to adults, who are often fixed in a single mode of sexual gratification, and this fundamental difference complicates fur-ther the alternation between cruelty and compassion which charac-terises adult-child relationships in Tournier, infusing Hugolian 'angélisme' with darker currents of physical desire and exploitation. In a text accompanying a volume of photographs by his friend Arthur Tress, Tournier notes the theme of the child in these pictures, in a characteristic play on ambiguous definition:

> *L'enfant.* C'est le témoin privilégié. Témoin: celui qui voit, qui sait, qui se souvient. Mais aussi: objet servant de preuve, subissant des épreuves, corps du délit. De tous les corps de délit, le corps de l'enfant est le plus charmant. L'enfant est l'objet privilégié du sadisme et de la nécrophilie. Mais il est aussi mémoire et espoir, car demain peut-être, devenu fort, il se vengera.[13]

Clearly, *Le Roi des aulnes* in particular is richly illustrative of these divergent roles of the child in an adult world. Éphraïm is the exemplary witness 'qui voit, qui sait, qui se souvient', and who will be exemplarily avenged by the slaughter of the sons of the oppressor in the closing pages. The boys at the Napola are 'corps du délit', objects of the sadism of Raufeisen who tramples them underfoot (*RA* 549), and of the necrophilia of Tiffauges who admires the 'plenitude' of the corpse of the decapitated Hellmut von Bibersee (*RA* 537-9). The morbid combination of tenderness and necrophilia can produce the sentimental sadism of Gilles de Rais: 'J'ai pitié de ces petits qu'on égorge. Je pleure sur leurs tendres corps pantelants. Et en même temps, je ressens un tel plaisir! C'est si émouvant, un enfant qui souffre!' (*GJ* 53).

It is in *Le Roi des aulnes* that the complex and disturbing compounds of pity and sadism, of idolatry, oppression and unavowed desire are most subtly explored. Tiffauges recounts in his diary the intense emotion he feels at a Holy Thursday service in Notre-Dame when an old priest ritually washes and kisses the feet of the choirboys: one of them, of particularly angelic appearance, can scarcely suppress a giggle at all this, which particularly endears him to the watching Tiffauges. The priest's gesture of child-worship redeems in Tiffauges's eyes what he sees as the Satanic pomp redolent of the Church's corrupt institutional power. It also, he says enigmatically, provides an answer to 'la question que posait Nestor, il y a vingt ans, l'avant-veille de sa mort' (*RA* 120). The only such question directly recorded which would seem to qualify is: 'Il doit y avoir un signe absolu alpha-oméga. Mais où le trouver?'(92), and indeed the ritual kiss could be seen as an answer to this quest for the marriage of opposites: the meeting of mouth and foot, of old age and childhood, of ornate robes and naked flesh, of solemnity and laughter. The more obvious reference, however, is to a conversation which arose from Abel's shocked realisation that the clergy choose choirboys primarily for their physical beauty, although (unlike Gilles) they would never admit it. Nestor is unmoved by this observation, preferring to reproach the priests with failing to realise that a child is beautiful when it is at once possessed and served, as when St Christopher carries the child away, while lifting it humbly above the waves. '[...] Nestor aurait voulu retrouver cette ambiguïté dans l'enfant de choeur, et voir s'agenouiller un prélat devant son petit thuriféraire'(86). The later scene witnessed by Abel in Notre-Dame is an obvious 'answer' to this wish. Nestor sketches himself in the role of St Christopher; Abel will finally act it out.

Nestor: Incubation, Inscription, Intertext

In this as in other ways, Tiffauges's life as a man appears to unfold in line with the dictates of a child, Nestor, who is the presiding genius of the 'Écrits sinistres'. The influence of this child-mentor on Abel's perception of his life is so profound that it is worth looking closely at the first moment in the text when Nestor's name is conjured up by the memory of Rachel's accusation:

> - Tu n'es pas un amant, tu es un ogre.
>
> O saisons, ô châteaux! En prononçant cette simple phrase, Rachel a fait surgir le fantôme d'un enfant monstrueux, d'une précocité effrayante, d'une puérilité déconcertante dont le souvenir prend possession de moi avec une impérieuse souveraineté. [...] Ma nouvelle écriture sinistre et le départ de Rachel m'avertissent d'une prochaine restauration de sa puissance. (22-3)

Rachel's departure, and her parting shot about Tiffauges's ogrish nature, signal the irrevocable predominance in Abel of an oral-anal sexuality over a genital one, an orientation which in turn refers back to the bulky figure, the huge appetite and the defecatory rituals of Nestor. The exclamation 'O saisons, ô châteaux!' which immediately follows Rachel's barbed remark is a quotation from a poem by Rimbaud - another 'enfant monstrueux, d'une précocité effrayante'.[14] The young-old Nestor, schoolboy of 1914, outrageously subversive of all order, with a gift for obscure and pregnant utterance, is thus momentarily superimposed on a figure from the previous generation, that of a young, revolutionary, homosexual poet, writing in the aftermath of the Franco-Prussian war of 1870 (the context, we recall, of the founding anecdote of *Le Vent Paraclet*). These ancestral subversive voices, real or fictional, from other epochs of Franco-German conflict serve as a paradigm and inspiration to Tiffauges's 'écriture' on the eve of yet another war with Germany. Rimbaud's voice is a fleeting, distant but powerful echo; Nestor's is the generator and inspirer of Tiffauges's text.

Nestor's determining power over Tiffauges's writing has been transmitted in three ways, of increasing depth, mystery and efficacy: through example, incubation and inscription. Firstly, and most mundanely, Nestor sets the example of an 'écriture sinistre' by incessantly writing and drawing in class with his left hand. Secondly, and more importantly, his right hand meanwhile enfolded Tiffauges's own left hand, imbuing it (Tiffauges will suggest) with a power which only later becomes manifest: 'Toute la force de Nestor, tout son esprit dominateur et dissolvant sont passés dans cette main, celle dont procèdent jour après jour ces écrits sinistres qui sont ainsi notre oeuvre commune' (55). The image used is that of an egg being incubated and hatched: '[...] [I]l a couvé dans sa grande main pesante et moite mon faible poing, ce petit oeuf osseux et translucide [...] Et le petit oeuf est éclos'(54-5). As with the recurrent image of metamorphosis from larva to butterfly in *Vendredi*, this biological metaphor of incubation represents the process of (re)birth, the emergence of a new form of the self, while placing the child Nestor in an idiosyncratic role as pseudo-parent and catalyst to this transformation. 'The child is father of the man' seems here to be realised - the child Nestor is, in a metaphorical but highly active sense, father to the man Tiffauges. A similarly biological metaphor is used by Nestor just a few pages later: 'J'ai planté toutes mes graines dans ce petit corps. Il faudra que tu cherches un climat favorable à leur floraison. Tu reconnaîtras la réussite de ta vie à des germinations et à des épanouissements qui te feront peur' (62).

Creative power is transmitted from pseudo-parent to pseudo-child by example and by incubation. The third mode of transmission, most important of all, is the process of inscription. Tiffauges's regret at not having kept any of the 'cahiers' in which Nestor wrote is outweighed by the awareness that he is himself a 'cahier' inscribed by his mentor, even if he can recall only fragments of Nestor's often impenetrable discourse. 'Cette période [...] que j'ai passée auprès de lui s'est inscrite si profondément en moi, les tribulations que j'ai traversées dans la suite s'y rattachent si manifestement qu'il est à peine nécessaire de distinguer dans mon bagage ce qui lui revient en propre et ce qui doit m'être imputé' (54). The 'écrits sinistres' and the story they tell are thus co-authored, 'notre oeuvre commune' (one is reminded of the classical euphemism for father - 'l'auteur de mes jours'). Tiffauges's voice is inhabited by the voice of the child-father, Nestor.

Guided by Nestor's voice, Tiffauges feels himself to be at once 'le dépositaire et l'exécuteur' of Nestor's destiny (68): '[...] [D]'une certaine façon il revit en moi, je suis Nestor' (204). This inheritance is not merely to be accepted passively (as *dépositaire*) but carries with it an obligation to act in accordance with its terms (as *exécuteur*). In effect, Nestor's voice has at least three functions. Firstly, there is the 'deposit' of Nestor's actual words, more or less accurately recalled, whose real weight and meaning is often recognised by Tiffauges much later (see for example the series of utterances recorded on pp. 62-3). Secondly, there are the instances when Nestor's voice intervenes in the inner reflections and debates of the narrator-protagonist, and here this surviving voice invariably addresses the 'executory' function, anticipating with exhortations or warnings the realisation of a destiny whose secrets it already knows:

'Un jour, Mabel, un jour, tu verras!' (65)

'Nous reverrons bientôt, Mabel, [...] les robes d'été et les culottes courtes! Tu peux fourbir ta machine à voler les cris et les sons, et ta boîte à capturer les images.
 Mais prends garde aussi, car les prémonitions ne vont pas tarder à te sauter au visage!' (161)

'Du calme, Mabel, retiens ta colère, fais taire tes imprécations. Tu sais bien maintenant que la grande tribulation se prépare, et que ton modeste destin est pris en charge par le Destin!' (194)

These moments when Tiffauges becomes as it were a medium for his dead friend's voice are signalled by the use of the 'tu' form, and of the sexually ambiguous pet-name 'Mabel'. Tiffauges's voice is thus inhabited by Nestor's voice, the voice at once of a child, and of a father-figure, and of a friend in an ambiguously gendered relationship.

To the voice remembered and the voice actively engaging in inner dialogue can be added a third mode of inscription: it is Nestor who is largely responsible for imprinting on Tiffauges's mind the curious anthology of texts and legends which provide him with many of the terms for interpreting his own life. Within the space of thirty pages four such intertexts are introduced.

Firstly, Nestor can recite by heart (ventriloquising, 'sans remuer les lèvres' (63)) whole pages from *Le Piège d'or* by James Curwood, a novel about the Far North and the wild giant of a man, Bram, who roams there with the wolves.[15] He thus provides the young Abel with a transcendent dream-country, 'le Canada', symbolic of a liberating release from present afflictions. 'Le Canada reste toujours, pour moi, cet au-delà qui frappe de nullité les dérisoires misères qui m'emprisonnent. Oserai-je écrire que je n'ai pas renoncé? Un jour, Mabel, un jour, tu verras!' (64-5). When Abel's pen falters ('Oserai-je écrire...') before confessing his continued attachment to this dream of 'un monde vierge et inhumain, blanc et pur comme le néant' (64), it is Nestor's voice which encourages him and promises its final realisation. Later, in the third section of the novel entitled 'Hyperborée' (the name given in Greek legend to an idyllic country situated in the Far North),[16] Abel discovers a cabin in a wood at some distance from his POW camp which seems to him the very embodiment of this utopia. 'Et il entendait à nouveau la voix sourde de Nestor [...]'(267). At the conclusion of the novel, this name will attach itself to another 'monde [...] inhumain', when Éphraïm reveals to him that 'le Canada' was the name given in Auschwitz to the store where the victims' clothes and possessions were placed. For the Jewish child too, Canada had once represented a mythic land of happiness and freedom, until he found its caricature in the 'trésor d'Auschwitz' (556). Tiffauges thus shares with Ephraïm this ghastly metamorphosis of 'une province de son rêve personnel' (556). Canada had been 'le refuge de son enfance nestorienne' (556),[17] but from this point on, as the human cost of this aspiration to 'purity' becomes manifest, Nestor's voice falls silent to be replaced by the voice of another child-mentor, Éphraïm.

The second intertext in this sequence is the legend of St Christopher, taken from the *Légende dorée* of Jacques de Voragine, chosen by Nestor for Tiffauges to read aloud in the refectory (68-72). A few pages later, Nestor tells Tiffauges the story of the Baron des Adrets and the refined sadistic pleasure he obtained from making his prisoners dance blindfold on a high platform until they fell to their death (80-2). The last of the legends to be introduced in this section is that of the conquistador Albuquerque who, in peril at sea, takes a young boy on his shoulders in the hope that God, taking pity on the child's innocence, would bring them both to safety. The episode is taken from Montaigne [18] and chosen by the Father Superior of the college as the starting-point of his sermon in the chapel service. While on this occasion Nestor neither tells the story nor has chosen it, it is nevertheless his immediate and intense attention to the text which lends it its importance in the eyes of Tiffauges (88). Nestor covets the manuscript of the sermon and finally manages to obtain it. He is thus once again the channel by which a crucial intertext is added to Tiffauges's personal anthology of significant narratives.

Three of these intertexts - St Christopher, Albuquerque, Curwood's Far North - will continue to be developed as points of reference as the narrative progresses. St Christopher and Albuquerque are linked in the Father Superior's sermon as phoric figures seeking salvation (89), and this link is consistently reinforced (e.g. 146, 469). Each is present through textual quotation in the closing pages: the Albuquerque story is explicitly requoted (576), the St Christopher one only slightly more discreetly in the final vision of Tiffauges sinking into the marsh under the weight of the child.[19] The only anecdote of the four which is not so obviously seminal is the one concerning the Baron des Adrets. After telling the story, 'Nestor n'ajouta aucun commentaire' (82). Nevertheless, Nestor's later commentary on its significance is immediately recorded: 'Il n'y a sans doute rien de plus émouvant dans une vie d'homme que la découverte fortuite de la perversion à laquelle il est voué. [...] Adrets [...] avait découvert l'*euphorie cadente*' (82). Each of these intertextual figures - St Christopher, Albuquerque, Bram, Adrets - present a reflection of some part of Tiffauges's being, and the Adrets-Tiffauges link is explicitly centred on the chance discovery of the perversion to which one is destined (reinforcing the notion of a life programmed to follow a pre-ordained pattern). This 'éblouissante découverte' (131) is vouchsafed to Tiffauges when he lifts up the unconscious body of his apprentice Jeannot, struck by a flying piece of metal in his garage. The link between this moment and the Adrets anecdote is reinforced by the use of the term 'euphorie' to describe Tiffauges's feelings, the self-conscious choice of the word being carefully highlighted on both occasions (131, 82). To link the episodes even more firmly, Tiffauges's first exclamation of wonder at the euphoria he feels, 'Je n'aurais jamais cru [...] que porter un enfant fût une chose si belle' (131) echoes the Baron's 'Je ne savais pas qu'un homme qui tombe fût une chose si belle' (81). But it also echoes, even more closely, Nestor's own ecstatic utterance, recorded just a few pages before the Adrets story, after carrying young Abel on his back in a playground battle of horses-and-riders: 'Je ne savais pas, petit Fauges, que porter un enfant fût une chose si belle' (78). This all serves to establish that Tiffauges shares his pre-destined 'perversion' with Nestor, and that it indeed forms part of the programming he has inherited from him. His 'phoric' vocation has nothing in common with Adrets's alternative perversion: indeed the latter's *euphorie cadente* could even be seen as opposite to *phorie*: the Baron stands apart to watch men fall to the ground, whereas Tiffauges gathers children up in his arms to raise them from the ground. The difference is pointed at key moments. When he has picked up a young boy roller-skater who has fallen, he props him up in order to photograph him. '"Il va tomber", prononce l'un des enfants. Il n'en est pas question' (172). Once the film is used up, 'je me relève avec mon frêle fardeau' (173). As after the garage incident with Jeannot, this incident is followed by a sensation of being borne aloft to an angelic paradise - the opposite to an 'euphorie cadente'. One final example: when he is pursuing Lothar in order to recruit him forcibly into the Napola, the boy takes refuge up a tree. Tiffauges, on horseback, pulls him down and catches him in his arms: 'l'enfant bascula dans ses bras' (468-9). The drama of the falling body is here one of contact and capture, not of detached spectacle as for the Baron. The Adrets reference functions then as an example of a quite different perversion; it is in its way as contrary to Tiffauges's as is Raufeisen's taste for walking on the prostrate bodies of the Napola cadets, a gesture which infuriates Tiffauges as the 'acte *anti-phorique* par excellence' (549). Thus Tiffauges's particular obsession with 'phorie' is set in perspective as only one of a range of possible 'perversions', and indeed is arguably thrown into a more favourable light as having at least the potential for expressing compassion, which is more than can be said either for Adrets's or Raufeisen's varieties of cruelty.[20]

It can be seen then that Nestor is not only a voice in his own right, but also a transmitter of intertexts, a channel for oral tradition, albeit of a very selective kind. To start with, Tiffauges wonders if Nestor's discourse consists wholly of quotations - 'J'ai d'abord cru qu'il ne s'exprimait que par des citations glanées dans ses lectures' (37). Although closer acquaintance convinces him that this is not the case, it remains the fact that, if one is to consider Nestor as Tiffauges's putative parent in the non-genetic ancestry of giants to which he lays claim, then the equivalent of the genetic inheritance is the oral transmission of insights, prophecies, legends and stories which can enable the descendant to perceive his identity and his destiny. The 'chromosomes' which tie Tiffauges into his timeless dynasty are made of language and coded with myth. The birth of this true identity starts, as we have seen, in a biological metaphor, with the 'incubation' of Tiffauges's left hand to empower it, when the time comes, to create in the *Écrits sinistres* an *écriture* emancipated from mere social intercourse. It is this language - language not of a rational, scientific or empirical kind, but in its mode of prophesy, poetry and myth - which informs Tiffauges's decoding of his life, and hence his choices, actions and ultimate fate. Tournier predicates a belief in language as a powerful magic: words, like symbols in the Kommandeur's theory of saturation and inversion (473), are no longer innocently transparent bearers of meaning, but seminal, active, dangerous, charged with power, and their most powerful transmitter is the voice of the child within. 'En vérité,' Tournier has declared, 'tout ou presque tout ce que j'écris est enfantin. Cela vient de mon inspiration mythique. Le mythe est enfantin à sa base, métaphysique à son sommet.'[21]

Le Roi des aulnes can thus be seen as exploring in some detail how a text, the 'Écrits sinistres', is shaped by the inner voice and presence of a formidable child, how it is programmed on multiple levels by example, incubation, inscription and intertextual transmission. It is possible to see this programming of the writing by the child within as a generative principle of Tournier's own writing. Let us recall his characterisation of his own childhood as a 'chaos brûlant' (*VPar*, 19) which required the whole of the rest of his life to explore. Let us recall in particular the tonsilectomy, 'l'Attentat, l'Agression', the 'crime qui a ensanglanté mon enfance et dont je n'ai pas encore surmonté l'horreur' (*VPar* 17), which he represents as the horrific invasion of his body by the surgeon's knife, with the complicity of his parents. In the closing pages of *Le Roi des aulnes*, in the burning chaos of the shattered and burning fortress of Kaltenborn, Tiffauges encounters the 'puéril Golgotha' (*RA* 578) of the three boys impaled on swords. It is the image of 'l'Attentat, l'Agression', in that it can be decoded as a nightmarishly amplified representation of the tonsilectomy, the 'crime qui a ensanglanté [l']enfance': one of the boys has a sword-point sticking out of his throat, another out of his mouth. The whole icon is accorded additional symbolic weight by association with the Crucifixion. It does not require any sophisticated Freudian analysis to suggest that this powerful and disturbing passage represents at one level an effort to 'surmonter l'horreur', to 'mettre en ordre et expliquer le chaos brûlant de l'enfance'. The generative scene of the tonsilectomy combined three human elements: the suffering of the child, the brutality of the surgeon and the complicity of the parents, and these three elements - the suffering of the innocent, and the sadism and complicity of those in authority - are powerful constituents of the whole narrative of *Le Roi des aulnes*. It is part of what Tournier sees as his 'immaturité inguérissable', his hybrid child-adult perspective, that he is bound to explore all three together, and that his writing as regards children oscillates alarmingly between the compassionate and the exploitative. What is at stake in this writing is how to deal with the pain of childhood and the guilt of adulthood. In this search for a kind of redemption, it is the child who will be the saviour.

The Child Saviour

In the intertextual sequence Albuquerque-St Christopher-Tiffauges, salvation, whether physical or spiritual, is sought in the service of a child. In 'Le Nain rouge', likewise, the dwarf Lucien, murderer and sadist, decides to offer his circus act free of charge to an audience composed wholly of children aged 12 and under (Rousseau's age of child maturity, we recall). At its conclusion he is overwhelmed by their ovation, 'cette tempête de douceur qui le lavait de son amertume, l'innocentait, l'illuminait' (*CB* 121). From being an adult, capable of inflicting sexual violence and humiliation, he is accepted into the family of children and thereby cleansed of his guilt.[22]

This absolution is available only to those who have a childlike element in their nature. Tiffauges is eligible because, as Tournier himself has asserted, he is not (temperamentally) an adult: 'il est caractérisé par une immaturité profonde et irrémédiable'(*VPar* 121).[23] Of Gilles, Blanchet says: 'Ce géant, ce maître de vingt forteresses, ce maréchal de France a le coeur d'un petit enfant'(*GJ* 91), and it is this which responds to the 'innocence enfantine' (15) which Gilles senses in Jeanne. Underlying this notion is a quotation from the Gospels: 'Il est écrit qu'on n'entre pas dans le royaume des cieux si l'on ne se fait pas semblable à un petit enfant.' Robinson, following on his sojourn in the grotto, recalls these words of Christ[24] and wonders how possible and desirable such a regression is. While he cannot return to a pre-adult sexuality, he does, as has been seen, undergo a series of symbolic rebirths, and notably after the explosion, his relationship to Vendredi reverts from that of adult master and mentor to that of dependent child in need of reassurance: 'Il ne devait plus lâcher cette main brune qui avait saisi la sienne pour le sauver [...]'(*VLP* 190). Tiffauges, under the orders of the child Éphraïm, fulfils exactly the terms of Christ's condition: 'Tiffauges obéit docilement, et ne fut plus dès lors qu'un petit enfant entre les pieds et les mains du Porte-étoile' (*RA* 578). In *Gaspard*, Taor's passion for sweets is already a mark of the same innocent immaturity. The intellectual aesthete Balthazar tells him:'[...] [I]l y a en toi une naïveté que j'admire, mais qui me fait peur. Lorsque tu dis "L'Enfant m'attend", je comprends surtout que c'est toi, l'enfant qui attend' (*GMB* 222). Taor will not find the Christ-child, but in serving children he will realise fully the child in himself, and thus know salvation. In rediscovering the child in themselves, these heroes become more like the children they revere. Robinson sheds beard and clothes to resemble Vendredi,[25] while Jaan is a younger version of Robinson himself - an exiled, red-haired Northerner.[26] The principle of redemption through the rediscovery of the child within the self is of course most perfectly encapsulated in the story of Barbedor (*GMB*): the king metamorphosed into his own young successor represents a perfect, magical realisation of this permanent longing in Tournier's work for the saving spirit of childhood.

This spirit of childhood is often associated with metaphors of lightness and aeration. In *Vendredi*, Vendredi's ariel spirit gradually asserts itself over Robinson's natural 'gravity' (see Chapter 5 above). Through the notion of 'lightness' it becomes associated with a whole series of experiences which enable Robinson to transcend his ponderous pre-occupation with administering the island. When he emerges from the grotto 'il n'était vraiment ni ankylosé ni affaibli, mais allégé plutôt et comme spiritualisé. [...] [I]l flotta comme un ludion' (109). The pattern is sufficiently significant for it to recur in *Gaspard*. Taor, emerging from the salt-mines, is in a similar 'spiritualised' state: 'Son extrême faiblesse était en partie compensée par sa légèreté. [...] Il flottait à la surface du sol, comme s'il eût été soutenu à droite et à gauche par des anges invisibles' (*GMB* 270). Robinson experiences later, in the 'combe', a similar sensation of lightness - 'Robinson sentit son âme légère s'envoler [...]'(*VLP* 126) - which convinces him that he is momentarily on 'the other island', in an alternative reality, or rather perhaps in an alternative relationship to reality. Later still, the free-floating meditation on myths in his final logbook entry, which is at the opposite pole to his once resolutely practical, earthbound focus, also takes place in an ambience of 'légèreté' and 'gratuité' - '*Ave spiritu* [...]'(230).

It is in *Le Roi des aulnes* that this motif of lightness is most directly associated with the child. Tiffauges is astonished to discover that when he lifts his wounded apprentice's inert body, the additional weight of the child provokes, paradoxically, a 'sentiment de légèreté, d'allégement, de joie ailée'(*RA* 133). This paradox of weight and lightness is developed in the series of 'phoric' episodes, culminating in those involving Hellmut and Éphraïm. When he finds himself staggering beneath the uncanny weight of Hellmut's corpse, it is, he concludes, because the body is headless: 'J'ai toujours soupçonné la tête dd n'être qu'un petit ballon gonflé d'esprit (*spiritus*, vent) qui soulève le corps [...] et lui retire du même coup la plus grande partie de son poids. Par la tête le corps est spiritualisé, désincarné, éludé. Décapité au contraire, il tombe sur le sol, soudain rendu à une incarnation formidable, doué d'une pesanteur inouïe' (*RA* 538-9). This polarity - body=flesh=weight, head=spirit=lightness - acquires its full significance with the advent of Ephraïm. When Abel first finds him by the road-side, 'il eut le coeur serré de le trouver si incroyablement léger, comme s'il n'y avait rien dans le ballot de tissus grossiers d'où sortait sa tête'(551). This is a wholly plausible observation of a strong man lifting for the first time an emaciated concentration camp victim, but Tiffauges gives it a metaphysical significance. Ephraïm, seemingly a head without a body, is thereby the antithesis to Hellmut, body without head, and accordingly stands for the lightness and life of the spirit as opposed to the heaviness and death of the flesh.[27] The only clear memory Ephraïm retains of his family's arrival at Auschwitz is of the barrage balloons, 'ballons captifs'(*RA* 555), surrounding the camp - quite possibly a playful extension of the same motif (the captive Ephraïm = head = 'petit ballon gonflé d'esprit' = 'ballon captif'). In the camp he receives lessons from a teacher who sets an essay topic on what would happen if universal attraction ended - that is, if there were no longer any *gravity*. The answer - that we would all fly to the moon - makes Ephraïm laugh. The paradox of lightness and weight returns in the final paragraph of the novel: 'il sentait l'enfant - si mince, si diaphane pourtant - peser sur lui comme une masse de plomb'(580). Ephraïm has become his eyes and his directing intelligence: the child is, in effect, Tiffauges's head. While the weight of the body (Tiffauges) is sucked down into the marsh, the 'diaphanous' head (Ephraïm) dematerialises into air (*'spiritus*, vent') to become a free-floating source of illumination.[28] This radical separation of head and body, of spirit and flesh encodes the moment of Abel's death, and of the redemptive liberation of the child spirit within him.

Presented in much simpler terms, a similar apotheosis of the child within can be seen in the penitence and atonement of Gilles. It is the threat of excommunication which brings him to accept his guilt, a threat which reduces him to the state of a lost child: 'L'Eglise est ma mère! [...] Je ne suis pas un enfant abandonné! Je ne veux pas avoir froid loin du sein de ma mère!'(*GJ* 131). Reinstated and repentant, he asks his judges to 'm'aimer comme une mère aime le plus malheureux de ses enfants'(133). His final statement to the crowd at his execution begins with the words: 'J'atteste que la foi de mon enfance est demeurée pure et inébranlable'(152). For all the crimes of his adulthood, he is, by implication, saved by the constancy of the child within.

In a page of *Le Vent paraclet*, Tournier elevates this redemptive persistence of the child within to an existential principle. His starting point is the standard recommendation to children 'd'être bien sages', reinterpreted in the light of a verse from Luke about the 'sagesse' of the young Jesus. 'C'est que la sagesse est un savoir vivant, presque biologique, une maturation heureuse, un accès réussi à l'épanouissement du corps et de l'esprit. [...] La sagesse est altération, mûrissement, mue'(*VPar* 290). If this 'wisdom' is thus defined as a capacity for growth and change, then (Tournier argues) adults cannot be wise, almost by definition, and the wisest beings are those who most retain their childhood openness: '[...] [L]es vies les meilleures ne connaissent pas de phase adulte. L'homme s'enrichit de chacun de ses avatars successifs. [...] Un enfant émerveillé reste caché jusque sous le masque du vieillard' (*VPar* 290). The child, then, represents for Tournier an ideal of Becoming rather than just Being. Its 'polymorphic' sexuality is for Tournier, as has been seen in Chapter 3, an ideal and enriching relationship to the physical and human environment. Its 'innocence' is the capacity to accept many new experiences undiscriminatingly and learn from them. 'L'enfant naturellement quitte l'adulte. Son mouvement spontané le porte vers l'extérieur, à la découverte et à la conquête d'une réalité riche et bariolée. D'instinct l'enfant obéit à une force centrifuge.'[29] This dynamic of discovery, conquest and metamorphosis drives all of Tournier's heroes out of the rut of predictably ordered lives - mariner, garageman, Saharan tribesman, Breton seigneur, even Indian princeling - towards unforeseen destinies, and is at the root of the patterns of initiatic narrative (described in the next chapter) which serve to articulate it. A kind of immaturity is necessary, a refusal to accept all the codes of adult, 'civilised' culture: we have seen above how Tournier speaks (boasts?) of his own 'immaturité inguérissable'...

The sign of this life-enhancing openness is laughter. Tournier finds in a quotation from Hugo this celebration of a child's laughter as a 'surnaturel positif, divin'(*VV* 183):

> Nul n'ira jusqu'au fond du rire d'un enfant;
> C'est l'amour, l'innocence auguste, épanouie,
> C'est la témérité de la grâce inouïe,
> La gloire d'être pur, l'orgueil d'être debout,
> La paix, on ne sait quoi d'ignorant qui sait tout.
> Ce rire, c'est le ciel prouvé, c'est Dieu visible.[30]

Besides being a spontaneous expression of vivacity and joy, the child's laughter is a potent weapon of demystification against the adult world. Robinson begins by deploring Vendredi's capacity for laughter: '[...] Son enfance le pousse à rire insolemment de mes enseignements' (*VLP* 147). He correctly sees it as an attack on the dignity and order he has so carefully cultivated, 'un rire redoutable, un rire qui démasque et confond le sérieux menteur dont se parent le gouverneur et son île administrée' (149). Once these structures are swept away however, he records at length in his logbook his yearning to share this salutary sceptical hilarity: 'Donne-moi le visage de Vendredi, [...] taillé tout entier pour le rire. [...]. Cet oeil toujours allumé par la dérision, fendu par l'ironie, chaviré par la drôlerie de tout ce qu'il voit' (217). Such laughter can 'dénoncer et dénouer ces deux crampes, la bêtise et la méchanceté...'(217). It is a tonic to a sick culture. Even the horrors of Auschwitz have not extinguished Éphraïm's capacity for laughter (*RA* 555), and Tiffauges, like Robinson, sees true fulfilment only in being taken over by its power: 'Ainsi moi, triste et emprunté, [...] je ne suis moi-même que harnaché par le corps d'un enfant, [...] couronné par son rire' (523).[31] As has been seen, Tournier plays on the double meaning of 'gravity'. In the sense of 'weight', its antidote is air, '*spiritus*'; in the sense of 'le sérieux menteur', its antidote is laughter. The child is the chief source of this double remedy of humour and spirituality, 'le comique cosmique', 'le rire blanc' which Tournier sees as characteristic of some of the philosophical writers he most reveres - Nietzsche, Valéry, Léon Bloy, Thomas Mann.[32]

'Un enfant en larmes caché par l'oeuvre qu'il porte' (*VPar* 11) - if we are right in seeing this as an emblem not just for *Le Vent Paraclet* but for all Tournier's writing, then the recurrent evocation of a child's laughter and its spiritual potency against 'la bêtise et la méchanceté' is its antidote. Whether he is writing of the child without, maltreated or adored, or the child within, it is possible to see in Tournier's work an effort both to exorcise the child's tears and to celebrate its radiant power for renewal, discovery and transformation.

When Rachel leaves Tiffauges, his apparent light-hearted resignation conceals the deep grief and sense of loss felt by a visceral inner self, 'le moi visqueux': 'Je le porte au fond de moi comme une blessure, cet être naïf et tendre, [...] si facilement abusé [...]' (*RA* 41).[33] In *Les Météores*, Alexandre finds in the pity he feels for his young lover Daniel an expression of a similarly unhealed emotional wound: 'Je viens de heurter la plaie ulcéreuse de mon 'petit chagrin' [...], en l'espèce la compassion que m'inspire le petit garçon orphelin que maman a laissé derrière elle. Narcisse se penche sur son image et pleure de pitié'(*Mét* 247). These psychic wounds left by the loss of comforting feminine-maternal contact are the marks of the 'enfant en larmes' living on within the adult self, which impel Tiffauges (like another weeping Narcissus) to 'chercher la trace [...] d'un petit fantôme inconsolable' (*RA* 41-2), that is of his own unhappy childhood self. This 'trace' is everywhere apparent in Tournier, as the founding emblem of *Le Vent Paraclet* suggests, and Tiffauges goes on to formulate one of the most fundamental impulses of Tournier's writing: 'Comme si je pouvais [...] prendre son malheur sur mes épaules d'homme, et le faire rire, rire!' (*RA* 42).

Notes to Chapter Six

[1] This quotation is taken from Tournier's 'discours de réception' at the Académie d'Arles, published in a volume of photographs by Lucien Clergue, *Mers, plages, sources et torrents, arbres* (Paris, Perceval, 1974), [p.1]. Let us note at once that Tournier is addressing *male* experience here.

[2] Interview with T. Zeldin, 'The Prophet of Unisex', *Observer* (30.1.83), 43. In Tournier's fictions, this rather stern and undemonstrative attitude characterises Robinson's mother (*VLP* 107) and Abel's father (*RA* 100).

[3] In *Le Vent Paraclet* (20), he wonders if this officially sanctioned aggression should be envisaged as a savage initiation rite, and compares it to circumcision, which he sees as a calculated device for reducing the capacity for erotic pleasure. These are in his view dramatic manifestations of a social attitude which is fundamentally uncaring about children and their real needs. This general point has already been touched on above, at the start of Chapter 3.

[4] Interestingly, as Davis has pointed out (*Michel Tournier: Philosophy and Fiction*, 188), a similar throat operation without anaesthetic features in Michel Leiris's *L'Age d'homme*, an autobiographical memoir published in 1946. Leiris likewise presents the episode as an 'agression', and the memory of it as so painful that it marked his whole view of life. See Leiris, *L'Age d'homme* (Paris, Gallimard (Folio), 1973), 104-5.

[5] The phrase 'chaos brûlant' ties this original emotional energy-source of childhood interestingly to the tarot figure of Chaos and of the volcanic imagery in *Vendredi*, referred to in earlier chapters.

[6] The point is suggested, but not developed, by Merllié (*Michel Tournier*, 31).

[7] A phrase of Jean Paulhan which Tournier puts into the mouth of the elderly and bookish Aristide Coquebin in 'La jeune fille et la mort': see Tournier's own footnote. On the child as a victim of exclusion, see Guichard, *Michel Tournier*, 56-72.

[8] For one critic, nevertheless, Amandine is the exception which in fact proves the rule: 'Amandine, grâce à son aventure dans l'autre jardin, pressent qu'elle est une petite femme promise à la maternité.' See Merllié, *Michel Tournier*, 124.

[9] 'L'étrange et mortel "déplaisir" d'Henri de Campion' (*VV* 44-51) and 'Émile, Gavroche, Tarzan' (*VV* 174-95).

[10] See also *TS*, 64-5. In the course of an illuminating discussion on Tournier's view of childhood and its quasi-sacred status, Lorna Milne observes that the insistence on the particular age of 12 comes from Tournier, not Rousseau. See Milne, *L'Évangile selon Michel*, 79-106 (90). The same disenchanted view of puberty is expressed in *Gaspard* by Balthazar's mentor Maalek (*GMB* 65).

[11] 'L'Aigle du casque' is the fourth and last poem in section XVII, 'Avertissements et châtiments', of Victor Hugo, *La Légende des siècles* (pp. 320-31).

[12] See 'Quand Michel Tournier récrit ses livres pour les enfants', *Le Monde* (24.12.71), 13.

[13] See Arthur Tress and Michel Tournier, *Rêves* (Brussels, Complexe, 1979), 42.

[14] The text of 'O saisons, ô châteaux' exists in two versions, in *Derniers Vers* and in *Alchimie du verbe*. See Rimbaud, *Oeuvres*, 179, 234.

[15] James Oliver Curwood, *The Golden Snare* (London, Cassell, 1918), translated into French by P. Gruyer and L. Postif as *Le Piège d'or* (Paris, Hachette, 1930). Tournier comments on his reading of Curwood in *VPar* 52-3. The name of Curwood's hero, Bram, is linked in *Le Roi des aulnes* to 'le brame', the full-throated howl with which Tiffauges gives vent to his existential pain. It may also evoke the name of Bran, an ancient Celtic deity of the Underworld associated particularly with alder trees: see Robert Graves, *The White Goddess*, rev. edn. (London, Faber, 1961), pp.51, 169-70, 191n. The Underworld in question, Graves specifies (p.89), is 'the icy Northern Hell of the souls of the damned, or of unbaptised infants'.

[16] The Hyperboreans were a mythical race, said to live in an ideal country 'beyond the North wind (Boreas)'. They are referred to by Herodotus and Pliny. See Pierre Grimal, *Dictionary of Classical Mythology* (Oxford, Blackwell, 1986), 221, and Robert Graves, *The White Goddess*, 284-5.

[17] The adjective 'nestorien' refers in theology to the beliefs of Nestorius, a fifth-century heresiarch who maintained that Christ had two separate and distinct natures, one human and one divine. This implication accords well with the idea of Abel evolving, under Nestor's tutelage, a second transcendental self indissolubly linked to a higher destiny. (See e.g. Petit, *Michel Tournier's Metaphysical Fictions*, 31-2.) This does not preclude another and more well-known association of the name Nestor, sometimes given to the oldest and wisest member of a group, after the sage Greek king of that name in Homer's *Iliad*.

[18] *Essais*, XXXIX ('De la Solitude'). The preacher cleverly links the gesture of Albuquerque to that of St Christopher, but there remains a difference: while Albuquerque seeks safety, the Saint seeks *salvation*. Tiffauges arguably finds both, in succession: Éphraim enables him to pass safely through the Russian lines, but then in the marshes, safety is readily sacrificed for salvation. 'For whosoever will save his life shall lose it: and whosoever will lose his life for my sake shall find it' (Matthew 16:25).

[19] The phrase 'pes(er) sur lui comme une masse de plomb' is directly repeated (pp.71, 580). A comparable episode, where the hero rows his unnaturally heavy passenger (Christ or an angel in disguise) across a river, figures in the legend of St Julian the Hospitaler, most well known in the version by Flaubert in his *Trois Contes*. A preface written by Tournier for the Gallimard (Folio) edition of this work is reprinted in *Le Vol du vampire*, 166-73.

[20] The Adrets story of prisoners made to fall from a tower to be impaled on lances stuck in the ground is, however, predictive in another sense of the fate of the three boys impaled on swords at the end of the novel. Whether they meet this fate after being made to fall from the overlooking window of the Kommandeur's office is not made clear.

[21] See interview with J.-J. Brochier, 'Dix-huit questions à Michel Tournier', *Magazine littéraire* no. 138 (June 1978), 11-13 (11).

[22] In 'La Reine blonde' (*GO*) it is Riad, a 12-year-old boy, who is able to exorcise the tangle of cruelty and guilt which gives the queen's portrait its maleficent power: here again, the child is the redemptive source of absolution and restored innocence. On the general theme of the child saviour in Tournier, see Bouloumié, *Michel Tournier*, 220-1.

[23] 'Tiffauges, comme Robinson, se retrouve à l'état d'innocence, c'est-à-dire à celui de l'enfant, c'est-à-dire en proie à un grouillement de perversions larvées.' See Tournier's interview with Jean Prasteau, 'Michel Tournier et l'ogre

de Rominten', in *Figaro littéraire* 1271 (28.9.-4.10.70), 22-3.

[24] *VLP* 112, 114: the biblical source is Mark 10:15 and Luke 18:17.

[25] In *Vendredi ou la vie sauvage*, as Tournier himself has asserted, 'le couple enfant-adulte se retrouve dans le couple Robinson (barbe et peaux de bique) et Vendredi (nudité et fou-rires). A la fin, la barbe et les peaux de bique tombent, et les deux amis, devenus semblables, se livrent à des jeux sauvages, inventant la musique, la poésie, le théâtre...' See 'Quand Michel Tournier récrit ses livres pour les enfants', 20. Guichard (*Michel Tournier*, 314) is surely right when she suggests that in this enterprise of rewriting, Tournier has in mind 'un lecteur idéal, sorte de clone de l'enfant qu'il a été doté de l'expérience de l'adulte qu'il est devenu'.

[26] 'Le petit mousse est un peu le clone de Robinson. C'est la grande différence avec Vendredi. Il est petit, il est roux. Comme Robinson, il vient du Nord. Il craindra les coups de soleil. Je n'avais pas pensé que le petit mousse pouvait être le clone de Robinson' (Tournier in interview with B. le Péchon, 21). This ending was a fairly late decision in the composition of the novel, and some of its implications seem not to have been anticipated by the author himself.

[27] Milne, by a rather different route, also views the Tiffauges-Ephraïm couple as a fusion of body and spirit. See *L'Évangile selon Michel*, 105.

[28] In the light of this moment from *Le Roi des aulnes* and of the notion of a 'chaos brûlant' within, a sentence from Nietzsche quoted by Tournier (*MI* 136) takes on a particular resonance: 'Il faut avoir un chaos en soi-même pour accoucher d'une étoile qui danse.'

[29] Preface to Jerry Mason (ed.), *La Famille des enfants* (Paris, Flammarion, 1977), 3.

[30] The quotation is from 'Petit Paul', the second poem of section lvii ('Les Petits') of *La Légende des siècles* (759).

[31] This gift of laughter from a child in the midst of carnage is given both to Idriss from Ibrahim ('le rire de son ami enseveli vivant'(*GO* 21)) and, in passing, to Gaspard, from a little boy who emerges from the carcass of a dead hippo (*GMB* 38).

[32] See Tournier's reflections on laughter and the comic in *Le Vent Paraclet*, 196-204. On the subject of the child's laughter and wisdom, see Kirsty Fergusson, 'Le rire et l'absolu dans l'oeuvre de Michel Tournier', *Sud* 61 (1986), 76-89. Tournier indicates that this theme of laughter as an antidote to the 'esprit de lourdeur' is inspired by his reading of Nietzsche: in his note on 'Le froid et ses vertus' (*CS*) he sums up Nietzsche's tonic message: 'Il n'y a de vérité que légère et chantante. La pesanteur est du diable'(*CS* 33). A. Bouloumié identifies some sources in Nietzsche's *Thus Spake Zarathustra*: see her article 'Inversion bénigne, inversion maligne' in A. Bouloumié and M. de Gandillac (eds), *Images et signes de Michel Tournier*, 17-41 (23-4).

[33] In a note on 'le moi visqueux' of Tiffauges, Tournier has written: 'C'est peut-être son passé d'enfant triste et désarmé qu'il traîne avec lui et qui explique une part de ses pensées et de ses actes.' See his 'Petit lexique d'un prix Goncourt: treize clefs pour un ogre', *Figaro littéraire* 1280 (30.11.1970), 20-2 (21).

7

The Initiatic Narrative

In one quite precise sense Tournier regards himself as an educational writer. He has written a number of stories for children, including versions of two of his major novels: *Vendredi ou les limbes du Pacifique* became in its simplified version, published four years later, *Vendredi ou la vie sauvage*, while a similarly rewritten version of *Gaspard, Melchior & Balthazar* was simply entitled *Les Rois mages*.[1] He has insisted on the great importance he attaches to this aspect of his work, and to the educative role of the kind of writing for children which can help to shape their 'sensibilité et [...] mythologie personnelles'.[2] In *Le Vent Paraclet* Tournier defines education (57) as 'initiation + information', while complaining that current educational practice seriously overemphasises the information function at the expense of that of initiation, i.e. the proper development of the emotions and the imagination. Clearly he intends his own writing for children to promote initiation in this sense.

In the light of these views, it is not surprising that for his first novel *Vendredi* (in both versions), he should choose *Robinson Crusoe* as his starting point. Rousseau, in his *Emile*, recommended Defoe's novel as the ideal educational book for his young pupil, and in abridged and simplified form it has become a children's classic down the ages. In many different versions this story has been used as a vehicle to transmit quantities of geographical, scientific and practical information to its young readers, as well as various kinds of edifying morality.[3] Tournier's version follows the tradition in that it provides a substantial amount of carefully documented information about the flora and fauna of an island in the South Pacific, as well as some plausible ethnographic details about Vendredi's Araucanian culture.[4] This informational aspect is, however, never free-standing: its presence in the narrative is justified in that it is seen as a constitutive element of a learning process which ends by transforming Robinson's relationship to the world. It is part, in fact, of his initiation firstly into his 'alien' surroundings and then into cultural otherness, leading finally to a transformation of self.

In a eulogy of Hans Christian Andersen's *The Snow Queen* as initiatic narrative, Tournier speaks of initiation as the 'thème littéraire dont l'apparition dans une oeuvre mobilise mon attention et ma sensibilité avec le plus d'urgence' (*VPar* 49). Suzanne Vierne, seeking to define the 'novel of initiation' makes a useful distinction between the 'roman d'éducation' and the 'roman d'initiation':

> Dans un roman d'éducation, on acquiert une sagesse, une manière de se conduire en vieillissant, et c'est une formation très rationnelle... Dans le roman initiatique, le héros acquiert assurément une formation... Mais ce n'est qu'un aspect d'une transformation plus large et surtout plus profonde. L'initié est devenu un autre homme, qui ne sera plus soumis au destin commun, celui de la condition mortelle.[5]

Many of Tournier's narratives can be read as studies in what Vierne calls, using an alchemical term, the hero's 'transmutation':[6] they are fictions of initiation rather than simply of 'éducation'. This transmutation is sometimes figured literally in the text, as in the apotheosis of Robinson on the final page of *Vendredi* as well as the less palpable and more allusive apotheosis of Paul at the end of *Les Météores*, as he attains the condition of ubiquity in the unfurling of 'l'âme déployée'. The term transmutation is all the more appropriate in that Tournier maintains the metaphoric link, implicit in alchemy, between the chemical transformation of matter and the spiritual transformation of the human subject, as was seen in Chapter 5. In *Vendredi* this founding metaphor is carried through the images of metallification and mineralisation already studied above, and in *Les Météores* the final passage also refers to a physical change in matter, 'sublimation', as a metaphor for Paul's spiritual renewal.[7]

This transmutation is the end-result of an initiatic process. Tournier's anthropological studies provided him with abundant material on initiation rituals, and it is instructive to identify their characteristic patterns in his narratives. We are dealing here with a process of change more radical than the progressive growth to maturity portrayed in the realist *Bildungsroman*. The *Bildungsroman* category is a broad one, but it can usefully be seen as a spectrum running from the realist to the more magical and fantastical. While novels such as Stendhal's *Le Rouge et le noir* or Dickens's *David Copperfield* place their hero's development primarily in the context of social, cultural and interpersonal factors, a different tradition, of metaphysical quest and mystic forces, informs works such as Novalis's *Heinrich von Ofterdingen* or Hesse's *Das Glasperlenspiel (The Glass Bead Game)*. The logic which is seen to govern the hero's evolution is radically different in these two traditions: the one is culturally and historically specific, and self-contained, while the other is seen as the manifestation of timeless patterns and depends on the acceptance of a transcendental system of some kind. Some of the greatest *Bildungsroman* writers combine elements of both logics - Thomas Mann and James Joyce arguably come into this category. In *Le Vol du vampire*, Tournier surveys works both from the more realist canon in France - *Le Rouge et le noir*, Balzac's *Le Père Goriot* - and from the more magical-metaphysical German tradition - Goethe's *Die Wahlverwandtschaften (Elective Affinities)*, as well as the aforementioned works by Novalis and Hesse.[8] His devotion to and expertise in German philosophy and literature suggests that he wished to pour into the contemporary French novel a strong draught of the idealism characteristic of these German novels, and his reworking of archetypal initiatic patterns involving radical transformations of the hero is an aspect of this emancipation from realist conventions in his texts.

Mircea Éliade defines initiation as: 'un ensemble de rites et d'enseignements oraux qui poursuit la modification radicale du statut religieux et social du sujet à initier. Philosophiquement parlant, l'initiation équivaut à une mutation ontologique du régime existentiel. A la fin de ces épreuves, le néophyte jouit d'une tout autre existence qu'avant l'initiation: il est devenu un *autre*.'[9] Let us consider in turn seven features of this initiation process as exemplified in Tournier's fiction: the journey, the mentor, bereavement, symbolic death and rebirth, sacrifice or mutilation of the body, fertility, and incorporation/spiritualisation of the beloved.

The Journey

The journey as a quest for illumination is a structural principle in most of Tournier's major narratives: Abel's from France to Prussia in *Le Roi des aulnes*, Paul's round the world in *Les Météores*, the several journeys of the Magi to Bethlehem or (in Taor's case) to Jerusalem in *Gaspard*, Idriss's from Africa to Paris in *La Goutte d'or*. The biblical Wise Men follow a star in the East, which brings them to the Christ-child. Abel likewise journeys eastward 'vers la lumière. *Ex Oriente lux*' (*RA* 250). The final stages of Paul's grand tour are eastward, from Japan to Vancouver to Montreal, to end in *East* Berlin. The initiatic orientation to the East is an archetypal one, related to the rising sun as a symbol of the life-force and of cyclical rebirth: at the end of *Vendredi*, 'du côté du levant le ciel... incandescent' betokens the promise of renewed life for Robinson and the child (*VLP* 253).[10]

The Mentor

The initiatic quest will generally offer the neophyte encounters with mentors, from whom he[11] can gather wisdom. Sometimes these will take the form of father-figures proffering counsel and encouragement. As Vierne observes, 'il y a toujours [...] une sorte de *parrain*, avec lequel le futur initié gardera des liens spéciaux, partagera des secrets'[12]. It is this pseudo-paternal role which is played by Van Deyssel in *Vendredi*, and by Nestor in *Le Roi des aulnes*. It is likewise in this role of 'père-jumeau' (as he calls it) that Paul would have wished to cast Alexandre: '[...] J'aurais eu beaucoup à lui dire, beaucoup à apprendre de lui' (*Mét* 387). Other figures such as the Kommandeur in *Le Roi des aulnes*, Shonïn in *Les Météores* or Prelati in *Gilles & Jeanne* are more objectively teachers, providers of systems of knowledge required by the initiate at a particular stage. A second type of mentor is to be found in the same generation as the initiate, more akin to a real twin than to a 'père-jumeau'. Vendredi and Jean are, for Robinson and Paul respectively, objects of passionate devotion as well as sources of insight: they provide an experience and a focus on the world which is intimately complementary.

Bereavement

For the neophyte the initiatic journey (real or metaphorical) is, as Vierne explains, generally preceded by a 'rupture avec le monde profane - qu'il s'agisse de l'univers maternel ou du passé personnel du myste. Et cette séparation est plutôt un arrachement.'[13] This 'isolation from the tribe' is enacted in Robinson's shipwreck and in Abel's equally involuntary conscription into the army which takes him away from the garage and from France. It functions too in the series of disasters which affect Paul's cocoon-like family environment, summed up in the chapter heading 'Les pierres foudroyées', and culminating in Jean's departure.

The journey itself leads characteristically through the realm of death, as a necessary prelude to eventual rebirth. Robinson, in his island 'limbo' between life and death, is aware that he must be supposed dead by all his family and friends. 'Il se sentait sombrer dans un abîme de déréliction, nu et seul, dans ce paysage d'Apocalypse, avec pour toute société deux cadavres pourrissant sur le pont d'une épave' (30). He must endure this passage through the landscape of Death before his first experience of renewal and rebirth at the end of Chapter 2. In the last chapter of the novel, this sequence is repeated. The pre-dawn landscape is death-marked - grey sea, colourless sky, waves toying with a dead crab, the birds icily silent. Within him is a poisoned well, 'une citerne sonore et noire d'où montait - comme un esprit délétère - une nausée qui lui emplissait la bouche de salive fielleuse' (248). This scene of malediction is the prelude to his discovery that Vendredi has left, as though the island itself was already stricken by the withdrawal of its fertility god. Robinson feels the weight of years descend on him, and the birds of carrion who spied on him in the opening chapters gather around him again (251), until the emergence of Jeudi and the sunburst of new life.

This passage through a deathly realm is the result of bereavement: Robinson is first bereft of all human company, and then of Vendredi, in whom for Robinson the whole of humankind had been summed up. Tiffauges's life is also punctuated at key moments by a series of bereavements. At the start of the narrative Rachel ejects him scornfully from her bed and her life, and he will go on to recount the loss of his 'père putatif' Nestor. He is present at the execution of his pseudo-twin, the German murderer Eugène Weidmann with whom he inexplicably shares the same date of birth, the same height and weight measurements and the same characteristic of left-handedness. According to Mme Eugénie the resemblance is striking: 'Ma parole, on dirait votre frère! Mais c'est vous, monsieur Tiffauges, c'est tout à fait vous!' (190). Tiffauges's revulsion at this execution is thus heightened by the sense that this is a vicarious execution of himself, a ghastly dramatisation of his own condemnation in the eyes of the whole of French society.[14] It is a formative experience, immediately preceding the Martine affair and his ejection towards Germany (Weidmann's country). Again at the end of the novel Tiffauges is a witness to brutal execution, this time of the three boys, in a setting that, even more than Robinson's island, justifies the epithet 'paysage d'Apocalypse'. It is only when the death of these, his pseudo-children, is added to those of pseudo-father (Nestor) and pseudo-twin (Weidmann) that Tiffauges's ordeal by bereavement is complete, and he is ripe for the revelation which is the initiate's reward.

There is an obvious parallel between Tiffauges's presence at Weidmann's execution and Gilles's similar revulsion and distress at the burning of Jeanne (*GJ* 45). Like Vendredi for Robinson, Jeanne sums up in her person all Gilles holds dear in humankind, and this ordeal of bereavement is decisive for his subsequent evolution.

The passage through the valley of the shadow of death is just as apparent in *Les Météores*: indeed, the shadow, while centred on Paul as the initiate hero, spreads across a whole central section of the text (Chapters 9-16) and functions as a kind of initiation of the reader also. In the Alexandre sequence - which we called sequence B in Chapter 1 - the death of his lover Daniel in Chapter 9 of the novel is followed by that of his dog Sam in Chapter 11, and these bereavements impel him to stage-manage his own death in Chapter 13. The intervening sequence A chapters are equally punctuated by death and loss. Alexandre's brother Edouard is bereft first of his new mistress Angelica in Chapter 10, then of both his Parisian mistress Florence and his wife Maria-Barbara in Chapter 12, which completes his devastation. Edouard's life is in a sense a failed initiation: while he suffers the ordeals necessary to the initiatic process, he does not have the character or the vocation to turn them to good account, and all his efforts to impose a heroic stamp on his life are doomed to failure. By contrast Paul, suffering similar bereavements in the loss of his mother and uncle and the flight of his twin, is called to a voyage of discovery and enlightenment. His journey, at its start, is still marked by the shadow of death. He goes first to Venice, where his two interlocutors, Signor Colombo and Hamida, insist on Venice's aura of mortality: 'Venise est un très bon endroit pour mourir' (432), 'La mort est sur cette ville. Comment ne sentez-vous pas la menace terrible qui pèse sur elle?' (458).[15] At El-Kantara he finds Deborah's two graves (symbolising the death of the twin relationship in its old form?) and the grieving widower, Ralph. Ralph is, like Edouard, devastated by his loss and incapable of further growth: it is another initiatic failure, placed as a foil to Paul's own resolute progression from here on.

Symbolic Death and Rebirth

Initiation traditionally involves the symbolic death of the subject, so that he can be reborn to some higher status. 'La mort initiatique est indispensable au "commencement" de la vie spirituelle.'[16]

One figuration of this ritual death can be a sojourn (like Jonah's) in the belly of a monster, whence derives the symbolism of the Harrowing of Hell, 'hell being regularly represented in iconography by the "toothed gullet of an aged shark"'.[17] The tunnel beneath Berlin into which Paul must descend is described as a 'boyau', whose first meaning is intestine (but which was commonly used to refer to trenches in the First World War). When the tunnel collapses, the surge of mud mixed with the debris of the metal supports which crush him is likened to jaws and steel teeth (*Mét* 603). When he relives the nightmare of that moment, he sees 'la gueule béante, hérissée des crocs d'un requin' (*Mét* 605).[18] Tournier is deploying here an archetypal ritual of passage into the body of Mother Earth: 'le novice est censé pénétrer dans le corps de la Grande Mère Chthonienne, monstre de formes diverses, mais pourvu en tout cas de dents menaçantes [...].'[19]

The theme of the descent underground as a symbol of death/rebirth is a significant feature of each of Tournier's first three novels, and has an important place in the initiatic pattern which the novels present. It can take the form either of a descent into the underworld or alternatively of a regression to the womb as with Robinson's descent into the grotto.[20] Tiffauges, we may recall, declares himself scandalised by how much less interested his fellow humans are in life before birth than in life after death (*RA* 13), and Robinson's temporary sortie out of his normal existence is in accordance with this curiosity. This excursion out of current time, back to a point of origin, has an evident initiatic function. It is the necessary prelude to the growth of the new Robinson, who will eventually break out of linear time altogether. At the final crisis-point in the initiatic structure of *Vendredi,* the ordeal of despair after Vendredi's departure, the grotto becomes the place of death as well as birth, in which he thinks to take eternal refuge: 'Là il lui suffirait de se mettre en posture foetale et de fermer les yeux pour que la vie l'abandonne, si total était son épuisement, si profonde sa tristesse'(*VLP* 252). It is precisely from this 'étroit orifice' that new hope and new life emerge in the shape of the cabin-boy Jaan. Likewise, the foetal position in which Jean-Paul consummate their ritual seminal exchange nourishes their bonding, but by its very infantile closure signifies a kind of sterility, the impossibility of growth: as in Robinson's grotto, birth and death are in close proximity.

In *Le Roi des aulnes* also, crucial turning points in the narrative take place underground: Nestor dies in a fire in the cellars of the school, after being sent to stoke the boilers, and it is similarly in a cellar that Tiffauges is seized as the supposed rapist of Martine. These are both infernal images, of death by fire and of nightmarish retribution,[21] and each marks a decisive stage in Tiffauges's development. Nestor's death signifies for Abel his coming-of-age, the moment when he must assume his own destiny, while the Martine affair leads directly to his involvement in the war. The first ejects him from the protective realm of Nestor's tutelage; the second will thrust him out of safe anonymity and ultimately out of France. A later passage underground has by contrast a benign aspect: it is by a covered trench ('ruelle souterraine', 'étroit boyau' (*RA* 265-6)) that Tiffauges will reach the refuge of the forest hut he calls 'le Canada', 'un mot qui plongeait dans son plus lointain passé' (267). Like Robinson's dive into the grotto, it is a symbolic and therapeutic revisiting of a starting-point, when he can touch the imprint of the 'mémoire profonde et secrète de son enfance' (282). The mythical status of a descent into the earth, what one might call inhumation, is progressively emphasised in *Le Roi des aulnes*, and is linked to the novel's presiding, titular legend. The first references to the Erlking evoke, naturally enough, the malevolent wood-deity of Goethe's ballad, whose attempted abduction of a boy leads to the child's death: this figure symbolises the malign aspect of the theme of *phorie* and in particular of *pédéphorie* (carrying a child). Later, however, after hearing Professor Keil give the name Erlking to an exhumed bog-corpse, Tiffauges begins to think of this legendary figure rather as an earth-spirit, sleeping underground, beyond time and history: '[...] Roi des Aulnes, immergé dans les marécages, protégé, par une lourde nappe de limon, de toutes les atteintes [...]'(531). His final sense of joy as, bearing Ephraïm on his shoulders, he is sucked down into the marsh derives in part from the implied conviction that he is symbolically becoming the Erlking, in this second, infinitely less malign aspect of timeless, subterranean sleeper, and that he is thereby entering a zone of refuge beyond reach of humankind.

Sacrifice or Mutilation of the Body

As Northrop Frye points out in an outline of the tradition of the quest-romance, 'Mutilation or physical handicap, which combines the themes of *sparagmos* [tearing to pieces] and ritual death, is often the price of unusual wisdom or power'.[22] '[...] Ce voyage,' writes Paul in *Les Météores*, 'devait me mener sous le mur de Berlin à seule fin que j'y subisse les *mutilations rituelles nécessaires* à l'accession à une autre ubiquité' (618 - my emphasis). Here Tournier is showing his hand, and making the self-consciously anthropological structure of his narrative explicit. This theme of bodily sacrifice as the price of vocation is clearly present too in *Le Roi des aulnes* and in the story of Taor in *Gaspard*.

Fertility

Bearing the mark of his ordeal on his body, Paul returns to La Cassine to preside there, taking the place of his deceased father. The old King has perished, and the new King comes, bringing a promise of new fertility, as in rituals described by Frazer in *The Golden Bough*.[23] Maria-Barbara's seemingly endless fertility dried up, we recall, with the birth of the twins, and the twin-cell itself is consistently presented as 'sterile'. The novel enters its 'valley of death', as Maria-Barbara, the symbol of fertility, is snatched from them, and Paul shatters the relationship between Jean and Sophie, with its fragile promise of new growth. Only by seeking the wisdom of the four corners of the earth and by pitting himself against the power of the underworld can Paul reclaim the winds, the breath of life.[24] The fertility ultimately achieved by Tournier's heroes has, however, nothing to do with procreation: it takes the form, rather, of a self enriched by becoming the channel of fertile exchange between earth and heaven, physical and supernatural: between island and sun (Robinson), marsh and star (Tiffauges), beach and wind (Paul).

Incorporation and Spiritualisation of the Beloved

The loss of the mentor through death (Nestor) or through sudden and definitive departure (Vendredi, Jean) is part of the ordeal for the initiate, but it is of course a necessary stage in his accession to higher status. While the physical presence of the mentor is withdrawn, his spirit remains as an indelible presence. The function of the mentor is always to enlarge the horizon of the initiate. On a prosaically literal level, Vendredi encourages Robinson to explore the island's coastline from the sea, and to conquer his fear of heights; Nestor takes Abel to normally inaccessible parts of the school at night, and lends him his bicycle for an excursion. Paul is obliged to trail breathlessly in Jean's wake as he leaves their bed to set off on a hectic run towards the ebb-tide (176-7). These geographical extensions are just the visible sign of the mental and spiritual outreach which it is the mentor's function to stimulate. Robinson, 'l'homme de la terre', is 'arraché à son trou par le génie éolien', Vendredi, and transformed from an earth-bound larva into a glittering butterfly, 'un être de soleil' (*VLP* 226). This metaphor of his development is manifested in the text by the transition from his pre-Vendredi larva-like state in the grotto to his post-Vendredi apotheosis at sunrise. In a still more explicit metaphor of this liberating extension of self, his totemic animal, Andoar, is sacrificed by Vendredi in ritual combat and the parts of his body opened to the elements. The mentor thus acts out for Robinson a spectacular parable of his own potential evolution: once Robinson has successfully decoded its meaning, in his logbook in Chapter 10 (*VLP* 227), Vendredi's task is complete and he can be evacuated from the text, to leave space for Robinson to grow to his full spiritual stature. Likewise, in *Le Roi des aulnes*, Nestor's body disappears in fire and smoke, but his voice remains interiorised in Abel's consciousness as a constant incitement to him to assume his (supposed) destiny, which will take him by stages on his initiatic journey eastward. Paul, in *Les Météores*, is also 'arraché à son trou'. He is launched on his travels by the double example of Jean and Alexandre, but he finally transcends both. With Jean's departure, his condition of bereaved twin approximates to that of Alexandre, the 'sans-pareil' in restless search of a partner. The scope of Alexandre's wanderings is limited however to the sites of his private empire, and once he leaves France he perishes; Paul's journeys, by contrast, span the globe. Similarly, while he starts his journey by trailing in Jean's footsteps, he overtakes him in Canada - a sign that his journey has developed its own dynamic, and that Jean's function as guide is redundant. Like Vendredi, Jean can now be evacuated from the text, his role in the initiation process complete.[25]

As we have mentioned, these mentors are not just teachers, but also the objects of the intense love of the initiate, so that their 'absorption' by the initiate is also an act of love. In *Le Roi des aulnes* in particular, this worshipful ingestion of the beloved can imply vampirism, as when Tiffauges euphorically sucks the blood from his hero Pelsenaire's wounded knee (31). Later, Tiffauges reverently eats the bodies of the three pigeons he has cherished, and insofar as the three birds and their impaling on the spit by the soldiers is a carefully contrived anticipation of the fate of the three boys impaled on swords, it suggests a metaphor of cannibalism, the process of eating what you love. Prior to this, in the final paragraph of the long first part of the novel, Abel describes in provocative terms his taking of the Eucharist: 'Communié ce matin avec des transports secrets [...] Fraîcheur revigorante de la chair pantelante de l'Enfant Jésus sous le voile transparent de la sèche petite hostie de pain azyme' (207). Here Holy Communion is associated not only with erotic titillation (desirable flesh beneath a see-through veil) but with Tiffauges's ogrish appetites for raw meat[26] - he resents the fact that the faithful are denied

Communion wine, whereby the flesh would be 'arrosée de son sang chaud'. While Tournier's formulation here has a certain shock value (enhanced by its placing at the end of a major section), it is based on a literal reading of transubstantiation, of the bread and wine as consubstantial with the flesh and blood of Christ, worshipfully eaten and drunk by those who love Him. It is part of Tournier's purpose, as we have seen in Chapter 4 above, to restore the part of religion concerned with the appetites and the senses. A more joyfully sensual scene of sacramental eating concludes *Pierrot ou les secrets de la nuit* when Pierrot and Arlequin share the loaf cooked in the shape of Colombine's body (*MA* 276). In the closing pages of *Gaspard*, it is granted to the heterodox fourth Wise Man, Taor, to be, instead of a witness to the Nativity like his three predecessors, a late participant in the Last Supper - not only seeing the Word made flesh, but tasting it. This ingestion of the essence of his Master in its original manifestation completes his initiation-quest, and leads directly to his apotheosis.[27]

The fleshly dimension is thus a significant ingredient in these relationships: Robinson and Vendredi examine and admire each other's bodies (221-2, 224-5), Nestor stresses bodily functions and transmits to Abel his own devotion to ingestion-digestion-defecation, while Jean-Paul's togetherness is constantly confirmed by erotic exchange. Nevertheless, Tournier's metaphysical dynamic always carries his heroes beyond this, towards a spiritual communion which is prepared by, and transcends, incorporation. As Paul's friend, the priest Thomas Koussek puts it, in religious terms, 'Le Christ doit être dépassé' (*Mét* 154). Referring to Jesus' words in St John's Gospel (Ch.14), he argues that Christ's task was to prepare the central event in Christianity, which was Pentecost, the coming of the Holy Spirit. Seeing himself as Christ's twin, he has a fixation on the body of Christ, as Paul discovers when he finds Thomas in the crypt of his church embracing a life-sized statue of Christ on the Cross. Salvation, and release from his anguish, comes to Thomas when he accepts the death of Christ as the necessary preliminary to the advent of the Spirit, accepts that the person of Christ is now replaced by a ubiquitous and benign power. This pattern, encoded in theological terms, provides the interpretative key for the ending, in which the person of the lost twin (now Jean) is replaced by Paul's sense of communion with 'les météores', a realm of meteorological phenomena saturated with the symbolism of the Holy Spirit: ubiquity, unpredictability, fire, wind, bird imagery. In the Bible, Christ's characterisation of the Holy Spirit in John 3:8 ('The wind bloweth where it listeth, and thou [...] canst not tell whence it cometh, and whither it goeth: so is every one that is born of the Spirit'[28]) anticipates the 'rushing mighty wind' of Pentecost (Acts of the Apostles 2:2), when the tongues of fire descend and the apostles are given the gifts of speech. Paul experiences a thunderstorm of wind and fire which is simultaneously outside and within himself: 'Puis la grande colère de l'orage a grondé dans ma poitrine et mes larmes ont commencé à rouler sur les vitres de la véranda' (*Mét* 621). He recognises that the wind 'bloweth where it listeth': 'Misère de la météorologie qui ne connaît la vie du ciel que de l'extérieur et prétend la réduire à des modèles mécaniques. Les démentis constants que les intempéries infligent à ses prévisions n'ébranlent pas son obstination stupide' (624). Only one who has undergone the initiatic process and who has attained the mage-like status of which his mutilation is the emblem can claim this higher knowledge: 'Il manque au physicien pour le savoir une dimension, celle précisément qui plonge en moi, articulant mon corps gauche déployé sur mon corps droit estropié' (624). His 'corps gauche'[29] is the body of Jean, appropriated and spiritualised, 'déployé sur la mer comme une grande aile sensible' (623), recalling the iconography of the Holy Spirit as a bird, as at the baptism of Christ. The process of 'sublimation' described in the final paragraph concerns the direct transformation of a solid into a gas, of snow into vapour. Here again Tournier has found an admirably concrete image for the process whereby, in the pagan version, the body of the twin is replaced by a magic knowledge of nature, and in the Christian version the body of Christ makes way for the Holy Spirit. In a remarkable balancing act physical science and metaphysics, Christianity and pantheism, the literal and the metaphoric are held in balance, to create a free space of interpretation which enacts the openness which the text, through Paul's voice, advocates.

Initiatic patterns, like the traditional lore of the elements, place the novelist of modernity in a relationship to archetypal patterns which can touch deep chords in the cultural consciousness of the reader. While the play of the elements can inform the relationship of characters to their environments, and by extension their whole temperament, the patterns of initiation can provide strong models for plot structure. Robinson's ascent of the ladder of elements in *Vendredi* combines both. The other feature of the magical mode of initiation which leads Tournier into a fantastic rather than realist mode of writing is that individuals become exemplary heroes, following a path of emancipation and transformation according to values and patterns which transcend them. We shall consider this subordination of character to pattern further in the final chapter. For the present, we can say that Tournier's fiction illustrates how, for the contemporary novelist, the anthropologist's records and interpretations of fundamental patterns of human behaviour and belief can be an inexhaustible source of reflection and of raw material: Tournier's contact with Lévi-Strauss and other anthropologists clearly nourished his fascination with the semiology of culture, and enriched the explorations of it which his novels embody. This anthropological underpinning carries a major advantage: it acts as a kind of alibi, enabling the novelist implicitly to lay claim to the authority of archetypal experience while stretching the bounds of realism to the utmost.

Notes to Chapter Seven

[1] The rewritten versions are 'simpler' in the sense that much of the explicit exposition of ideas has been sifted out. To those readers alert to the play of ideology and symbol which remains implied in these distilled texts, they may seem not simpler, but denser. See Michael Worton, 'Michel Tournier and the masterful art of rewriting', *PN Review* 41 (vol.11, no. 3: 1984), 24-5 and 'Ecrire et ré-ecrire: le projet de Tournier', *Sud* 61 (1986), 52-69.

[2] *Le Vent Paraclet*, 56. For Tournier's views on this subject, see e.g. 'Quand Michel Tournier récrit ses livres pour les enfants', *Le Monde* (24.12.71), 13,20 ; 'Les Enfants dans la bibliothèque', *Le Nouvel Observateur* 369 (6-12.12.71), 56-7; 'Point de vue d'un éducateur', *Le Monde* (20.12.74), 20.

[3] For an extensive survey of this fictional genre, see Erhard Reckwitz, *Die Robinsonade: Themen und Formen einer literarischen Gattung* (Amsterdam, B.R. Grüner, 1976). In the chapter on *Vendredi* in *Le Vent Paraclet*, Tournier shows that he is very aware of the metamorphoses which this story has undergone, and acknowledges a particular debt to Jules Verne's *L'Ile mystérieuse* (*VPar* 219).

[4] Tournier's enthusiasm for ethnographic detail can be traced to his studies at the Musée de l'Homme (*VPar* 227). See also 'Claude Lévi-Strauss, mon maître', *Figaro littéraire* 1420 (26.5.73), 15,18. In an interview with Jean Prasteau, Tournier confirms this in some detail: 'Je me revois encore dans le hall de M. Leroi-Gourhan, m'exerçant sous sa direction au maniement du boomerang... Et la pêche au cerf-volant... Encore un emprunt à mon professeur. On le pratique dans les îles Salomon.' See 'Comme Robinson, Michel Tournier a trouvé son île déserte', *Figaro littéraire* 1127 (20-26.11.67), 24-5.

[5] Simone Vierne, *Jules Verne, mythe et modernité* (Paris, P.U.F., 1989), 120.

[6] Vierne, *Jules Verne*, 11; see also her *Rite, roman, initiation*, 2nd edn. (Grenoble, 1987), 66 (hereafter referred to as *Rite*).

[7] Most of the major critical works on Tournier deal, in various ways, with the initiatic aspect of Tournier's fictions. Bouloumié asserts with good reason that Tournier 'renoue avec une longue tradition mythique où le héros plonge, au cours d'un voyage initiatique, dans les ténèbres de la mort, pour en surgir autre, égal aux dieux' (*Michel Tournier*, 155). Elsewhere she discusses *Vendredi*

both as an initiatic and as an alchemical novel: see her *Vendredi de Michel Tournier*, 124-49.

[8] This is not to suggest that the more magical-metaphysical tradition is not present in French fiction, in writers such as Villiers de l'Isle-Adam and Huysmans. It has arguably been undervalued in importance, while it is the realist wing which has been the more influential and highly-considered.

[9] Éliade, *Naissances mystiques* (Paris, Gallimard, 1959), 10.

[10] Vierne (*Rite*, 38) refers to Jung and Frobenius as attesting to this recurrent, archetypal orientation to the East.

[11] The overwhelming weight of tradition, in anthropology and literature, makes the subject of this kind of initiation male, not female: see e.g. Vierne, *Rite*, 60.

[12] Vierne, *Rite*, 61.

[13] Vierne, *Rite*, 17 (a 'myste' is a candidate undergoing initiation). On the function of exile in Tournier, see Rosello, *L'In-différence chez Michel Tournier*, 153-60.

[14] A similar motif of the execution of a pseudo-twin is used by Stendhal in *Le Rouge et le noir* (Part I, Ch.5), when the young Julien Sorel inexplicably finds in church a newspaper cutting relating to the execution of one Louis Jenrel, whose name happens to be an anagram of his own. In both cases, the reader is implicitly invited to regard the 'coincidence' as a sign of the exceptional destiny of the hero. See Stendhal, *Le Rouge et le noir*, ed. P.-G. Castex (Paris, Garnier, 1973), 24-5.

[15] The powerful link between Venice and death, celebrated in Thomas Mann's novella *Der Tod in Venedig* (*Death in Venice*), is explored in Tournier's preface, entitled 'Venise ou la tête coupée', to a volume of photographs by Fulvio Roiter, *Venise hier et demain* (Paris, Chêne, 1973).

[16] Éliade, *Naissances mystiques*, 16. See also Vierne, *Rite*, 7,19.

[17] Northrop Frye, *Anatomy of Criticism* (Princeton, Princeton University Press, 1957), 190. The Harrowing of Hell, when Christ leads the souls of the damned out of Hell, is traditionally situated between the Crucifixion and the Resurrection. The reference to Paul's 'corps crucifié' (*Mét* 603) as he undertakes his 'descente aux enfers' (*Mét* 599) might also suggest this analogy.

[18] A similar metaphor of the underground labyrinth as the body of a monster pervades Zola's *Germinal*, where Etienne Lantier's equally near-fatal ordeal also prepares a final sense of regeneration.

[19] Vierne, *Rite*, 20. See also Eliade, *Naissances mystiques*, 81-4, 111-12. Such regression, says Eliade (111), may be safe or it may be dangerous, involving the risk of being torn apart in the monster's mouth or the *vagina dentata* of the Earth Mother. A broader view of the motif is given by Bachelard in the chapter headed 'Le complexe de Jonas' in *La Terre et les rêveries du repos* (129-82).

[20] 'Selon Paracelse, "celui qui veut entrer dans le royaume de Dieu doit retourner au sein de sa mère, ou même cohabiter avec elle". Le *regressus ad uterum* est parfois présenté sous la forme d'un inceste avec la Mère.' (Eliade, *Naissances mystiques*, 121-2, where he refers to his earlier study *Forgerons et alchimistes* (Paris, Gallimard, 1956, 159)). This notion of regression clearly coincides with Robinson's experiences and concerns in the grotto, as well as casting a new light on the biblical injunction to become like a child in order to enter the kingdom of God, whose implications were discussed in the previous chapter.

[21] Tiffauges goes on to suffer a 'nuit d'enfer' in prison, obscenely false

accusations of the 'diablesse' Martine and six hours of ferocious interrogation in 'une pièce exiguë, surchauffée, laide et banale comme l'enfer' (*RA* 197-8).

[22] Northrop Frye, *Anatomy of Criticism*, 193. He quotes the examples of Woden's willingness to give up an eye to learn powerful secrets, of the crippled smith Hephaistos and of Jacob's wound in his struggle with the angel.

[23] Sir James Frazer, *The Golden Bough*, abridged edn. (London, Macmillan, 1929), 269.

[24] 'Dans l'ivresse de l'extase nous sommes montés sur le char des vents. Vous, mortels, vous ne pouvez apercevoir que notre corps... L'extatique est le cheval du vent, l'ami du dieu de la tempête...' So speaks the *muni* (ecstatic) in the *Rig-Veda*. Quoted in M. Eliade, *Le Chamanisme et les techniques archaïques de l'extase* (Paris, Payot, 1951), 365-6.

[25] This interpretation suggests that it is pointless to wonder, as some critics have done, what becomes of Vendredi once he has left on the *Whitebird*, or indeed of Jean at the end of *Les Météores*. They are written out of the text for structural reasons, and in a text which focuses on the evolution of the (undoubted) central character, their subsequent fate is not of intrinsic interest.

[26] The word 'fraîcheur' is used throughout the novel in connection with Tiffauges's desire for flesh, especially of young boys. The epigraph from Perrault's 'Le Petit Poucet', placed at the head of Chapter 4, consolidates the link to the myth of the Ogre.

[27] In terms of the anthropological logic of ritual-initiation, the novice may be required to eat the flesh of another man in order to acquire his wisdom or strength.

[28] A more standard modern translation, as in the New English Bible, reads 'The wind blows where it wills'.

[29] Just as it was Tiffauges's left hand that revealed a new dimension to his being in the 'Écrits sinistres', the epiphany of new insight is again associated with the left side, the shadowy, hidden wing of human life.

8

The Escape from History

There is in Tournier a profound aversion to history. He is a spokesman for that voice in the human psyche which refuses to accept that it is limited in its significance and range by the parameters of time and space of a single life lived. His writing is a revolt against chronological and topological localisation.

His fictional output has progressively favoured the 'conte', where time and place are unspecific and often fabulous, over his earlier, more historically specific mode of fiction. Even in his more realist works the prestige of the historical framework is constantly challenged. This challenge is carried first and foremost by the attitude of the hero. Robinson becomes addicted to the ahistorical limbo into which the accident of shipwreck has led him, and refuses re-entry into the stream of history when the arrival of the *Whitebird* makes this possible. Specifically, the events of the American War of Independence are viewed with the supercilious disdain of one now accustomed to a cosmic perspective. In *Les Météores*, the events take place between the 1930s and the 1960s, as the *prière d'insérer* reminds us. However, that roller-coaster period of French and European history does not shape the story. It is the source of occasional brutal intrusions which disrupt the characters' lives - the death or deportation of the women around Edouard, Paul's involvement in the Berlin Wall crisis - but in the absence of any sense of historical continuity in the novel, these calamities appear as instruments of destiny designed to encompass the personal collapse of the one (Edouard) and the eventual apotheosis of the other (Paul). Maria-Barbara's arrest and deportation is wholly unprepared - no previous hint has been given of her Resistance activity - with the result that it has the appearance of a natural disaster, akin to the storm which destroys the similarly enclosed idyll of Ralph and Deborah. The most historically rooted of all Tournier's novels is *Le Roi des aulnes*, where the specifics of military and civilian life of the period have often been carefully researched. Yet even here it can be seen that the authoritative voice of the historiographer implicitly yields to the self-centred view of Tiffauges.

The narrative of *Le Roi des aulnes* can be seen as a dialogue between self and history. It would be convenient to see the diary mode of the 'Écrits sinistres' as the voice of self, and the third-person narrative as the voice of history. In reality the relationship between the two modes is more subtle than that, as can be seen for example in the opening pages of Part VI of the novel, headed 'L'Astrophore'. Here an initial segment of five paragraphs of third-person narrative (527-31) soon gives way to a two-page diary entry (532-4). On closer examination, however, the juxtaposition of point of view is not as obvious as this might suggest, and the transition from one mode to the other is carefully prepared.

The opening paragraph of narrative ('Les derniers combats de l'année 1944 eurent pour enjeu en Prusse-Orientale la ville de Goldap [...]') is wholly historical in its discourse, setting out the military situation and the cruel dilemma of the civilian population, forced to delay their flight until the last possible moment. It could, without amendment, be included in a non-fictional work on the Eastern Front. The second paragraph presents the testimony of Tiffauges, 'témoin de ce lamentable exode', and in particular an incident in which a horse is impaled on the shaft of a cart in the crush of vehicles: this is history as anecdote, as 'fait divers', micro-history rather than the macro-history of the first paragraph, and now centred on Tiffauges as focalising character.

The third paragraph focuses attention on Tiffauges's reactions to what he sees. He is 'impressionné par le spectacle de l'exode', mentally compares it to that of the French in 1940, which now seems positively idyllic by comparison ('un embarquement pour Cythère'), and recalls a prayer from the Bible. In the spectacle of the impaled horse he senses some symbolic or heraldic figure whose meaning remains obscure. The paragraph ends with the still more shocking sight of a human body which has been trampled into the mud and crushed out of all recognition: this new horror is 'dépourvu de toute aura symbolique'. There are thus three important developments here. Firstly, Tiffauges has moved from being a mere witness to being the subject of the narrative, in his reactions and reflections. Secondly, there is a momentary movement to abstraction, as the record of historical situations and incidents gives way to a play of memory (of 1940), of intertextual- mythological reference (Cythère, Bible) and of symbolic-heraldic figures. Thirdly, this movement is itself called into question as it is confronted with a vision of brutally mangled flesh which seems wholly resistant to incorporation within some symbolic system of meaning.

The fourth and fifth paragraphs repeat this movement from *témoignage* to reaction to symbolic intuition. He meets hundreds of his fellow-countrymen, liberated prisoners of war, now making their way westward on foot, shod with boots of rags and paper. From his polished jackboots they take him to be German, and he does not disabuse them, recognising the gulf which had always divided him from his fellow Frenchmen. As he returns to the castle he is haunted by the image of the Erlking, buried deep in the marsh, out of reach of the vagaries of history.

The narrative logic of this concluding evocation of the Erlking is far from clear. It does not arise naturally or directly from the encounter with the French POWs, but erupts irrationally and spontaneously both as an icon of his visceral allegiance to Germany and as a dream of eternity, beyond history. One further observation can be made regarding the final sentence which proposes the Erlking image: 'Il eut bientôt oublié cette rencontre [with the POWs], car il appartenait désormais à cette Prusse qui croulait autour de lui, mais il fut hanté jusqu'à son arrivée au château par l'image du Roi des Aulnes [...]' (531). It is the last sentence before the return to the diary mode of the 'Écrits sinistres', and it could easily be recast in the first person to become part of such a diary entry: 'J'ai vite oublié cette rencontre, car j'appartiens désormais à cette Prusse qui croule autour de moi, mais j'ai été hanté jusqu'à mon arrivée au château', etc. Thus a smooth transition to diary mode is assured, with the final switch to first-person writing emerging as the crystallisation of a focus and a voice which has already unobtrusively taken control of a narrative section which started out as impersonally historical.

It can be seen from this brief analysis of one small section that while Tiffauges's voice is most directly mediated through the diary, it is by no means confined to it. The narrative sections enact their own dialectic between a conventional, notionally authoritative and independent view of history and the play of personal emotion, memory, intertextual and cultural reference which constitutes Tiffauges's 'reading' of that history and his place within it. The gap between self and history which any such reading must seek to bridge becomes itself an insistent preoccupation of the discourse. This figure of the gap emerges implicitly or explicitly at three points in the short section under consideration. Firstly, the mangled body represents the sense in which the brute and bloody facts resist assimilation into the abstractions and symbolic patterns which Tiffauges cultivates.

Secondly, Tiffauges recognises the 'distance infranchissable' separating his essential self from the group to which, historically and culturally, he belongs. Finally, this independence from history is extended to mystic identification with the Erlking as a being who is protected from history, secure within a dimension beyond time where such ephemeral events are irrelevant.

The tension between these two poles of Self and History does not function simply as a play of alternative (impersonal/personal) narrative modes. It operates within the supposedly impersonal narrative, as a struggle for narrative authority, with the voice of Tiffauges striving to take control of the creation of meaning in the text.[1] It implies a debate about the political relationship between self and history. The historiographical discourse starts with the public and collective dimension, and carries the conventional implication that history, as a context to the individual and transcending the individual, is largely beyond individual control. History sets limits to what we do, and substantially determines our lives: it is the house through which we move. Events in the novel, such as the fire at Saint-Christophe, Tiffauges's arrest, the outbreak of war, his capture and internment and so on - events over which he had no practical control - can be seen conventionally in this light. History is the cause, and individual life significantly its product.

The 'Écrits sinistres', however, as the main carrier of the voice of Self, set out from the very start to develop the reverse view. 'Je crois, oui, à ma nature féerique, je veux dire à cette connivence secrète qui mêle en profondeur mon aventure personnelle au cours des choses, et lui permet de l'incliner dans son sens' (13). In a metaphor which evokes magnetic attraction or gravitational pull ('l'incliner dans son sens'), Self ('mon aventure personnelle') is accorded precedence over History ('le cours des choses') which it can divert onto its own path. The trajectory of history is shaped, in this view, by the force of self, rather than the other way round, and the vocabulary of the passage undermines the would-be rational empiricism of historiography: 'féerie' is substituted for causality, the power of personal conviction ('je crois, oui') for empirical evidence, and the play of hidden powers and affinities ('connivence secrète') for the collective determinisms of public history.

It follows that the self that can change history is not limited by history, that it must by its 'féerique' nature transcend history. Tiffauges goes on, in these opening pages, to claim that he possesses supernatural power due to the 'antiquité vertigineuse de [ses] origines'. 'Quand la terre n'était encore qu'une boule de feu tournoyant dans un ciel d'hélium, l'âme qui la faisait flamber, qui la faisait tourner, c'était la mienne' (13). In a swift escalation of the gravitational metaphor of 'l'incliner dans son sens' he now instals himself as the Supreme Being, the Principle of Creation, in a breathtaking egocentricity which literally sees the cosmos as revolving around him. The 'Écrits sinistres' will continue to emphasise the extent to which Tiffauges explains the destruction around him as instrumental in the working out of his own destiny. After the fire at Saint-Christophe he is astonished that others are blind to the 'relation évidente, éclatante qui unissait cet incendie et mon destin personnel' (103), and when the whole of Europe faces the conflagration of war, he alone knows, 'et pour cause', why it must be so (206). Near the end of the novel, the collapse of the Eastern Front and the devastation of Prussia are to be understood, through the diary, as necessary steps to his pre-ordained rise to power: 'Il n'en fallait pas moins pour soumettre ce pays et ses enfants aux exigences de mon impérieuse tendresse' (534).

The source of the power over history to which he lays claim, and the key to his sense of special destiny, lies in his conviction that he belongs to 'la race ogresse', a dynasty of beings that stands outside history and is untouched by time. Ogres, like other monsters, are, we are informed, sterile (14), which constitutes another mark of their atemporality: their line is not bound by the succession of generations produced by procreation and governed by genetic history.[2]

The novel pursues the dialogue between Tiffauges - ogre, monster, exceptional being - and the claims of race and history. When he goes to Germany, his chosen land, he encounters in Nazi ideology a preoccupation with the relationship between race and history as expounded, for instance, by the fanatical eugenicist Dr Blättchen, whose life work is the classification of racial characteristics. Blättchen's thesis is that heredity, the inheritance of blood, counts for everything, while the cultural context counts for little. Aryan superiority is genetically guaranteed. Tiffauges's reaction to this line of thought is mixed. On one level he recognises that Blättchen's bloodthirsty enthusiasm for the extermination of racially inferior types could readily apply to the likes of him (431-3). However, Tiffauges himself claims a special, pre-ordained status for the members of his own 'race', marked out by certain physical and behavioural characteristics, and his notion of the mass of ordinary, lesser mortals being 'punished' for failing to recognise and honour this privileged destiny which he incarnates ('le châtiment prévu et mérité de la plèbe veule' (234)) is not so far removed from Blättchen's advocacy. Admittedly his non-genetic definition of his own 'race' is radically different to Blättchen's concept, in that it rejects any allegiance to science or physiological causality in favour of a mysteriously metaphysical and supernatural continuum. That said, each claims for his race of the elect a superior transcendent vocation which has its roots in the distant past and which places them beyond ordinary moral accountability in the historical present. Tiffauges comments penetratingly on Nazism's rejection of time and historical progress: 'L'hitlérisme est réfractaire à toute idée de progrès, de création, de découverte et d'invention d'un avenir vierge. Sa vertu n'est pas de rupture, mais de restauration: culte de la race, des ancêtres, du sang, des morts, de la terre...' (413-4). The tone of the comment is neutral, not hostile, and the reader is left to reflect on Tiffauges's own abiding obsession with all the cult elements he mentions: his 'race' and his 'ancestors', blood, death, earth... Thus behind Tiffauges's interpreting voice the constituent elements of his ideological complicity with Nazism are developed, a disturbing mirror-image which will enable him to see Weidmann, Goering and eventually Hitler himself as avatars of the ogre type to which he himself is assigned from the opening line of the text.[3]

   This non-genetic genealogy of ogres develops as a shadowy dynasty, pursued further and further back in time. Since he is as eternal as the world, Tiffauges declares, he can have only 'un père et une mère putatifs, et des enfants d'adoption'(14). The putative parent he finds in Nestor 'dont je procède indiscutablement'(37), while he himself plays a variety of paternal and maternal roles, benign and malign, towards children, culminating in his adoption of the orphaned Ephraïm. This pattern matches Robinson's rejection of the patriarchal model (see Chapter 3), and his acceptance of the path indicated by the pseudo-father (Van Deyssel), the enclosing presence and multiple roles of a pseudo-mother (Speranza) and pseudo-twin (Vendredi), crowned by the gift at last of an adoptive orphaned child. Beyond Nestor, the immediate 'progenitor' and source of an alternative authority structure in the school, stand Weidmann and Rasputin, execrated respectively by the representatives of public order and the writers of history. The development of Tiffauges's 'alternative dynasty' is linked in this way to the rejection of society's value-structures and of the history it tells itself. Like Nestor sitting at his raised desk in one corner of the classroom gazing out through the only pane of clear glass, Abel will throughout occupy a place at the edge of institutions and their history, and his attention will be fixed elsewhere, on a dimension they know not of. The indefinable age of Nestor, 'adulte nain' or 'bébé géant'(36), suggests a being over which time has no certain hold. 'Rien d'étonnant dès lors,' concludes Abel, 'que Nestor - dont je procède indiscutablement - échappât comme moi-même à la mesure du temps...'(37). Death itself has no dominion over Nestor, since his being passes into Tiffauges ('il revit en moi, je suis Nestor' (204)). As was seen in Chapter 6, not only is Nestor's voice inscribed in his consciousness, it becomes the transmitter of intertexts which broaden the alternative dynasty of forbears outside the limits of history into fiction, myth and legend. The descendance suggested in Nestor's intertexts represents the non-genetic equivalent of transmitted characteristics. Tiffauges is programmed with the actions and traits of his 'forbears', and destined (as supposed rapist and collaborator) to share the calumny poured on Weidmann or Rasputin.

By this whole process, the frontiers of history as an exclusive and privileged domain of causal explanation are exploded, and it becomes merely a sector in the wider hinterland of human culture - and not even the most fertile one. This annexation of history by myth is parodied 'en abîme' by the spurious theories of Professor Keil, when he names the bog-corpse the 'Erlking' and suggests a fanciful parallel with the Last Supper. The dedication of the novel to the memory ('mémoire diffamée') of Rasputin takes its significance from the acute sense of the injustice of history. Tournier's novel is symbolically redemptive of Rasputin, in taking another victim of public calumny who adopts and heals a child in times of war. The historical discourse which simply demonises a Rasputin or a Gilles de Rais is injected with elements of fiction and myth until an entirely new story emerges. Tournier's constant and multiple intertextuality, his insistence at the end of *Le Médianoche amoureux* on the sacrality of repeating and reflecting what has already been created, is another way of refusing history. The specificity, the here-and-nowness of the text is compromised by allusions, quotations and self-quotations which make it a place of dialogue between past ages, writers, thinkers and traditions. In this sense it shares a post-modern taste for assembling ready-made components in an attempt simultaneously to recapitulate history and to deny its power. On the opening page, Tiffauges asserts that his interest is in his origins, not in the after-life: 'L'en-deçà vaut bien l'au-delà, d'autant plus qu'il en détient probablement la clé' (13). This is a declaration of allegiance to a quest that will move through the novel against the flow of time. The tracing of Tiffauges's 'forbears' moves backwards from persons actually encountered, Nestor and Weidmann, to distant forbears, Albuquerque, Saint Christopher, Abel, the Erlking. Thus within the inexorable chronology of the historical setting of the war, the novel pursues an ever-broadening anti-historical perspective which finally eclipses the accidents of history to impose its own patterns and meanings. Tiffauges himself refers to his 'pèlerinage dans le passé'(314), and the paradox of the two time-scales of the novel, one historical and progressive, the other mythical and retrogressive, is summed up in Keil's phrase 'Mais plus nous avançons dans le temps, plus le passé se rapproche de nous' (296).

This stance allows Tournier to strike at several targets at once. It represents an attack on historical discourse as privileging the political and military over the anthropological and cultural, and as reinforcing prejudices which Tournier so much deplores (see Chapter 2).[4] At the same time, Tiffauges's construction of an alternative and eternal 'family' represents a fantasy escape from enslavement to the propagation of the species which inhibits a healthy and rich erotic freedom (see Chapter 3).

The unusual degree of historical detail in the novel thus only throws into greater relief the refusal of history embodied in Tiffauges and which underlies the whole dynamic of the text. Tiffauges proclaims on the opening page that his being is not limited in time or space, and his whole ambition is to establish these superhuman credentials, to find them confirmed in the signs he reads around him. How far the text wholeheartedly endorses this egomania is an open question, but undeniably, on the final page and at crucial moments before, it espouses Tiffauges's vision and projects the reader beyond the historically specific moment into an alternative realm of higher realities. If the reader accepts the full seriousness of this closure, and the weight placed on it by the cumulative over-determination which leads up to it, then the subject of the text emerges as not so much the specificity of a character in history, but the quest pattern itself as a manifestation of some transcendent shaping destiny.[5]

'Au milieu de ces incertitudes, un mot s'impose [...]: intemporel' (*RA* 37). The aspiration to timelessness is a constant in Tournier's heroes. Robinson stops the water-clock to escape the servitude of linear time. 'Ce fut d'abord pour descendre dans les entrailles de l'île, comme on plonge dans l'intemporel. Mais n'est-ce pas cette éternité lovée dans les profondeurs de la terre que l'explosion a chassée au-dehors, et qui étend maintenant sa bénédiction sur tous nos rivages?'(*VLP* 220). When history intrudes in the shape of the *Whitebird*, it is rejected and the order of eternity restored. Likewise, in *Les Météores*, 'la cellule gémellaire se veut intemporelle, et donc incréée tout autant qu'éternelle, et elle récuse de toutes ses forces les prétentions géniteuses qui peuvent s'élever à son endroit. Il n'y a pour elle de paternité que putative' (Mét 464).[6] Again, characteristically, the aspiration to timelessness involves a rejection of physical descendance, of the enslaving linear sequence of generations. This aspect is spelt out in Vendredi, in Robinson's vision of the heavenly twins, the Dioscuri: 'C'est qu'ils ne sont pas les chaînons d'une lignée qui rampe de génération en génération à travers les vicissitudes de l'histoire': they are instead 'êtres tombés du ciel [...], issus d'une génération verticale, abrupte' (VLP 232). Robinson himself will be shown as acquiring their eternal youth and inhuman, metallic beauty in the final pages. In similar terms, Paul in Les Météores reproaches the fugitive Jean with forgetting the fundamental truth of their timeless twinship, 'notre jeunesse [...] éternelle, inaltérable, inoxydable' and of allowing himself to be sucked into the 'courant des générations' (Mét 422).[7]

Implicit in Tournier's writing is an ontology which sees human life as an episode in the journey of a being from one eternity to another. The origins of being are linked to astral symbolism, and to the notion of a primal cell which will explode into life. Tiffauges refers to himself as the primal ball of fire at the origins of the universe, while Paul, visibly inspired by the myth of the Dioscuri (Castor and Pollux) describes the original twin-cell of Jean-Paul in astronomical terms. They too are 'jumeaux tombés du ciel' who, if they had not fallen into time and history, 'seraient inaltérables comme une constellation'(Mét 197).[8] In the case of Vendredi, where the hero is unaware at the outset of his cosmic destiny, these notions are nevertheless present in the prologue. He is enclosed in the cell of the ship's cabin, free-floating like the twin-cell of the Gemini, from which he will be ejected onto the earth. The new life into which he will be launched is, as it were, genetically programmed by the astral tarot predictions. In Gaspard, a star is of course the first manifestation of Christ's presence to the Magi. On each occasion, this initial perception of stellar eternity is followed by a disastrous fall into time.[9] Thereafter the initiatic narrative moves towards a redemptive apotheosis which suggests that the painful passage through history and the realm of death gives access to a higher mode of being, synthesising the stellar/ eternal/sterile and the earthly/timebound/fertile. Thomas Koussek provides a theological version of this three-stage, dialectical process in speaking of the passage from the impersonal ruah of the Old Testament, through the earthly ordeal of the life of Christ, to culminate in the gift of the Holy Spirit, a wind now rendered fertile by having acquired 'un certain poids de couleur, de chaleur et de douleur' from its passage through 'le corps du Bien-Aimé' (*Mét* 161).[10] This exemplary initiatic progression is of course mirrored in Koussek's own conversion to the Holy Spirit, after a period of tortured identification with the figure of Christ. This figure of a celestial status reclaimed after an enriching passage through human experience is symbolised at the end of each text: Robinson stands on the island but gazes at the sun, Tiffauges sinks into the mire, his eyes fixed on a star, Paul confined to his chaise-longue embraces in spirit the play of the elements. In this apotheosis the aspiration is not only to timelessness but also to ubiquity: by a supreme mythomania, the self absorbs the cosmos. The refusal of imprisonment within history is also the refusal of localisation in space.

It is intriguing to note that this three-phase dialectic also informs the account which Tournier has habitually given of his own development as a writer. '[A]yant abandonné la philosophie en 1950, je me suis aussitôt acharné à trouver mon chemin de passage au romanesque, tout en gardant naturellement mon arsenal philosophique. [...] Je me suis mis à l'école la plus romanesque qui soit, le naturalisme. Une école qui vous fait sentir l'odeur des choses et des gens [...]'.[11] 'Donc faire oeuvre littéraire. Mais ne jamais oublier que je venais d'ailleurs, et rester dans le monde des lettres un homme d'ailleurs' (*VPar* 179). He thus characterises himself, in semi-mythological terms, as a being from the ethereal world of metaphysical speculation descending into the realist's world of things and people, that of the 'roman à la Zola, avec de l'épaisseur, des odeurs, avec du crime, avec des personnages, de l'adultère, de l'argent [...]'.[12] There, as one marked out as exceptional by his own sense of his origins, he strives to achieve a synthesis of the earthly (naturalism) and the celestial (metaphysics), to become a 'naturaliste mystique'.[13] This initiatic drama of a passage through the earthbound realm of naturalism towards the ideal synthesis of the *conte* is enshrined in the structure of *Le Médianoche amoureux*, as analysed in Chapter 1. Critics should perhaps treat with some caution a writer's account of his own evolution which falls so readily into his preferred pattern of the initiatic hero.

The Metaphysics of Destiny

In *Le Vent Paraclet*, Tournier speaks of the synthesis he wished to achieve between the sense-impressions of naturalism and the hard-core of metaphysics in the following terms: '[...] [J]e voulais faire sentir sous ces vertes frondaisons et ces bruns labours le roc de l'absolu ébranlé par le lourd tam-tam du destin' (*VPar* 179). Tournier's fictions constantly present themselves as *exemplary*, in the sense that the human lives they recount are not seen as merely individual and accidental but as realisations of a pattern which transcends them and which it is an important purpose of the narrative to suggest or to reveal. This is in turn linked to Tournier's preference for human and mythological prototypes: the castaway, the ogre, the twin, the saint. With such subjects, the account of a single life may be used to discover truths about an exceptional but potentially exemplary mode of being in the world, from which ordinary mortals may learn, after the manner of Plutarch's *Lives* or medieval hagiographies. In each case Tournier's fiction describes a particular dialogue, or dialectic, between the external world and the character's own sense of special destiny. The character often claims, explicitly or implicitly, to be decoding a language of signs and events in his own ongoing experience. This semic pattern progressively underlines and authenticates the priorities he is inspired to adopt and his particular sense of 'vocation', of being called to fulfil a special destiny which only gradually reveals itself.[14] A major question underlying the narratives is always that of deciding how far this can be interpreted as the character's self-projection into the universe around him, or how far evidence is offered of some transcendental endorsement of the destiny the character claims for himself.

The minor episode of the twin clocks in *Les Météores* will serve as an example of this issue. Paul describes how he and his brother are each given a kind of cuckoo clock, and these identical models are hung side by side on the wall (*Mét* 173). For no obvious reason, Jean's clock always strikes first - a slight mechanical difference would be the normal explanation (as the text indicates), but Jean clearly sees in this phenomenon a special significance, a 'je ne sais quoi' which he refuses to explain. The brothers likewise possess barometers in the form of a chalet, from which two figures emerge, predicting rain or fine weather respectively. Here again, Jean's barometer seems to offer predictions well ahead of Paul's, so that there is often a wide discrepancy between them.

On one level this variance, in the same direction in each case, could be seen as a coincidence, which Jean seizes on out of his own psychological need for any discrepancy which will separate him from his twin. As he recounts later, he struggles and fails to find just such a differentiation in photographs, or in a supposedly independent choice of clothes (279-83). Finally, most disastrously of all, the relationship with Sophie which Jean intends to differentiate him definitively from his brother is jeopardised by her inability to distinguish the twins sufficiently to prevent Paul from entering the same intimacy with her. If we view the episode therefore in this light, the cuckoo clock/ barometer discrepancies can be seen as a motif which has only the significance which Jean, with his particular preoccupations, assigns to it. This psychological, character-centred interpretation does not, however, exhaust the weight which this episode acquires from the thematic structure of the text. It is in fact doubly charged. In the first place, it functions as a microcosmic anticipation of their macrocosmic journey which structures the whole final sequence. In this, the 'je ne sais quoi' of chronological discrepancy is writ large, Jean's presence in each place anticipating Paul's by a short period. Secondly, the juxtaposition of chronology and meteorology in the two devices of clock and barometer transparently encapsulates a major preoccupation of the text, especially when one notes that the often contradictory predictions of the two barometers imply a schism more radical than that implied by a minor difference in chronological time. The episode acquires its full significance not in terms of the particular viewpoint of a given character, but only when it is treated as an artifice required by the text's structure, a calculated node in a carefully constructed network of significance. As Tournier himself has observed: 'Certains romanciers se plaisent à dire que leurs personnages leur échappent et qu'ils se contentent de les suivre - chez moi, c'est différent, c'est le mécanisme mythologique et symbolique qui est si contraignant qu'il détermine entièrement l'action des personnages.'[15]

In fact the emphasis in the text shifts from psychology (that of twinship, or of the lone homosexual male) to the metaphysical, as the themes of space, chronology and meteorology come to dominate more and more. In the chapters of the intertwined sequences A and B (as defined in Chapter 1 of this study), there is some dispersal of interest among different kinds of lives within the Surin family, loosely linked to a historical period (war and occupation). In contrast, sequence C is monolinear. In this final section there is no continuing story to rival that of Paul: the accounts of other relationships - Ralph/Deborah/ Hamida in Venice and Africa, Selma/Olivier in Iceland, Kumiko/Urs in Japan and Canada - are no more than passing episodes designed to provide the hero with some particular insight or to add a particular colour to the mosaic of meaning which the whole text is laying out.

This whole sequence is highly teleological, in that Paul is driven forward by a lack, an absence in his life in the conviction that, if the proper route is followed, this aching void will be wondrously filled. Paul's most important interlocutors are not the personages he meets on the road, Hamida, Selma or Urs, but the absent Jean and even, perhaps, the spirit of his dead uncle Alexandre. This dialogue with the disembodied is impervious to contemporary history, which erupts into the text only once more, in the Berlin chapter, before Paul's final conversion to a half-disembodied self. The psychology of a life as it is recognisably lived gives way to a cosmic mysticism, in which Paul is presented as realising his extraordinary and unconfined ambition to 'assurer [sa] mainmise sur la troposphère elle-même, dominer la météorologie, devenir le maître de la pluie et du beau temps. Rien de moins!' (*Mét* 449). In the intoxicating accumulation of terms of power-fantasy (*mainmise, dominer, maître*) as well as in the final exclamation, the text itself appears to leave space for an ironic reaction to the preposterous unreality of such an aspiration. This reading is further reinforced by the flippant tone of the expression 'la pluie et le beau temps' ('faire la pluie et le beau temps' means, colloquially, 'to wield great influence'). Yet the final paragraphs of the novel suggest the realisation of this aspiration, without any obvious ironic dimension. Paul claims, by virtue of his mutilated, opened body, a special intuitive bond with the great body of the heavens, a direct contact with that principle of natural energy which constantly confounds the mechanical models of scientific meteorologists. The text thus ends as it began, with an evocation of a weather pattern, but with the process seen symmetrically in reverse. At the start of the text, the wind arriving from Newfoundland homed in finally on (among others) Michel Tournier reading on the beach and on the sleeping twins and their mother, so that the subject of the discourse moves from the presiding forces of nature - 'courant de perturbations', 'des masses d'air océanique', 'un souffle d'ouest-sud-ouest' (9) - to the human creator and protagonists of the tale to be told. The cumulative energy generated in the verbs of the second sentence conveying the wind's impact - *découvrit, fit claquer, rabattit brutalement, tourna huit pages, souleva un nuage, mouilla d'embruns, fit bouffer et danser, emballa, arracha* - seems designed to launch the fiction by establishing the wind and the elements as the true source of the narrative's trajectory, a source which must become manifest again at its conclusion. In the concluding chapter the movement is reversed, as the narrative quits the human and the mundane to re-enter the elemental and the cosmic, as Paul's horizon of perception dilates, extending outwards from his own body to his immediate surroundings, then to seascape and skyscape, finally to encompass the heavens. Even the direction of the wind is symmetrically opposite - East-North-East - to that blowing on the opening page.

It would be easy for a reader of a rationalist turn of mind to dismiss this ending as theosophic obscurantism: either (one might argue) it is a cripple's delusion of grandeur, which demeans it, or we are asked to believe that his aspiration to become 'le berger des nuages et des vents'(449) is actually realised, which implies an acceptance of his elevation to the status of a natural deity. What however authenticates this apotheosis in terms of the narrative - what in short allows Tournier to get away with such a (literally) fantastic ending - is the extent to which it has been prepared by the elaborate construction of the narrative leading up to it. As with *Vendredi* and *Le Roi des aulnes*, the ending is over-determined - that is, it is the product of several converging causal systems. Aside from the symmetry of opening and closing pages, the major narrative equations finding their resolution here are clearly twofold. The first is concerned with the possibility of realising, or imagining, a lived synthesis between the endogamous plenitude of the closed cell of the twins and the exogamous restlessness of the *sans-pareil* seeking the ideal partner to fill his emotional void (Alexandre, Edouard). The synthesis between these two conditions is accomplished through the intermediate condition of the bereaved twin, his insight purchased with grief and suffering. The second synthesis to be achieved is that between chronology and meteorology, between the abstract order created by the human intellect and the unregulated freedom of natural energy: it is suggested that Paul, who had long been concerned vigilantly to police and preserve the closed order of twinship, absorbs into his own being the disruptive impulse of Jean-le-Cardeur, and thus brings these two opposite but equally essential principles into balance. Both syntheses are eloquently implied in the simile of the fluttering flag by which Paul characterises this ultimate equilibrium: 'Car je suis désormais un drapeau claquant dans le vent, et si son bord droit est prisonnier du bois de la hampe, son bord gauche est libre et vibre, flotte et frémit de toute son étamine dans la véhémence des météores' (624). The opposition between *prisonnier* and *libre* relates to the conditions of closure (the twin-cell) and openness (the mode of being of the *sans-pareil*, to which Jean also aspires). At the same time, the flagpole symbolises location, geographical and chronological fixity as opposed to the 'véhémence des météores', whose free flow of energy is not to be predicted and constrained within artificial divisions of space and time.

The ending of this novel, or of other fictions by Tournier, does not therefore ask to be judged in terms of realist convention or of psychological plausibility: it stands or falls as part of the whole ideological backbone of the text which determines it. And just as the narrative is governed by a multiple ideological structure which only gradually reveals itself to the reader, the lives of the characters are governed by a 'destiny' whose direction they perceive only bit by bit. It is Alexandre who underlines and reflects on this sense of 'destin' in his own life, in a revealing paragraph, which is worth quoting in full:

> Ce qui fait le charme de ma vie, c'est qu'arrivé à l'âge mûr, je continue à me surprendre moi-même par les décisions ou les options que je prends, et ce d'autant plus qu'il ne s'agit pas de caprices ou de tours de girouette, mais bien au contraire de fruits longuement cultivés dans le secret de mon coeur, un secret si bien gardé que je suis le premier étonné de leur forme, substance et saveur. Il faut bien sûr que les circonstances se prêtent à l'éclosion, mais elles s'y prêtent souvent avec tant d'empressement que le beau et lourd mot de *destin* vient tout naturellement à l'esprit. (222)

A noteworthy feature of this observation is the shift in thinking that leads up to the 'heavy', and italicised, word *destin*. The emphasis at first is, uncontroversially enough, on the notion that Alexandre is sometimes the first to be surprised by his own decisions, and by the deep-rooted motives which they reveal within himself. The causality of behaviour initially suggested here is a psychological one, and its mystery derives only from Alexandre's lack of self-knowledge, from the unpenetrated recesses of the heart and its secrets. In the final sentence of this paragraph, however, there is an important transition. When Alexandre writes 'Il faut bien sûr que les circonstances se prêtent à l'éclosion', then this is consistent with what he has just said: for the inner secrets of the heart to find expression as decisions and options in real life, favourable circumstances are required - but these remain merely a catalyst, not the cause. His final comment, however, on the unnatural readiness of circumstances to respond to his needs suggests the word *destin* and throws into doubt all that precedes it: the suggestion here is that there is a kind of *complicity* in events which is encouraging him along some predetermined path of development. The model of the causality of behaviour suggested here - and it applies to most of Tournier's major characters - is that of a destiny which derives its power by linking the darkest, most impenetrable inner urges of a character to a sequence of external events and circumstances which seem so favourable to this inner dynamic and its needs that its full flowering seems ineluctable, and indeed ordained by some higher dispensation.

Alexandre goes on to complain, in a tone of mock grievance, that the signals which 'destiny' sends him in his life are anything but subtle: they are 'farces', 'bouffonneries', 'grimaces' (222). Elsewhere, in this and other Tournier texts, the references made to this overriding pattern of destiny are frequently light-hearted - but humour in Tournier often wells up when a fundamental point is being touched on.[16] In Vancouver, Urs light-heartedly recounts how Jean has set off 'en hippie' for the Rockies. 'Oh, nous nous reverrons! Nous avons rendez-vous le 13 août, chez moi, à Berlin. Et tel que je le connais il y sera, mais je me demande ce qu'il inventera pour semer le désordre sur les rives de la Spree! Walter Ulbricht et Willy Brandt n'ont qu'à bien se tenir!'(553). The 'désordre' which Urs predicts will shake the leaders of the twin German states turns out, of course, to be the building of the Wall, which will begin precisely on 13 August (579). What is striking here is not so much the accuracy of the prediction - the reader becomes used to omens and anticipations which from time to time intimate the presence of 'destiny'. It is, rather, the suggestion that the 'désordre', whatever form it takes, will be an invention of Jean, that Jean is in fact somehow responsible for the Berlin Wall. Fantastic though this notion is - and it is not elaborated - it is in tune with two features of Tournier's writing. Firstly, the existence of Jean in the text has been etherealised to the extent that he has now become a kind of cosmic principle of disorder, at work within Paul's destiny. In this sense, although Paul fails to meet Jean in person in Berlin, the promised rendezvous is kept: Jean *is* present, in the brutal division of the city (image of the twin-cell separated by a 'coup de hache'[17]), in the forcible removal of people from their homes (a reflection, writ large, of Paul impelled to leave La Cassine because of his brother's insistence on differentiation) and even in the crushing weight of the collapsing tunnel, which could be read as Jean's final revenge for the stifling closure of the twin-cell whose integrity Paul fought to maintain. Secondly, this idea of the Wall being in some way brought about by Jean is comparable to the way Tiffauges regarded the fire at Saint-Christophe school and even the outbreak of the World War as elements contrived to further his own personal destiny. The epic quest of the hero, be he phoric giant or bereaved twin, usurps history, and interprets even the most far-reaching historical events as pawns in its own personal - and cosmic - destiny. Paul's story, and those of Tiffauges and of Robinson, are at once sub-historical and supra-historical, stories of the 'secret du coeur' and of the constellations of destiny.

The whole conception of *Le Roi des aulnes* is likewise fundamentally anti-historical. The novel develops a systematic interplay of symbols and symbolic meanings which overlays the historical and chronological material and seems to aspire to a monolithic, metaphysical meaning which overrides it. This symbolic decoding is expressed through a multiplicity of binary pairs: Erlking/St Christopher, 'nomade'/'sédentaire', horse ('ange anal')/stag ('ange phallophore'), 'symbole'/'diabole', the pagan ancestor (Atlas)/the Christian ancestor (Adam) and so forth. What makes this novel dense and demanding to read is the way in which all of these different binary units are developed together. They feed off each other and refer to each other, and often seem cunningly interrelated. The reader is thus led into a labyrinth of symbolic meaning, and introduced to a view of the world which is dependent on a particular loaded vocabulary, a set of special definitions which have to be digested along the way. The binary pairs and other elements of the code remain, however, dynamic and unpredictable, subject to complex combinatory procedures which seem to aspire to an exhaustive, systematic world-view which is never finally vouchsafed.

The Kommandeur warns Tiffauges in the text of what can happen when codes and symbols reach saturation point in a culture: 'Mais vous ne voyez pas encore où mène cette prolifération redoutable de symboles. Dans le ciel saturé de figures se prépare un orage qui aura la violence d'une apocalypse, et qui nous engloutira tous!' (*RA* 478). Earlier, he warns of the 'mécanique des symboles' (*RA* 473), the sinister power of emblems which are not content to remain as flags or banners but take possession of the standard-bearer. The Third Reich is presented as a society consumed and destroyed by the appalling power of the symbols and rituals it has generated, and which by the end have taken complete control of its destiny.

This is an image, too, of the relationship between reader and text. In the sequence of episodes of ever-increasing violence and brutality which the novel presents, the culmination comes with the horrific spectacle of three boys impaled on swords, presumably by the invading Soviet troops. In *Le Vent Paraclet* (129-30), however, Tournier develops what may seem a surprising argument regarding this climactic episode. He asserts firstly that 'les vrais ressorts du roman' are not psychological or historical, and are not to be understood in terms of what he calls a 'causalisme banal'. The logic of the text derives rather from myths, symbols, even heraldry. 'C'est ainsi [...] qu'il ne faut pas demander *qui* à la fin du roman a empalé les trois enfants [...] Qui? Mais tout le roman, bien sûr, la poussée irrésistible d'une masse de petits faits et notations accumulés sur les quatre cents pages qui précèdent!'.[18] He cites three such premonitory elements: Nestor's mysterious utterance 'Il faudrait réunir d'un trait alpha et oméga' (*RA* 63), the three pigeons impaled and roasted on a spit, prefiguring the fate of the boys, and the Kommandeur's theory whereby in a malign inversion the symbols which were carried come now to carry their bearers, so that the once sword-bearing boys are now held aloft by swords. It is interesting to note that these three elements are not of the same order: the first is an injunction, the second an analogous parallel, the third a generative theory. Nestor's sentence is so gnomically unspecific that it can hardly be taken as a precise prediction of this outcome. Even if it is seen in this light, what is the force of 'il faudrait'? Is Nestor to be seen not only as predicting the grisly massacre, but as deeming it in advance as necessary or even desirable? The second premonitory element, the fate of the pigeons, implies a comparable question: is this low-intensity anticipation intended to suggest that the ritual killing of the Jungmannen is ineluctable, or even that it is as normal an event as hungry soldiers on the run slaughtering and cooking a few birds that come to hand? The Kommandeur's thesis suggests that there is a 'mécanique des symboles' (*RA* 473) which accounts for the derangement of the Third Reich as it falls prey to the power of its own symbolism. Tournier, for his part, speaks of an architecture of his text by which successive figures are drawn from 'une logique profonde' (*VPar* 129). The advice by the author to the reader is to view the 'puéril golgotha'(578) not as a crime imputable to human hands, but as the outcome of the inner dynamic of the narrative, and this way of reading suggests a profound analogy between the 'mécanique' of political symbols in history and the 'logique profonde' of narrative. The Kommandeur and the author occupy a similar posture. The Kommandeur stands outside the history in which he has participated, and analyses its processes for the benefit of Tiffauges, while the author stands outside the novel he has written and guides his readers in their decoding of the text. The Kommandeur's political stance is a somewhat ambiguous one: he is presented as an intensely traditionalist Prussian aristocrat who is to the very end enthusiastic in his eloquent evocation of the legends and symbols of ancient Germanic heroism in speeches designed to inspire the young SS recruits in their endeavours. While lucidly perceiving that the insane logic of Nazi culture and propaganda can lead only to disaster, he never formulates a moral condemnation of the regime. His indictment centres principally on the crime of *lèse-symbole*. While he is arrested by the authorities following the attempt on Hitler's life, we are never told whether he was implicated in this act of resistance. Tournier, for his part, seems likewise to wish to discourage, or even disqualify, the possibility of moral judgment on the part of the reader by moving the focus away from issues of human responsibility towards a 'deep logic' of cultural process or, more simply, something like classical Fate - at all events a determinism which decrees that people will live and die according to patterns which transcend them.

The episode of the killing of the three boys is potentially a critical point in the relationship of reader to text. Do we accept that it is an inevitable product of the novel's cumulative 'logic' and that we must accordingly suspend historical judgment, psychological explanation, moral reaction and become dazzled passengers on the nightmare roller-coaster of the narrative? In seeking to persuade us to do so, is Tournier surrendering to the formidably seductive power of his own fictional machine? It is arguable that the complicity of the narrative voice with Tiffauges is such that his destiny must finally be seen as exceptional in some transcendental terms, that we are asked to view him as much more than a misguided megalomaniac, and that an archetypal pattern of redemption requires first a simulacrum of the crucifixion as a vision of total abasement before the release from history into a kind of plenitude and grace. The reader is arguably invited to accept an ahistorical perspective and an overriding transcendental pattern within which this event is presented as part of a necessary 'logic' of myths and symbols which Tournier sees as governing the text. This is the imperative sense of Nestor's 'il *faudrait* réunir...', and of Tournier's 'il ne *faut* pas demander qui...' (my italics).

This is not to conclude, as some shocked early reviewers did, that the novel is devoid of moral perspective. The pages which unflinchingly relay Ephraïm's account of Auschwitz and of Dr Mengele's experiments there, leaving Tiffauges 'abreuvé d'horreur'(*RA* 554-60), remind the reader unequivocally of where Nazi ideology led, and offer Tiffauges an infinitely malign reflection of many of his own obsessions. What is the relationship of the presence of moral sensibility here, and its absence as regards the deaths of Haïo, Haro and Lothar? From Tiffauges's point of view, the latter are somehow ennobled by their insertion into symbolic and archetypal patterns: they represent a point of closure of an evolving pattern which he has been decoding throughout the novel. Objectively their deaths can be justified as gallant casualties in a patriotic war, deaths in which Tiffauges has no hand, despite his morbid obsession with blood and martyred young flesh. Auschwitz is however only just offstage, literally obscene (*obscenus* originally meant off-stage), its horror apparently unpredicted, and this discovery, embodied in the person of Ephraïm, is not closure but opening of new insight, marking the beginning of the countermovement away from contemporary history which is suggested in the last three pages. The narrative perspectives on the two images of horror are quite different. For all that the impaled boys' postures are described in detail, the scene remains irresistibly stylised, partly because of the iconographic over-determination which has generated it and partly because the three boys were never more than names and bodies, deprived in the text of any voice or any personality. They are, as it were, designer-made to be anonymous units in a kaleidoscopic pattern of symbols. Ephraïm, by contrast, is talkative, bossy and teasing by turns, intensely realised as a character, echoing the mocking tone and independent-mindedness of Rachel from the opening pages. This journey from one Jew to another, from the woman who first designates Tiffauges as flesh-eating ogre to the child who enables him to accede to the role of St Christopher, is another and more humane way of interpreting Nestor's bidding to 'réunir d'un trait alpha et oméga'. Meanwhile, the ambivalent stance of the narrative towards the ethics of history is swept aside in the metaphysical transcendence of the closing pages.

There is in Tournier a philosopher enamoured of systems, and seeking the gratification of a fundamental pattern of polarities which might promise an exhaustive account of human experience. There is also in Tournier a delinquent writer enamoured of dissidence and individualism, a counter-utopian suspicious of the totalitarian aspect of all system building. His novels offer accounts of the catastrophic consequences of a reliance on a closed system. Robinson's administered island explodes under the pressure of his own desire and emotional repression, and of Vendredi's unassimilable laughter; Franz, the calendar-child in *Les Météores*, cannot live with the unpredictability of the seasons. Jean seeks out always that 'je ne sais quoi' which disrupts the 'jeu de Bep', the closed and perfect system of twinship in which the I and the Other are indistinguishable. Paul's reflection on the rhythm of the tides reflects his frustration with a system that should be astronomically predictable, but which is in practice frustratingly capricious, 'une horloge prise de folie, victime de cent influences parasitaires [...] qui défient et bouleversent la raison'(*Mét* 175). *Le Roi des aulnes*, as we have seen, replaces the normal causal logic of historiography by a symbolic account of events, and finally dethrones the authority of history altogether in favour of a cluster of myths and archetypes, which one could also call 'influences which defy and overturn reason'. Moreover, on a moral level, Tournier clearly enjoys the way in which the theological notion of atonement defies and overturns the normal logic of human morality, to make Tiffauges and even Gilles, scandalously, eligible for salvation. In *Gilles* in particular, he pushes beyond this doctrine of the infinite availability of forgiveness towards the heresy whereby it is the greatest sinner who is in fact closest to God and to salvation. Bachelard ascribes this way of thinking to the alchemist, playing with the fundamental dialectic of all values: good and evil. 'Ne vaut-il pas mieux, avant de tendre au bien, d'aller d'abord *au fond* du mal?' The process in question is, Bachelard says, one of 'se perdre *pour* se sauver'.[19] Hence it is Prelati, the alchemist, who is made its main spokesman in *Gilles*. In general, Christianity, orthodox and heretical, provides Tournier with a rich store of paradox with which to breach the closed systems of rational explanation: Koussek's insistence on the powerful presence of the abstract in the Holy Spirit, the Magi's experience of the power of weakness at the Nativity, the supremely spiritual significance of the most physical act of eating, in the Eucharist which concludes *Gaspard*.

Tournier's account of his career as a philosopher turned naturalist novelist could more interestingly be rewritten in terms of a system-maker turned system-destroyer. It is the itinerary of an intellectual who could find only in imaginative fiction the liberties he sought: the licence to build and destroy systems simultaneously; to suggest transcendental patterns of destiny and initiation while maintaining an ironic detachment from the inescapable urge to order experience; and to deploy an eclectic mythology which can suggest pattern without any specific commitment other than that to openness and freedom.

There is in Tournier's writing in many aspects a refusal of containment, a dynamic of expansion. His most characteristic movement is from the particular to the general, whereby the individual becomes the manifestation of the universal: the present moment becomes a window into eternity, the present place a gateway to the cosmos, the child becomes the Child (or a star), the partner's bodily presence is disqualified to allow them to become a medium between the hero and the universe (Vendredi, Jean, Jeanne). Constriction, the 'glass cage', is the most consistent target of Tournier's invective, whether it be confinement within a family, a racial culture, a single mode of sexuality or dogmatic religious belief. His writing exudes a Gidean commitment to what the earlier writer called 'disponibilité', openness to all new experience.[20]

In fictional form, this same process of expansionism and 'éclatement' can be seen at work. The relatively monolithic structure of *Vendredi* gives way to more loose-limbed successors, *Le Roi des aulnes* and *Les Météores*, where unity of form is progressively under strain from the diversity of materials they are asked to contain. Thereafter Tournier will only occasionally (perhaps in *La Goutte d'or*) seek to achieve a high degree of integration of form, and that mostly in small-scale works, such as 'Pierrot'. *Gaspard* and *Le Médianoche amoureux* move away from the unitary novel form, with their loose constellations of smaller fictions, elements in an open exchange of meaning.

The refusal of ideological closure is balanced, and focused, by a very conscious commitment to artisanal construction, as we saw in Chapter 1. There we found that the dominant forms were those of symmetry (binary) and synthesis (ternary), and these formal alternatives can be seen as opposite poles of attraction, to closure (symmetry as stasis) and to openness (synthesis as dynamic evolution) - in other words, to the would-be perfect system, and to the organic processes which destabilise and challenge it.

The fascination of Tournier's *oeuvre* may derive precisely from the sense in which it seems at once to promise and withhold a unitary pattern of meaning, what one critic has called 'the frustrated promise of intelligibility'.[21] The formidable ideological networks which it is possible to create from the intersections between his texts cannot finally be integrated, because they rest on paradox. The aspiration is to a series of impossible syntheses - between a reaffirmation of the physical and an Assumption into the sphere of metaphysics, between the body as a locus for erotic pleasure and an escape from gender, between a revitalised understanding of Christianity and an escape from cultural specificity, between a resolute and deviant individualism and a dissolution into the cosmos. What is important in Tournier is less the answers he provides - which may be questionable, inconsistent, whimsical, preposterous or mythomaniac by turns - but the questions which he asks of our culture and of the stories it tells itself.

Notes to Chapter Eight

[1] This is just one aspect of a complex play of authority in Tournier's novels between author, narrative voice and character. One critic, Margaret Sankey, speaks of the 'complicity' between narrator and hero in *Le Roi des aulnes*, while another, Mariska Koopman-Thurlings, shows how in Tournier the character is liable to be made a mouthpiece for the ideas of the author, or eclipsed by the (meta)discourse of the narrative voice. See Sankey, 'La parodie: l'exemple du *Roi des aulnes*' in Bouloumié and Gandillac (eds), *Images et signes de Michel Tournier*, 325-40 (329); and Koopman-Thurlings, 'De la forme et du fond: le redoublement discursif', *Images et signes*, 279-93 (284, 292).

[2] See the discussion of this 'refus (impossible) d'avoir été engendré' in Rosello, *L'In-différence chez Michel Tournier*, 135 ff.

[3] In *Le Salut par la fiction?*, the most extended study so far published on *Le Roi des aulnes*, Liesbeth Korthals Altes observes that while Tiffauges vehemently rejects the theories of the 'Nazi Mephistopheles', he nevertheless shares some fundamental values with Nazi ideology (70). She sees the ethical stance of the whole novel as profoundly ambiguous. 'Ce roman laisse effectivement intacte la séduction esthétique de la mort et de la souffrance (ce qu'on appelle communément sadisme) qui fascine Tiffauges et les Nazis' (184).

[4] *Le Roi des aulnes* obviously offers a very heterodox view of the period 1938-1945, especially in the eyes of a French readership largely still accustomed, in 1970, to the heroic and officially promoted mythology of 'la France résistante' which de Gaulle represented in his person. Tournier's novel can be seen as in tune with a process of revaluation and demythologisation of this period which gained momentum after the end of de Gaulle's presidency in 1969. See Alan Morris, *Collaboration and Resistance Reviewed: Writers and the* mode rétro *in post-Gaullist France* (Oxford, Berg, 1992).

[5] For a Marxist critique of Tournier's abandonment of history and historical thought, see Christa Bevernis, 'Michel Tournier: l'oeuvre et son message', *Philologia Pragensia*, vol.26, no.3-4 (1983), 197-203.

[6] Jean, whose words these are, nevertheless goes on to declare 'J'ai trouvé un père'. He has chosen Ralph as a pseudo-father, for fear his twin should seek to take on the 'rôle paternel dont Edouard se trouvait [...] dépossédé' (464). The figure of the substitute father is, as has been seen, a significant one in Tournier's fiction and in the initiatic patterns which often underlie it.

[7] The urge to deny the oppressive power of heredity is implicit in Tournier's note on the word 'atavisme', defined as the appearance of a hereditary trait derived not from one's father or mother but from a more distant ancestor (*PL* 30-1). He concludes that 'l'hérédité qui pèse sur moi se trouve, grâce à l'atavisme, divisée en un nombre infini d'ancêtres, et par là pulvérisée, réduite en poussière, réduite à rien'. Elsewhere (*MI* 127-8), in the face of the two determining forces of heredity and environment, it is precisely in the experience of identical twins that he finds evidence of a third factor of human freedom and choice.

[8] See also *Mét*, 422, for a development of this astronomical image.

[9] The analysis of the narrative structure of *Les Météores* in Chapter 1 above shows how, on this textual level also, Paul 'falls into time'.

[10] This three-stage process, in *Les Météores* and elsewhere, has been compared not only with the three persons of the Trinity (as in Milne's detailed study, *L'Evangile selon Michel*) but with Spinoza's three types of knowledge - an unintentional parallel, according to the author himself (see *VPar* 235). Another

critic has identified the three sequences of chapters in *Les Météores* (discussed in Chapter 1 above) with the three ages of history as defined by the 12th-century thinker, Joachim de Fiore. See Petit, *Michel Tournier's Metaphysical Fictions*, 52-8, and also Milne, 166-7.

[11]   Interview in Ezine, *Les Ecrivains sur la sellette*, 225.

[12]   Interview with B. le Péchon, 28.

[13]   Tournier labels himself thus in the obituary he offers for himself, 'Nécrologie d'un écrivain' (*PP* 245).

[14]   It is legitimate to speak here of *his* vocation, since all the significant examples of such characters are male. Joan of Arc in *Gilles & Jeanne*, for instance, does not take over responsibility for the narrative at any point, and her destiny is viewed primarily in terms of her impact on Gilles and *his* destiny.

[15]   In an interview with Jean-Louis de Rambures, 'Je suis comme la pie voleuse', 166.

[16]   Tournier often speaks of what he calls 'l'humour blanc', a 'comique cosmique: celui qui accompagne l'émergence de l'absolu au milieu du tissu de relativités où nous vivons' (*VPar* 198).

[17]   This expression, repeatedly used by Paul, links the partition of Berlin to the division of the twins: see pp.388, 420, 587.

[18]   An earlier draft of the same argument begins with the assertion that 'l'horrible fin des trois Jungmannen [...] ne doit pas être imputée à l'armée rouge, comme une lecture superficielle pourrait le laisser croire'. See the note on 'Pal' in his reader's guide, 'Petit lexique d'un prix Goncourt: treize clefs pour un ogre', 22.

[19]   See Bachelard, *La Terre et les rêveries de la volonté*, 249, 250. This seductive argument occurs notably also in Chapter 25 of Thomas Mann's *Doctor Faustus*, when, in a passage influenced by Dostoevsky, Adrian Leverkühn, in a conversation with the devil, speaks of 'a sinfulness so damnable that it causes the doer to despair absolutely of salvation' as being 'the truly theological path to salvation'. ['Eine Sündhaftigkeit, so heillos, dass sie ihren Mann von Grund aus am Heile verzweifeln lässt, ist der wahrhaft theologische Weg zum Heil.'] See Mann, *Doktor Faustus* (Frankfurt a.M., Fischer Taschenbuch, 1971), 248. [I am indebted to Professor Raymond Furness for this reference.]

[20]   Bouloumié perceives in what she calls 'cette transgression généralisée des limites et des interdits' the doorway to the sacred, in Tournier's universe. See her *Michel Tournier*, 248.

[21]   The phrase is used by Davis (*Michel Tournier*, 93), with regard to *Les Météores*.

Epilogue:
Tournier's Signature

Je reconnais sa signature dans le filigrane de ce texte surprenant.

RA 68

We have already had occasion to comment on the significance of names of the characters in Tournier's fictions. Even when a name is already a given element in the story to be (re-)told, as is the case with Vendredi, its etymology (*Veneris dies*) is scrutinised and exploited, and in his volume of essays on modern painters, *Le Tabor et le Sinaï*, Tournier enjoys playing with the names of his subjects.[1] Where names are part of the invention of the fiction-maker, it is evident that he takes great care in their choice or their construction; the constituent elements of names in combination such as Abel Tiffauges or Thomas Koussek give rise to explicit and implicit ramifications of meaning through intertextuality (biblical or historical) or through playful homophony or transformation ('coup sec', 'ma belle', 'p'tit Fauges', 'T(r)iefauge'...).[2] They are designed as nodes which tie together divergent textual strands.

If such elaborate play is made with the names of characters, may it not extend to that of the author himself? In the musical masterpiece which (as we mentioned in the opening chapter) has been taken by Tournier as a structural model, J.S. Bach's *The Art of Fugue*, Bach uses the four notes corresponding (in German nomenclature) to the four letters of his surname as a theme in his counterpoint at several key structural points, thus inscribing his own name into the texture of his musical creation.[3] In less solemn vein, Tournier, in a footnote in *La Goutte d'or* (216), attributes several of his quotations to a writer called Edward Reinroth - whose name is more or less a composite of Tournier's own second name (Edouard) and his surname written backwards.[4]

Given this predilection for playing, seriously or lightheartedly, with names in his fiction, Tournier can hardly have failed to reflect on his own name and its potentialities. Tiffauges, we recall, reads about St

Christopher in *La Légende dorée* of Jacques de Voragine: in the article on 'Saint Michel, Archange' in the same work, we read: 'Michel veut dire: qui est semblable à Dieu'.[5] This definition could be seen as leading directly to Balthazar's intense preoccupation with the sentence from Genesis, 'Dieu fit l'homme à son image et à sa ressemblance', in which he sees 'ressemblance' as standing for a total likeness ('corps et âme') while 'image' is the merely superficial likeness which is all that remained after the Fall (*GMB* 47). From this one can derive the quest of Tournier's heroes for God-like status, whether it be Tiffauges's claim to embody the 'âme qui [...] faisait tourner [la terre]' (*RA* 13) or Paul's sense of being the axis of an 'âme déployée' which encompasses everything.

More particularly, Jacques de Voragine says of St Michael: 'C'est lui, dit-on, qui frappa l'Egypte des sept plaies, qui partagea les eaux de la mer Rouge [...]', which places him as the central instrument of destiny in the biblical narrative which underpins (as we saw in Chapter 4) the whole final episode of *Le Roi des aulnes*. The article on St Michael ends with a disquisition on angels, and specifically with a reference to the Angel of the Lord who was in the burning fiery furnace with the three children, and brought them succour.[6] Obviously, however, the major iconic image of St Michael is that of his victory over the Dragon, deriving from the account in Revelation 12 in which Michael casts out the dragon which was about to devour the man-child destined to rule the world. This story, taken from the Apocalypse narrative evoked earlier by the Kommandeur as a confusion of indecipherable symbols (*RA* 474), emerges nevertheless as one of the narrative strands encoded in this densely layered ending and links the central figure of the saviour (Tiffauges) of the child (Éphraïm) with the name of Michael.

It is not only in *Le Roi des aulnes* that St Michael's presence can be detected. While in Defoe's *Robinson Crusoe* the fateful shipwreck takes place early on 30 September, in Tournier's *Vendredi* it occurs late on 29 September - which happens to be St Michael's Day. The prophetic tarot reading of the 'prologue' which is the germ of the narrative is thus placed wholly under the aegis of Michael. At the end of the novel, the figure of the archangel is more visibly present. Robinson, his chest like a 'bouclier d'airain', is bathed and ennobled by the sunlight which bestows on him 'une armure de jeunesse inaltérable' and 'un masque de cuivre' (*VLP* 254).[7] The image of a creature of light in knightly armour mediating between earth and heaven (and associated again with the task of protecting a male child) irresistibly evokes the warrior

Saint.

In *Gilles & Jeanne*, the Saint is no longer a subtext, but is named. When Jeanne first hears an other-worldly voice, she identifies it as 'la voix d'un ange, et singulièrement celle de Saint Michel' (GJ 23), and in due course she is hailed by Gilles as 'Jeanne la victorieuse sous l'étendard de saint Michel'(GJ 48), presumably the standard described earlier (20-1) depicting an angel presenting the 'fleur de lys' to the Saviour. A striking iconic image is presented, at the end of the first section, of the angelic Jeanne standing calmly on the back of a galloping horse: 'Et elle semblait planer en effet sur des ailes invisibles au-dessus de la bête qui martelait rageusement la terre de ses quatre fers' (16). In this juxtaposition of the 'angel' and the raging beast subdued beneath her feet, the iconography of St Michael and the Dragon seems once more to be powerfully suggested.

In each case, St Michael is presented as a presiding prototype of the hero. In his ascent through the Hugolian ladder of being (see Chapter 5) Robinson achieves a superhuman, angelic status and takes on the appearance of the warrior saint. Tiffauges is intertextually implicated in the Saint's apocalyptic battle and his rescue of the child, while Jeanne is inspired by the saint's voice and rides under his banner, having herself (in Gilles's eyes at least) the appearance of an angel. The figure of the saint presides at the frontier of the natural and the supernatural; he is the hero of the end of time and of the transcendence of history.

Tournier's surname is if anything even more fertile as a generative element. It is instructive to notice how often the verbs 'tourner', 'tournoyer' and a lexicon of terms of turning, of revolving, of circular movement surface at significant points in the texts. The opening line of *Vendredi* describes the oscillation of the lantern hanging from the ceiling of the captain's cabin. In this 'prologue' printed in italics, the word 'circulaire'(12) is, as we have noted earlier, emphasised by being printed in roman type, when Van Deyssel is describing the ideal existence of the Cité solaire. When Robinson has apparently attained this ideal in Chapter 10, he speaks of the circular movement of time having speeded up to the point where it appears motionless, representing a 'révolution' in his life in both the literal and metaphorical senses (*VLP* 219).[8] A more concrete image of this paradox of rapid revolution and near immobility is offered in *Le Roi des aulnes*, in the description of Nestor's gyroscope - 'Le petit appareil [...] tournoyait autour de son point fixe' (*RA* 59). For Nestor it is an 'absolu de poche'(61), a symbol of an ideal autonomy of the self and of its emancipation from society and history. 'Le gyroscope a le don d'échapper au mouvement terrestre, et c'est pourquoi il paraît tourner. En vérité, c'est nous qui tournons autour de lui' (60).[9] This figure of revolution, of circular movement, generates a series of significant images in the text. In the playground Nestor becomes his own gyroscope as he spins round ('il se mit à tourner sur lui-même avec une vélocité [...] surprenante' (77)) while Tiffauges, perched on his shoulders, sends their adversaries flying with his outstretched arms. Much later in the novel we find a malign caricature of the same figure, when the Kommandeur characterises the swastika as 'cette araignée en perte d'équilibre, tournoyant sur elle-même et menaçant de ses pattes crochues tout ce qui fait obstacle à son mouvement [...]' (474). The benign counter-image to the swastika is the star of the final sentence of the novel 'qui tournait lentement dans le ciel noir' (581), and this image in turn is a symmetrical pendant to the initial Genesis of the self predicated on the first page of the novel: 'Quand la terre n'était encore qu'une boule de feu tournoyant dans un ciel d'hélium, l'âme [...] qui la faisait tourner, c'était la mienne' (13). Repeatedly, the figure of 'tournoiement' emerges to provide an ontological metaphor of the self, its origins, its paradox of stability and movement, its potential for good or ill, its spiritual essence.

In *Les Météores*, the same figure is immediately present in the meteorological map of the opening page: 'un courant de perturbations circulant de Terre-Neuve à la Baltique', matched by the evocation of the powerful anticyclone on the final page. These swirling 'météores' generate the wind which 'tourna huit pages des *Météores* d'Aristote que lisait Michel Tournier sur la plage' (*Mét* 9), which provides the metaphor of salvation through the Holy Spirit and which infuses Paul with vitality as he responds to its power like a fluttering flag (624). Paul reacts with special excitement to devices which turn in the wind, such as the anemometer at the Venetian weather-station ('un petit moulin à vent [...] tournoie avec une allégresse communicative, puérile et infatigable' (445)), or the wrecked windmill in the garden at El-Kantara ('On imaginait en fermant les yeux [...] un petit moulin à vent - [...] une éolienne tournant gaiement dans l'air vif' (476)). Here again, the figure of 'tournoiement' functions in this novel as an ideal image of the self as creatively and uninhibitedly responsive to its environment.[10]

The wind, and circular motion - these are central to a passage in *Le Pied de la lettre* which, in the light of this play of signifiers, could be read as an unstated and intriguing self-portrait. In this passage a reflection on the word *implosion* brings Tournier to the image of the cyclone: 'Le cyclone est une dépression atmosphérique très circonscrite que les vents ne parviennent pas à combler, parce qu'ils sont entraînés dans un mouvement giratoire effréné autour de l'oeil du cyclone. C'est une belle image de l'homme possédé par un rêve ardent, lequel au lieu de se réaliser purement et simplement reste irréalisé, et devient le moteur d'un mouvement giratoire vertigineux des choses autour de l'homme et de l'homme lui-même autour de son âme'(*PL* 105).

One further example of this figure of gyratory movement will suffice here. The pivotal point in the story of 'Barbedor' comes when the king picks up a feather of the bird which has been visiting him and balances it in the palm of his hand. It swivels, compass-like, and when it comes to rest, he sets off in the direction in which it points him. Thus the king is guided to the magical solution of his problem, and the pivotal instrument which liberates him from the limits of a single life-cycle is 'la plume', which is also the instrument of the writer.

It is in *Le Médianoche amoureux*, itself constructed around the theme of fiction, that Tournier links his name most clearly to the power of language. At the conclusion of the opening section, 'Les amants taciturnes' which provides a frame for all the rest, Nadège and Oudalle recognise that their marriage has been saved by the stories they have heard. Once, observes Nadège, religion supplied 'un édifice à la fois réel - l'église - et imaginaire, peuplé de saints, enluminé de légendes' (*MA* 49) within which people could live securement. In the absence of such certainties, what the fictions have provided for Nadège and Oudalle, as exemplary 'destinataires' of these texts, is a new 'maison de mots où habiter ensemble'(*MA* 48). They have just watched the delicate sand-sculptures of two human figures being inexorably washed away by the incoming tide, a parable of human transience. But, in response to the sculptor's gestures of worship and adoration, they turn - 'nous nous sommes retournés'(*MA* 28) - to see the apparition which he is hailing: over the whole scene towers the edifice of the Mont Saint-Michel silhouetted in the rising sun. Constructed to manifest the old certainties of religious faith, it celebrates the prestige of Tournier's name-saint (i.e. 'mon saint, Michel'...). Now it is metaphorically superseded by a new 'house of words', the abiding mansion of literary construction. In a pivotal movement, the couple avert their gaze from what is shifting and transitory -the figures of sand and tide - to fix it on the abiding and luminous heritage of language. Like Nadège and Oudalle, the reader has been guided, like a literary pilgrim, along a path of words through darkness to a new optimism based on the power of storytelling. With breathtaking faith in the power of words and a characteristically ironic arrogance, the author clearly invites us to complete the equation by accepting as the patron saint of the new temple of words a new Michel...[11] Thus, through an elaborate play of names, an *oeuvre* much concerned with apotheosis comes to rest - however provisionally and semi-seriously - on the apotheosis of the author himself.

Notes to Epilogue

[1] See *TS* 40 (Doutreleau), 47-8 (Hélion), 52 (Jenkins) and 91 (Lévêque). Tournier's name-play can be punning and/or etymological. In general, as has rightly been observed, '[l]e recours à l'étymologie est presque devenu un tic d'écriture chez Tournier. Ce jeu est d'autant moins innocent que le sens étymologique est en général convoqué comme sens "propre", comme origine dont le langage courant aurait déchu.' See Rosello, *L'In-différence chez Michel Tournier*, 154n. If further evidence were needed of this etymological passion, it can be found in abundance in Tournier's *Le Pied de la lettre: trois cents mots propres*.

[2] On the significance of names of Tournier's characters, see in particular Bouloumié, *Michel Tournier*, 41-56; Bouloumié, 'Onomastique et création dans *Les Météores* de Michel Tournier', *Revue d'histoire littéraire de la France* 88,6 (1988), 1,096-112; and Michael Worton, *Tournier: La Goutte d'or*, 39, 68-73. When we learn from Françoise Merllié (*Michel Tournier*, 19, 183) that the main character of *Le Roi des aulnes* was called Olivier Cromorne in an earlier draft, we glimpse an alternative network of name-play: the word denotes an ancient wind instrument producing a raucous sound (like the hero's 'brame'?), and derives directly from the German *Krummhorn*, which in turn suggests a crooked antler like the malformed 'bois asymétriques' of a stag killed by Goering (*RA* 330). Sound associations could yield Cro-Magnon (a species of primitive man), or 'homme morne', in addition to the 'croc-morne' and 'croque-mort' suggested by Merllié. The name was eventually allocated by Tournier to the park-keeper in 'Tupik' (CB). Rosello (*L'Indifférence chez Michel Tournier*, 69n) also mentions a (presumably unpublished) book of photographs by Tournier entitled *Idola Cromornia*.

[3] Until this, his valedictory work, Bach had never used his own name as a musical motif. In the view of Werner Breig (in his scholarly note for a recording of the work by Musica Antiqua Köln on Archiv 413642-2) this signature would thus seem to denote something more solemn than a mere *jeu d'esprit* or 'mason's mark'.

[4] See Worton, *Tournier: La Goutte d'or*, 73. The same pseudonym (now spelt Reinrot) recurs in *MI* 208 and *PL* 87.

[5] Jacques de Voragine, *La Légende dorée*, 2 vols (Paris, Garnier-Flammarion, 1967), II, 232.

[6] See the discussion in Chapter 1 of Stockhausen's *Gesang der Jünglinge* and its relation to *Le Roi des aulnes*.

[7] Hutton (*Tournier: Vendredi*, 39) refers in this regard to St Paul's call to 'put

on God's armour', in Ephesians 6:10-18. Paul's apocalyptic language here, of battles against principalities, powers and rulers of darkness, is wholly in keeping with the idea of a St Michael prototype. The imagery of knighthood is anticipated earlier in *Vendredi*, in Robinson's consecration as 'chevalier solaire' touched by 'deux épées de feu' (*VLP* 216).

[8] Tournier's definition of the word 'révolution' in *PL* 158 identifies both aspects ('1. Mouvement régulier en circuit fermé. [...] 2. Changement historique brutal et irréversible') and their linkage in Nietzsche's theory of Eternal Return.

[9] The microcosm of the gyroscope could also be read as a representation *en abîme* of the novel itself, as a sphere of created meaning independent of - and at odds with - the world around it. In that case Nestor's statement 'c'est nous qui tournons autour de lui' can be read metatextually as an ironic recognition by the character of his subordination to the machinery of the narrative, and the 'poussée formidable', the 'effort irrésistible de torsion' which Tiffauges feels when he picks up the gyroscope would translate the effect Tournier would wish his fictional 'absolu de poche' to have on the reader.

[10] A windmill features as early as the first paragraph of the novel, where the wind 'emballa l'éolienne de la ferme des Mottes' (9). The counter-image could be seen in the revolving shafts of light from the three lighthouses whose rhythms obsess the unstable Franz and draw him to his death (79). For further evidence of Tournier's fascination with windmills and their symbolic significance, see 'Les moulins de Beauce' (*CS* 55-7).

[11] Milne (*L'Évangile selon Michel*, 255) goes so far as to see Tournier appropriating the role of God himself, in his Trinitarian aspect.

Select Bibliography

A. Writings of Michel Tournier

Note:
Tournier's books are all published in Paris, except where otherwise stated. The details given are for the first edition, and then for the edition used, where this is different. For the shorter fictions included in *Le Coq de bruyère, Gaspard, Melchior & Balthazar* and *Le Médianoche amoureux*, reference is made to these volumes.

Of Tournier's numerous articles and interviews in the press, only those I have drawn on in the preparation of this study are listed. Articles and prefaces incorporated in volumes such as *Le Vol du vampire* and *Petites proses* are not listed separately.

1. Books

a) Fiction

Vendredi ou les limbes du Pacifique (Gallimard, 1967; Gallimard/Folio, 1972).

Le Roi des aulnes (Gallimard, 1970; Gallimard/Folio, 1975).
Les Météores (Gallimard, 1975; Gallimard/Folio, 1978).
Le Nain rouge (Montpellier: Fata Morgana, 1975).
Le Coq de Bruyère (Gallimard, 1978; Gallimard/Folio, 1982).
Gaspard, Melchior & Balthazar (Gallimard, 1980; Gallimard/Folio, 1982).
Gilles et Jeanne (Gallimard, 1983; Gallimard/Folio, 1986).
La Goutte d'or (Gallimard, 1986; Gallimard/Folio, 1987).
Le Médianoche amoureux (Gallimard, 1989; Gallimard/Folio, 1991).

b) Books for Children

Vendredi ou la vie sauvage (Flammarion, 1971; Gallimard/Folio Junior, 1984).

Amandine ou les deux jardins (Éditions G.P., 1977).
La Fugue du petit Poucet (Éditions G.P., 1979).
Pierrot ou les secrets de la nuit (Gallimard/Enfantimages, 1979).
Barbedor (Gallimard/Enfantimages, 1980).
L'Aire du muguet (Gallimard/Folio Junior, 1982).
Que ma joie demeure (Gallimard/Enfantimages, 1982).
Les Rois mages (Gallimard, 1983; Gallimard/Folio Junior, 1985).
Sept contes (Gallimard/Folio Junior, 1984).

c) Non-fiction

Le Vent Paraclet (Gallimard, 1977; Gallimard/Folio 1979).
Le Vol du vampire: notes de lecture (Mercure de France, 1981; Gallimard/ Idées, 1983).
Petites proses (Gallimard/Folio, 1986).
Le Tabor et le Sinaï: essais sur l'art contemporain (Belfond, 1988).
Le Miroir des idées: traité (Mercure de France, 1994).
Le Pied de la lettre: trois cents mots propres (Mercure de France, 1994).

d) Non-fictional Texts with Photographs or Drawings

Mythologie [engravings by Trémois], ([s.l.]: Pamela Verlag (Oeuvres graphiques contemporaines), 1971).
Miroirs: autoportraits [photographs by Édouard Boubat] (Denoël, 1973).
Des clefs et des serrures: images et proses (Chêne/Hachette, 1979).
Rêves [photographs by Arthur Tress] (Brussels: Complexe, 1979).
Vues de dos [photographs by Edouard Boubat] (Gallimard, 1981).
Journal de voyage au Canada [photographs by Edouard Boubat] (Laffont, 1984).[Revised edition of *Canada: Journal de voyage* (Ottawa: La Presse, 1977).]
Le Vagabond immobile [drawings by Jean-Max Toubeau] (Gallimard, 1984).
Le Crépuscule des masques: photos et photographes (Hoëbeke, 1992).

2. Articles

'Des éclairs dans la nuit du coeur', *Nouvelles littéraires* 2253 (26.11.70), 1, 6.
'Petit lexique d'un Prix Goncourt: treize clefs pour un ogre', *Figaro littéraire* 1280 (30.11.70), 20-2.

'Quand Michel Tournier récrit ses livres pour les enfants', *Le Monde* (24.12.71), 13,20.

'La Dimension mythologique', *Nouvelle Revue française* 238 (Oct.1972), 124-9.

'Clés pour l'histoire', *Quinzaine littéraire* (16-30 April 1973), 25-6 [review of Gilles Lapouge, *Utopie et civilisations* (Paris: Weber, 1973)].

'Le bilingue, surhomme ou infirme', *Le Monde (des livres)* (3.5.73), 20-1.

'Claude Lévi-Strauss, mon maître', *Figaro littéraire* (26.5.73), 15,18.

'Point de vue d'un éducateur', *Le Monde* (20.12.74), 20.

'La Leçon que nous donnent les pays pauvres', *Paris-Match* no.1432 (6.11.76), 102.

'Le Fantastique et le mythe: deux réalités', *Bulletin de l'Académie Royale de langue et littérature françaises* [Belgium], LVI, 3-4 (1978), 307-16.

3. Interviews

'Quand Vendredi éduque Robinson...' [with J.-P. Gorin], *Monde* (18.11.67), 10.

'Comme Robinson, Michel Tournier a trouvé son île déserte...' [with Jean Prasteau], *Figaro littéraire* 1127 (20-26.11.67), 24-5.

'Michel Tournier et l'ogre de Rominten' [with Jean Prasteau], *Figaro littéraire* 1271 (28.9-4.10.70), 22-3.

'Plaidoyer pour un ogre' [with Quentin Ritzen], *Nouvelles littéraires* (26.11.70), 6.

'Portrait d'un ogre' [with Guy Dumur], *Nouvel Observateur* 316 (30.11.-6.12.70), 44-6.

'The offal truth: Michel Tournier and the perversions of fine literature' [with Nina Sutton], *Guardian* (10.2.71), 8.

'Les Enfants dans la bibliothèque' [with Jean-François Josselin], *Le Nouvel Observateur* 369 (6-12.12.71), 56-7.

'*Les Météores*, chef-d'oeuvre ou provocation? Michel Tournier répond aux critiques', *Figaro (littéraire)* 1509 (29.4.75), 15.

'Michel Tournier:"Dans le mythe se conjuguent roman et philosophie"' [with Xavier Delcourt], *Quinzaine littéraire* 251 (1-15.3.77), 25-6.

'Une logique contre vents et marées: entretien avec Michel Tournier' [with Alain Poirson], *La Nouvelle Critique* 105 (June-July 1977), 47-50.

'Michel Tournier: Je suis comme la pie voleuse', in Rambures, Jean-Louis de, *Comment travaillent les écrivains* (Paris: Flammarion, 1978), 163-7 (first published as 'De Robinson à l'Ogre: un créateur de mythes' in *Monde* (24.11.70), 28).

'Dix-huit questions à Michel Tournier' [with Jean-Jacques Brochier], *Magazine littéraire* 138 (June 1978), 11-13.

'An interview with Michel Tournier' [with Penny Hueston], *Meanjin* 38 (1979), 400-5.

'Entretien avec M. Tournier' [with Brigitte le Péchon], *Recherches sur l'imaginaire dans la littérature française contemporaine depuis 1945* [séminaire de Georges Cesbron], vol.5 (1978-9) (Angers: Université d'Angers, 1979), 6-29.

'Montre-moi ta bibliothèque, je te dirai qui tu es' [with Vera Kornicker], *Figaro* (20.8.79), 18.

'Ce qu'ils pensent de Flaubert (enquête)', *Quinzaine littéraire* 324 (1-15.5.80), 21-2.

'Une conversation avec Michel Tournier' [with Alison Browning], *Cadmos* 3me ann., no. 11 (Autumn 1980), 5-15.

'Michel Tournier', in Jean-Louis Ezine, *Les Ecrivains sur la sellette* (Paris: Seuil, 1981), 223-8.

'Un roi mage en liberté' [with Jérôme Le Thor], in *Gaspard, Melchior & Balthazar* (Paris: Tallandier (Cercle du nouveau livre), 1981), 3-27.

'Qu'est-ce que la littérature?' [with Jean-Jacques Brochier], *Magazine littéraire* 179 (December 1981), 80-6.

'The Prophet of Unisex' [with Theodore Zeldin], *Observer* (30.1.83), 43.

4. Prefaces

Roiter, Fulvio, *Venise hier et demain* (Paris: Chêne, 1973). [Preface entitled 'Venise ou la Tête coupée'.]

Clergue, Lucien, *Mers, plages, sources et torrents, arbres* (Paris: Perceval, 1974).

Mason, Jerry (ed.), *La Famille des enfants* (Paris: Flammarion, 1977).

Goebbels, Joseph, *Derniers carnets: journal 28 février - 10 avril 1945* (Paris: Flammarion, 1977).

Staël, Germaine de, *Essai sur les fictions* (Paris: Ramsay, 1979).

Appelt, Dieter, *Morts et résurrections de Dieter Appelt* (Paris: Herscher, 1981).

Thorn-Petit, Liliane, *Portraits d'artistes* (Paris/Luxemburg: RTL Edition, 1982). [Preface entitled 'Quand le peintre parle'.]

Müller, K.R., *François Mitterrand* (Paris: Flammarion, 1983). [Preface entitled 'Pouvoir de l'image et image du pouvoir'.]

Haffner, Sebastian and Venohr, Wolfgang, *Profils prussiens* (Paris:

Gallimard, 1983). [Preface entitled 'La Prusse: une vue de l'esprit'.]

5. Translations from German

Les Archives secrètes de la Wilhelmsstrasse [*Akten zur deutschen auswärtigen Politik*], vols 1-4 (Paris: Plon, 1950-3).

Remarque, Erich-Maria, *L'Etincelle de vie [Der Funke Leben]* (Paris: Plon, 1953).

Remarque, Erich-Maria, *L'Ile d'Espérance [Eine Zeit zu leben und eine Zeit zu Sterben]* (Paris: Plon, 1954).

Lutz, Emil, *Les Mains d'or [Die goldenen Hände]* (Paris: Plon, 1954).

Frank, Herbert, *L'Enfant muet [Der Stumme]*, (Paris: Plon, 1955).

Lange, Kurt, *Des Pyramides, des Sphinx, des Pharaons [Pyramiden, Sphinxen, Pharaonen]* (Paris: Plon, 1956).

B. Critical works on Tournier

1. Books

Austin de Drouillard, Jean-Raoul (1992), *Tournier ou Le retour au sens dans le roman moderne*, Berne: Peter Lang (Publications universitaires européennes).

Bevan, David (1986), *Michel Tournier*,Amsterdam: Rodopi.

Bouloumié, Arlette (1988), *Michel Tournier: le roman mythologique, suivi de questions à Michel Tournier*, Paris: Corti.

Bouloumié, Arlette (1991), *Vendredi ou le limbes du Pacifique de Michel Tournier*, Paris: Gallimard (Foliothèque).

Bouloumié, Arlette and Maurice de Gandillac (eds) (1991), *Images et signes de Michel Tournier: actes du colloque de Cerisy, 1990*, Paris: Gallimard.

Cloonan, William (1985), *Michel Tournier*, Boston: Twayne.

Davis, Colin (1988), *Michel Tournier: Philosophy and Fiction*, Oxford: Clarendon Press.

Fischer, Manfred (1977), *Probleme internationaler Literaturrezeption: Michel Tourniers* Le Roi des aulnes *im deutsch-französischen Kontext*, Bonn: Bouvier.

Guichard, Nicole (1989), *Michel Tournier: autrui et la quête du double*, Paris: Didier.

Hutton, Margaret-Anne (1992), *Tournier: Vendredi ou les limbes du Pacifique*, Glasgow: University of Glasgow French and German Publications.

Jay, Salim (1986), *Idriss, Michel Tournier et les autres*, Paris: La Différence.

Korthals Altes, Liesbeth (1992), *Le Salut par la fiction? Sens, valeurs et narrativité dans* Le Roi des aulnes, Amsterdam: Rodopi.

Koster, Serge (1986), *Michel Tournier*, Paris: Veyrier.

Krell, Jonathan F. (1994), *Tournier élémentaire*, West Lafayette, Indiana: Purdue University Press.

Merllié, Françoise (1988), *Michel Tournier*, Paris: Belfond.

Milne, Lorna (1994), *L'Évangile selon Michel: la Trinité initiatique dans l'oeuvre de Tournier*, Amsterdam: Rodopi.

Petit, Susan (1991), *Michel Tournier's Metaphysical Fictions*, Amsterdam: John Benjamins (Purdue University Monographs in Romance Languages).

Poirier, Jacques (1983), *Approche de...* Le Roi des aulnes *(Michel Tournier)*, Dijon: L'Alei.

Roberts, Martin (1995), *Michel Tournier:* Bricolage *and Cultural Mythology*, Stanford: ANMA Libri (Stanford French and Italian Studies 79).

Rosello, Mireille (1990), *L'In-différence chez Michel Tournier*, Paris: Corti.

Salkin Sbiroli, Lynn (1987), *Michel Tournier: la séduction du jeu*, Geneva: Slatkine.

Scheiner, Barbara (1990), *Romantische Themen und Mythen im Frühwerk Michel Tourniers*, Frankfurt a.M.: Peter Lang.

Stirn, François (1983), *Vendredi ou les limbes du Pacifique*, Paris: Hatier (Profil d'une oeuvre).

Worton, Michael (1992), *Tournier: La Goutte d'or*, Glasgow: University of Glasgow French and German Publications.

Yaiche, Francis (1981), *Vendredi ou la vie sauvage de Michel Tournier*, Paris: Pédagogie moderne (Lectoguide).

2. Special Issues of Periodicals
(Articles cited in the text are listed separately below)

Sud (numéro hors série, 1980).
Sud no. 61 (1986).

Magazine littéraire 138 (June 1978).
Magazine littéraire 226 (January 1986).

3. Articles and Reviews

Bevernis, Christa (1983), 'Michel Tournier: l'oeuvre et son message',

Philologia Pragensia, vol.26, no.3-4, 197-203.

Bougnoux, Daniel (June 1972), 'Des Métaphores à la phorie', *Critique* 301, 527-43.

Bouloumié, Arlette (1991), 'Inversion bénigne, inversion maligne', in A. Bouloumié and M. de Gandillac (eds), *Images et signes de Michel Tournier*, Paris: Gallimard, 17-41.

Cesbron, Georges (1979), 'Notes sur l'imagination terrienne du Corps dans *Vendredi ou les limbes du Pacifique*', *Revue de l'Université de Bruxelles*, 357-65.

Chabot, Jacques (July 1976), 'Un frère jumeau du monde', *Études* 345, 49-71.

Clavel, André (1977), 'Un nouveau cynique: Tournier le jardinier', *Critique* vol.33, no.361-2, 609-15.

Deleuze, Gilles (1969), 'Michel Tournier et le monde sans autrui', in *La Logique du sens*, Paris: Minuit, 402-23 [added as 'Postface' to the Gallimard/Folio edition of *Vendredi ou les limbes du Pacifique*, 257-83].

Fergusson, Kirsty (1986), 'Le rire et l'absolu dans l'oeuvre de Michel Tournier', *Sud* 61, 76-89.

Gascoigne, David (July 1980), 'Noble savages: an introduction to the work of Tournier, Grainville, Decoin', *Literary Review*, no. 20, 13-14.

Gascoigne, David (1990), 'Michel Tournier', in Michael Tilby (ed.), *Beyond the Nouveau Roman. Essays on the Contemporary French Novel*, Oxford: Berg, 64-99.

Gascoigne, David (1992), 'Michel Tournier, *Le Roi des aulnes* [lecture expliquée d'un extrait]', in Catherine Henry (ed.), *Ecritures autobiographiques et romanesques*, Dublin: University College Dublin ERASMUS publication.

Koopman-Thurlings, Mariska (1991), 'De la forme et du fond: le redoublement discursif', in *Images et signes de Michel Tournier*, Paris: Gallimard, 279-93.

Maclean, Mairi (July 1987), 'Human Relations in the novels of Tournier: polarity and transcendance', *Forum for Modern Language Studies*, 23,3, 241-52.

Maclean, Mairi (April 1988), 'Michel Tournier as misogynist (or not?): an assessment of the author's view of femininity', *Modern Language Review*, 83.2, 322-31.

Mansuy, Michel (1978), 'Trois chercheurs de paradis: Bosco, Tournier, Cayrol', *Travaux de linguistique et de littérature de l'Université de Strasbourg*, XVI.2, 211-32.

Nettelbeck, Colin (1984), 'The Return of the Ogre: Michel Tournier's *Gilles et Jeanne*', *Scripsi*, 2.4, 43-50.

Petit, Susan (1984), 'The Bible as inspiration in Tournier's *Vendredi*', *French Forum*, 9, 343-54.

Purdy, Anthony (1984), 'From Defoe's *Crusoe* to Tournier's *Vendredi*: the metamorphosis of a myth', *Canadian Review of Comparative Literature* 11, 216-35.

Purdy, Anthony (December 1980), '*Les Météores* de Michel Tournier: une perspective hétérologique', *Littérature* 40, 32-43.

Redfern, W.D. (1985), 'Approximating Man: Michel Tournier and play in language', *Modern Language Review* 80, 304-19.

Sankey, Margaret (1981), 'Meaning through intertextuality: isomorphism of Defoe's *Robinson Crusoe* and Tournier's *Vendredi ou les limbes du Pacifique*', *Australian Journal of French Studies*, 18,1, 77-88.

Sankey, Margaret (1991), 'La parodie: l'exemple du *Roi des aulnes*', in A. Bouloumié and M. de Gandillac (eds), *Images et signes de Michel Tournier*, Paris: Gallimard, 325-40.

Shattuck, Roger (1983), 'Why not the best?', *New York Review of Books*, 30,7 (28.4.83), 8-15.

Vray, Jean-Bernard (1980), 'L'habit d'Arlequin', *Sud* (special issue on Tournier), 149-66.

White, J.J. (1974), 'Signs of Disturbance: the semiological import of some recent fiction by Michel Tournier and Peter Handke', *Journal of European Studies*, 4, 233-54.

Worton, Michael J. (Fall-Winter 1982), 'Myth-reference in *Le Roi des aulnes*', *Stanford French Review*, 299-310.

Worton, Michael (1984), 'Michel Tournier and the masterful art of re-writing', *PN Review* 41 (vol.11, no.3), 24-5.

Worton, Michael (1986), 'Ecrire et ré-ecrire: le projet de Tournier', *Sud* 61, 52-69.

York, R.A. (1981), 'Thematic construction in *Le Roi des aulnes*', *Orbis Litterarum*, 36.1, 76-91.

C. Other Works Consulted

Alexandrian, Sarane (1977), *Les Libérateurs de l'amour*, Paris: Seuil.

Aristotle (1982), *Météorologiques*, 2 vols, ed. P. Louis, Paris: Belles Lettres.

Bachelard, Gaston (1943), *L'Air et les songes: essai sur l'imagination du mouvement*, Paris: Corti.

Bachelard, Gaston (1942), *L'Eau et les rêves: essai sur l'imagination de la matière*, Paris: Corti.

Bachelard, Gaston (1988), *Fragments d'une poétique du feu*, Paris: P.U.F.

Bachelard, Gaston (1968), *La Psychanalyse du feu*, Paris: Gallimard (Idées, 73) [first published 1949].

Bachelard, Gaston (1948), *La Terre et les rêveries de la volonté*, Paris: Corti.

Bachelard, Gaston (1948), *La Terre et les rêveries du repos*, Paris: Corti.

Bachelard, Gaston (1967), *La Poétique de l'espace*, 5th edn., Paris: P.U.F.

Baudelaire, Charles (1975), *Oeuvres complètes*, ed. C. Pichois, 2 vols, Paris: Gallimard (Bibliothèque de la Pléiade).

Beauvoir, Simone de (1986), *Le Deuxième Sexe*, 2 vols, Paris: Gallimard (Folio/essais), [first published 1949].

Beecher, Jonathan (1986), *Charles Fourier: the Visionary and his World*, Berkeley: University of California Press.

Bénichou, Paul (1977), *Le Temps des prophètes: doctrines de l'âge romantique*, Paris: Gallimard.

Brandi, Daniel (1980), *La Guerre de 1939-45 dans les romans de Camus, Céline, Gracq, Simon, Tournier: la guerre transposée*, doctoral thesis, Univ. de Paris-IV.

Bruckner, Pascal (1975), *Fourier*, Paris: Seuil (Ecrivains de toujours, 98).

Bunyan, John (1926), *The Pilgrim's Progress*, London: Constable.

Curwood, James Oliver (1930), *Le Piège d'or*, Paris: Hachette, [translation of *The Golden Snare*, London: Cassell, 1918].

Custance, John (1954), *Le Livre de la sagesse et de la folie* (Paris: Plon, [translation of *Wisdom, Madness and Folly: the philosophy of a lunatic*, London: Gollancz, 1951].

Defoe, Daniel (1965), *Robinson Crusoe*, Harmondsworth: Penguin.

Diderot, Denis (1935), *Supplément au voyage de Bougainville*, ed. G. Chinard, Geneva: Droz.

Eliade, Mircea (1951), *Le Chamanisme et les techniques archaïques de l'extase*, Paris: Payot.

Eliade, Mircea (1959), *Naissances mystiques: essai sur quelques types d'initiation*, Paris: Gallimard.

Fairchild, Hoxie Neale (1928), *The Noble Savage: A Study in Romantic Naturalism*, New York: Columbia University Press.

Flaubert, Gustave (1973), *Trois contes*, Paris: Gallimard (Folio).

Frazer, Sir James (1929), *The Golden Bough*, abridged edn., London: Macmillan.

Frye, Northrop (1957), *Anatomy of Criticism*, Princeton: Princeton University Press.

Genette, Gérard (1972), *Figures III*, Paris: Seuil.

Genette, Gérard (1982), *Palimpsestes: la littérature au second degré*, Paris: Seuil.

Gide, André (1958), *Romans, Récits et soties, Oeuvres lyriques*, Paris: Gallimard (Bibl. de la Pléiade).

Gould, Cecil (1975), *Leonardo: the Artist and the Non-artist*, Boston: New York Graphic Society.

Goulet, Alain (1985), *Fiction et vie sociale dans l'oeuvre d'André Gide*, Paris: Minard (Lettres Modernes).

Goulet, Alain (1994), *Lire* Les Faux-Monnayeurs *de Gide*, Paris: Dunod.

Graves, Robert (1961), *The White Goddess*, rev. edn., London: Faber.

Grimal, Pierre (1986), *Dictionary of Classical Mythology*, Oxford: Blackwell.

Hugo, Victor (1964), *La Légende des siècles*, ed. A. Dumas, Paris: Garnier.

Hugo, Victor (1969), *Les Contemplations*, ed. L. Cellier, Paris: Garnier.

Jacques de Voragine (1967), *La Légende dorée*, 2 vols, Paris: Garnier-Flammarion.

Klossowski, Pierre (1974), *Les Derniers Travaux de Gulliver, suivi de Sade et Fourier*, Montpellier: Fata Morgana.

Larousse Dictionary of Mythology (1959), London: Paul Hamlyn.

Libis, Jean (1980), *Le Mythe de l'androgyne*, Paris: Berg International.

Mann, Thomas (1971), *Doktor Faustus*, Frankfurt a.M.: Fischer Taschenbuch.

Mansuy, Michel (1967), *Gaston Bachelard et les éléments*, Paris: Corti.

Marcuse, Herbert (1966), *Eros and Civilization: A Philosophical Enquiry into Freud*, 2nd edn., Boston: Beacon Press.

Morris, Alan (1992), *Collaboration and Resistance Reviewed: Writers and the* Mode Rétro *in Post-Gaullist France*, Oxford: Berg.

Ovid (1928), *Métamorphoses*, ed. G. Lafaye, Paris: Belles Lettres.

Perrault, Charles (1967), *Contes*, ed. G. Rouger, Paris: Garnier.

Perrot, Jean (1976), *Mythe et littérature sous le signe des jumeaux*, Paris: P.U.F.

Reckwitz, Erhard (1976), *Die Robinsonade: Themen und Formen einer literarischen Gattung*, Amsterdam: B.R. Grüner.

Rendel Harris, J. (1906), *The Cult of the Heavenly Twins*, Cambridge: Cambridge University Press.

Rimbaud, Arthur (1987), *Oeuvres*, ed. S. Bernard and A. Guyaux, rev. edn., Paris: Garnier.

Robert, Marthe (1981), *Roman des origines et origines du roman*, Paris: Gallimard (Tel).

Rogers, Pat (1979), *Robinson Crusoe*, London: Allen & Unwin.

Sachs, Maurice (1979), *Le Sabbat*, Paris: Gallimard (L'Imaginaire).

Schérer, René (1970), *Charles Fourier*, Paris: Seghers.

Spencer, M.C. (1981), *Charles Fourier*, Boston: Twayne.

Stendhal (1973), *Le Rouge et le noir*, ed. P.-G. Castex, Paris: Garnier.

Vallès, Jules (1973), *Jacques Vingtras, I: L'Enfant*, Paris: Gallimard (Folio).

Vandegans, André (1964), *La Jeunesse littéraire d'André Malraux*, Paris, Pauvert.

Vierne, Simone (1987), *Rite, roman, initiation*, 2nd edn., Grenoble: Presses universitaires de Grenoble.

Vierne, Simone (1989), *Jules Verne: mythe et modernité*, Paris: P.U.F.

Voltaire (1964), *Dictionnaire philosophique*, ed. R. Pomeau, Paris: Garnier-Flammarion.

Voltaire (1964), *Lettres philosophiques*, ed. R. Pomeau, Paris: Garnier-Flammarion.

Watt, Ian (1967), *The Rise of the Novel: Studies in Defoe, Richardson and Fielding*, London: Chatto & Windus.

White, John J. (1971), *Mythology in the Modern Novel*, Princeton: Princeton University Press.

Zazzo, René (1960), *Les Jumeaux, le couple et la personne*, 2 vols, Paris: P.U.F.

Zazzo, René (1984), *Le Paradoxe des jumeaux, précédé d'un dialogue avec Michel Tournier*, Paris: Stock, Laurence Pernoud.

Index